rick stein's seafood lovers' guide

rick stein's
seafood lovers' guide

recipes inspired by a coastal journey

BBC

For Jill, Edward, Jack and Charles

food photography by
james murphy

location photography by
craig easton

This book is published to accompany the television series
entitled *Rick Stein's Seafood Lovers' Guide*.
The series was produced for BBC Television
by Denham Productions.
Producer and Director: David Pritchard
Executive Producer for the BBC: Jeremy Gibson

First published by BBC Worldwide Limited in 2000
80 Wood Lane, London W12 0TT

ISBN 0 563 55152 6

Commissioning Editor: Vivien Bowler
Project Editor: Rachel Copus
Copy Editor: Jane Middleton
Art Director: Lisa Pettibone
Designer: Paul Welti
Home Economist: Debbie Major
Stylist: Antonia Gaunt

The white crockery featured in the food photographs was
provided by Divertimenti and Cucina Direct.
Recipe for warm salad of samphire, asparagus and crab
(page 25) previously appeared in *BBC Good Food
Magazine*.

Set in Helvetica Neue extended
Printed and bound in Great Britain by Butler and Tanner
Limited, Frome and London
Colour separations by Radstock Reproductions Limited,
Midsomer Norton
Jacket printed by Lawrence Allen Limited, Weston-super-Mare

contents

introduction

Don't it always seem to go that you don't know what you've got till it's gone

JONI MITCHELL, 'Big Yellow Taxi'

I'm humbled, after travelling around the world looking at beautiful sunsets on beaches without end and wandering through exotic markets filled with fish and spices, I thought a journey around our own coast would be mundane. How wrong could I have been? I have spent much of the last two years on a series of trips around the coast of the British Isles and Ireland looking for the best seafood, where to buy it and eat it and how it is caught. I found much to enjoy and much to depress me but above all I found a long coastline of matchless beauty. From the rustling shingle beaches along the south coast of England to the soaring cliffs silhouetted against a cold northern sky off the Shetlands, and the falling off the edge of the world feel on lonely stretches of sand in Connemara, these sceptred islands are truly precious stones set in a silver sea.

The people who fish around the coast too are special, gritty, determined, intelligent and stoical people plying a dangerous and fast-declining trade as our fishing stocks are ever more depleted. The terrible conundrum of fishing – the hunter chasing vanishing prey – tinged everywhere I went with melancholy.

But there was hope too, clear signs that a change in attitude is afoot and moments of great joy finding hardly known fish that tasted so good and recipes that astonished me.

I feel I have to justify my exuberance for seafood at a time when its very existence is threatened by over-exploitation. My answer is that the more we love seafood and the more we know about it, the greater will be our diligence in preserving it and the more we will prefer to eat it ourselves rather than see it trucked overland to the fish markets of Spain and France. There's no reason why fish conservation shouldn't work. I just have this nagging doubt that it won't if we don't care enough.

So this is my present effort to fight the cause – a book designed to take you to the best seafood in Britain and Ireland. It's not been a thoroughly exhilarating trip. I was moved at one stage to suggest that there are probably more good seafood restaurants in Brittany than on the coasts of these islands. There's too much showy cooking which falls flat, not enough sensible reliance on good local seafood plainly cooked. However, there are some very good restaurants and suppliers out there, and signs that things are getting better.

Finally, I must stress that the guide is a personal not comprehensive selection of the best among fishmongers, fish processors and restaurants. Those places not in the book are not necessarily excluded because they weren't good enough, I may just not have been there. I've devoted my attention to the coast, to anywhere within the sound of seagulls. At the end of the listings for each region I've also included some restaurants where fish is not a speciality, but where I feel they still do it extremely well. So, I've broken the rules a bit, but generally I feel that there is something particularly exciting about finding good seafood by the sea.

- major town or city
- where to buy and eat the best fish

Orkney Islands

Firth
KIRKWALL
Stromness
St Margaret's Hope

THURSO

WICK

Lochinver
Achiltibuie
Ullapool

Peterhead

Colbost Portree
INVERNESS
Aberdeen
Stonehaven
Inverbervie

Skye

Sound of Sleat

Dee

THE WEST COAST
OF SCOTLAND &
THE ISLANDS

FORT WILLIAM
Duror
Port Appin
Cairndow

Tay

DUNDEE Arbroath
Perth
Peat Inn Crail
Anstruther
Gullane
Edinburgh

THE EAST COAST
OF SCOTLAND &
THE ORKNEYS

Colonsay

Tarbert
Glasgow
Fairlie
Troon

Clyde

BERWICK-UPON-TWEED
Holy Island
Seahouses
Craster

Tweed

Greencastle Ballycastle
Glenarm
LONDONDERRY
Toomebridge
Bangor
BELFAST
Killyleagh
Portaferry

NORTHERN
IRELAND & EIRE

Isle of Man

DUMFRIES
CARLISLE

Newcastle upon Tyne
Sunderland

MIDDLESBROUGH
Staithes
Whitby
Northallerton
Scarborough

Morecambe
Blackpool
Lytham St Anne's

Harrogate
LEEDS

KINGSTON UPON HULL

Leenane

Galway
Kilcolgan
Ballyvaughan Burren

Shannon

Dublin Howth
Dun Laoghaire

Anglesey
LIVERPOOL
HOLYHEAD

MANCHESTER
SHEFFIELD

Grimsby

EAST ANGLIA &
THE EAST COAST

LIMERICK

Dungarvan

CAERNARFON

NOTTINGHAM

Trent

Burnham Market
Cromer
KING'S LYNN
NORWICH
Hambleton
Barnby Lowestoft
LEICESTER
Southwold
Dunwich
Snape
Woodbridge Aldeburgh
Harwich

Castletownbere
Cahersiveen
Skibbereen
Cork Cobh
Midleton
Shanagarry
Kinsale
Skull
Castletownshend
Baltimore

Aberdovey
ABERYSTWYTH

WALES &
THE NORTH-
WEST COAST

BIRMINGHAM

CAMBRIDGE

Gt Ouse

Maldon
West Mersea

FISHGUARD
Letterston
Neyland

Abergavenny

Severn

OXFORD

Thames

Leigh on Sea
Southend
Bray London
Whitstable

Swansea
Penclawdd Cardiff

Bristol
Barrow Bath
Gurney Rowde

East Grinstead

Hythe DOVER
Sandgate
Rye
Hastings

Braunton
Taunton

Lymington
SOUTHAMPTON
Portsmouth
Seaview
Bembridge
Shanklin
Milford on Sea

Brighton
Hove

THE WEST COUNTRY

Broadhembury
Chagford
EXETER
Bridport
Kenton Burton Bradstock
West Bay
Torquay
Brixham
Weymouth
Bournemouth

THE SOUTH COAST

Port Isaac
Padstow
Indian Queens
Fowey
Charlestown
St Mawes
PLYMOUTH

St Ives
Newlyn
Falmouth
Porth Navas
Porthleven

Isles of Scilly

Walls

*Shetland
Islands*

THE CHURNING FRENZY OF THE SEA IN WINTER IS ROMANTIC AND STIRRING BUT THESE ARE DANGEROUS TIMES FOR FISHERMEN.

INSET RIGHT: SAFELY HOME TO NEWLYN, CORNWALL.

the west co

I set out on a bleak, bitingly cold December's afternoon, the wind cutting through my jersey, to walk that part of the coastline I know best, just south of Padstow. I started near Trevose Head down from my old house, looking out towards the dark-grey jagged rocks called the Quies, where we fish for mackerel on balmy summer days. Even the dog looked a bit uncertain, with the wind blowing his fur hard against him, though happy to

untry

be taken for a walk. I had a question to answer to myself. Every time I get off the plane in Australia I go straight down on to the beach in Manly and it's warm, even if it's raining, it's warm and the sea smells warm, I always think, why would anyone want to live anywhere else than that comfortable part of the world?

The dog and I went down the sandy tamarisk-fringed lane to Boobies Bay with the surf getting louder and louder, glimpses of the slate-blue sea and the smell of cold salt. The surf was smashing over the rocks and spume blowing over the thick tufts of grass. Everyone had gone home from the summer and left the spray and me, so it seemed. I passed the rocky beach where we used to collect cowrie shells and coloured glass as children and when my boys were young we did the same – fifty pence for a piece of rare blue glass and much wailing when they brought blue plastic and it wouldn't do. In the watercress-covered stream above the beach, there was some grey polystyrene moulded into pebble shapes by the sea, made almost natural. I walked on up to Trevose Head. I dreaded this part of the walk because I had to pass a deep, round hole near the cliff's edge caused by the erosion of soft strata of rock by the sea. As usual, I found myself veering a long way from the edge yet still with an anxious fascination to go closer and peer down into the sickening depth.

The answer to my question was clear; the comfort of a warm climate with plenty of sun is not, quite, enough. I realized I like the smell of the wind in winter; I like the cloudy gloom of an early darkening afternoon just before Christmas. If there's such a thing as collective memory this sort of experience is where it lies, a mutual understanding in all of us who inhabit these cold northerly islands, a sense of belonging. The Cornish have an expression – where you 'belong to be'.

O the opal and the sapphire of that wandering western sea
from 'Beeny Cliff' by Thomas Hardy

THE VIEW FROM THE TOP: THROUGH MISTY DAYS AND LONG DARK NIGHTS THE TREVOSE HEAD LIGHTHOUSE, 250 FT ABOVE SEA-LEVEL, WARNS SHIPPING OF THE TREACHEROUS ROCKS BENEATH THE SWIRLING SEA.

The churning frenzy of the sea in winter is romantic and stirring but these are tough times for fishermen. Fishing is the most dangerous commercial activity carried out in Britain and to me this makes the seafood from the cold months particularly exquisite. Knowing that the catches of the small fishing boats of the West Country are so hard won makes me appreciate the splendour of the area's seafood all the more. It's all to do with the respect I have for what the fishermen experience in order to catch the fish. I think the more you know about the way food is gathered the more you value it. The West Country has perhaps a greater variety of species than anywhere else due to its unique position: jutting out into the Atlantic towards the Bay of Biscay and enjoying the benefits of the warm Gulf Stream and plankton-rich water. There's an almost Mediterranean ring to many of the varieties of fish landed: red mullet, John Dory, red bream, black bream, trigger fish, grey mullet and even rarities like scorpion fish, used in the Mediterranean for fish soup and bouillabaisse.

It's an area of small boats and local inshore fish. Sadly, the numbers of these vessels have declined greatly as a result of the Government's plan to reduce the size of the fishing fleet by decommissioning – paying fishermen to scrap their boats. With ever declining stocks fishermen have to invest in ever bigger boats to catch the same amount of fish but small owners often haven't the capital to

WHEN THE FISHERMEN'S
WORK IS DONE, THE
BOATS TURN TOWARDS
THE SHORE AND,
ESPECIALLY ON A CALM
DAY, THE HARBOUR IS A
SCENE OF COMPLETE
TRANQUILITY ONCE
MORE.

invest and so decide, literally, to burn their boats instead. But it's from those small local boats that the best fish comes – I know, I buy it. What is unsettling is the thought that decommissioning just leads to the same amount of fish caught by fewer, far more efficient super-trawlers with the loss of thousands of jobs.

There's no doubt that those in charge of conservation would prefer to survey a much smaller fleet of large trawlers landing in a few 'designated' ports. No one could then land fish at Port Isaac or Bere Regis out of boats like the *Sea Jade*, the *Girl Maureen* and the *Blue Hooker*.

The West Country is one of the best places to study the demise of what I would call 'fishing families' and their replacement by more commercially viable bigger trawlers. I have long had an image in my head of what this means. In the 1970s, massive winter catches of mackerel were made by a fleet of largely Scottish trawlers off the coast of Cornwall. The fish were removed from the sea in hundreds of tons by a fleet who sold the catch straight into the holds of a chain of Eastern-bloc factory ships moored just off Falmouth. These were known as Klondikers referring to the almost gold rush frenzy of fishing.

The fishing was rich, but the Cornish hand-lining fishery was decimated. I recall a remark from one of the Scottish fishermen at the time, he said that he couldn't understand why some enterprising local didn't get some money

VISITORS WONDER AT
THE UNFAMILIAR
SIGHTS AND SMELLS
OF WORKING BOATS,
BUT THE INSTINCTS
AND SKILLS OF SEA-
FISHING ARE IN THE
BLOOD OF LOCAL
FISHERMEN.

WORK DOESN'T STOP
WHEN THE BOATS
RETURN SAFELY TO
HARBOUR. NETS AND
EQUIPMENT NEED
CONSTANT REPAIR
AND ATTENTION AND
MUST BE STOWED
READY FOR THE NEXT
TRIP TO SEA.

together, buy a massive trawler and do the same thing. He felt they seemed to show a complete lack of enterprise. But was it lack of enterprise or an understanding of natural conservation? I should certainly prefer to eat mackerel still mottled with green and blue and landed on a cold winter's morning from a hand-liner in Cadgwith, than one defrosted from an iced chamber of millions of long-frozen, long-dead fish. When I was last in that fairytale thatched village, a fisherman looked down at me from the deck of his fishing boat, winched onto the pebbly shore, and held up a magnificent large brill, all slimy from the sea and said with immense pride 'better fish than Padstow'.

But let me not be too gloomy. We have great fish in the West Country and some great suppliers. Just wander round the quay in Porthleven to John Strike's Quayside Fish shop and check out those pearly skinned ray wings or the sensational un-dyed local-smoked haddock. Or go and talk to Phil Bowditch in Taunton about John Dory and plaice. These people really know what's good. Have a chat to Matthew Stevens in St Ives about where he buys his fish and he'll tell you about the families of the fishermen who trawl for his fish in St Ives Bay. He has such an infectious enthusiasm. He picked up a fillet of codling which had a firm, plump look of freshness that I knew would translate into wild joy in a restaurant in London when cooked and served with the understanding it deserved. He spoke of the startling translucence of squid when it is just out of the water and picked a large one up to show me exactly what he meant. We talked in his small, spotless filleting unit above the town. Anyone who goes to St Ives can appreciate the limpid quality of the light there so valued by artists like Ben Nicholson, Barbara Hepworth, Terry Frost and Patrick Heron.

Like everywhere else, the best fish comes from small day boats which go out early in the morning, returning in the evening and selling their catch on the market the next morning. The West Country is blessed with a number of small fish markets in places such as Looe, Brixham, Bideford and Plymouth. Fish especially worth seeking out are turbot, sea bass and Dover sole. The lemon sole of the south coast in early spring are, I think, some of the best fish in the world. Just try buying some from the curiously named Nicole's Yorkshire Fisheries in St Marychurch, Torquay in early March. Take them home whole, grill them and serve with the parsley butter on page 184 to see what I mean.

Red mullet from off Land's End in late September and October is another pleasure unknown to those used to buying in supermarkets deep-frozen specimens from far-off countries. And the lobsters of the north coast of Cornwall, along with those of the west coasts of Scotland and Ireland, are unequalled anywhere else. Go to Dennis Knight's of Port Isaac and order your lobsters live for an opportunity to agree with me. Another treat not to be missed is the astonishing brown crabs from a 30-mile stretch of coast around Start Point near Brixham. They weigh up to 3 kg and, apart from the King Crabs of Alaska, are the largest crabs in the world. Their flavour doesn't suffer at all from their awesome size. You can buy them from Browse Seafoods, whose owners, Graham and Kay Browse, are a delight, having a natural care for the quality of the crab they dress. Graham showed me upstairs to the crab-picking room and explained that the boys do the claws and brown meat – the easy bits – and the girls the 'toes' (legs) and bodies – they have sharper eyes and concentrate better. Maybe the boys are day dreaming about catching those monsters.

If you never understood how fantastic a fresh pilchard could be contact Nick Howell at British Cured Pilchards Ltd in Newlyn. He can tell you when they're available because he buys them straight off the boats for salting. I bought his salted pilchards, done in the same way for hundreds of years, brined and tight-packed in barrels. I grilled them, flaked them and sprinkled them on a bruschetta with tomato, onion, garlic, olive oil and parsley. Eaten on their own they're too salty and oily but used like this – as you would salt anchovies – they are quite special. Thinking of oily fish, in Bideford Bay there's a run of herring that only occurs in October; they're held to be a unique species. Go and see for yourself – even if they're not unique in reality, you'll still swear they are when you taste them.

I could write lots on the subject of eating seafood at restaurants in the area

FISHING FOLK HAVE BEEN SALTING FISH TO IMPROVE THE KEEPING QUALITY SINCE ANCIENT TIMES. THE PILCHARD WORKS AT NEWLYN PRESERVES A FINE TRADITION AS WELL AS A PARTICULARLY FINE FISH.

but I've decided only to be nice, it won't do for me to criticise fellow restaurateurs – heaven knows it's a difficult enough job as it is. As I said earlier, I have been surprised on my journey around Great Britain and Ireland as to how few really good fish and seafood restaurants there are. At least it can be said when using the guide pages at the end of each chapter, that you won't be encumbered with too many decisions!

But there's certainly reason to hope that things will get better. I have to state again that this is not a comprehensive guide to restaurants, more a selection of places I admired when nosing around. But I have enjoyed some dishes – a simple platter of tempura fish in No 7 Fish Bistro in Beacon Terrace, Torquay (01803 295055), pieces of fresh and perfectly cooked cod, monkfish, salmon, prawns, and spring onions with three dips: a tartare sauce, a teriyaki marinade and a plum and ginger sauce. This was served on a black hexagonal plate – not exactly the height of fashion, but the Japanese way does highlight the pale colours of the fish and the lovely crisp, thin batter. Torquay on a clear blue November day seemed a jolly place after I'd come out of that restaurant right onto the harbour – heartened, I'll own, by sharing a bottle of Muscadet Chateau de Cléray which seemed to go to the heart of the vine for its earthy flavour.

salt pilchard bruschetta

I must confess to having put a very similar recipe to this in one of my earlier books, *Fruits of the Sea*, but I had to write it using anchovies instead of salt pilchards because I knew nobody would be able to get hold of them. Now you can. They are available from Nick Howell at British Cured Pilchards Ltd in Newlyn, Cornwall (see page 31). The fact is that these bruschetta are fine made with anchovies but you can't beat the real thing. The flavour of these uncompromisingly salted and pressed pilchards is in the same spectrum as the greenest and bitterest olive in brine, or Malaysian dried shrimps – the sort of flavour that initially makes you think, 'How could anyone eat that?' but then, as a background to other familiar flavours, it becomes the essence of the dish. It's a bit like perfume: when you smell the individual aromas of a great perfume, some are frankly quite offputting but, balanced in the correct proportions, they are essential. And if you haven't read *Perfume* by Patrick Süskind, then you must, it's great.

SERVES 4

4 SALT PILCHARDS, SCALES REMOVED

1 LOAF OF CIABATTA OR OTHER RUSTIC WHITE
BREAD, CUT INTO SLICES 1 CM ($^1/_2$ INCH) THICK

3 GARLIC CLOVES, PEELED

85 ML (3 FL OZ) EXTRA VIRGIN OLIVE OIL

6 VINE-RIPENED TOMATOES, THINLY SLICED

1 SMALL RED ONION, HALVED AND VERY
THINLY SLICED

3 TABLESPOONS COARSELY CHOPPED FLAT-LEAF
PARSLEY OR BASIL

FRESHLY GROUND BLACK PEPPER

METHOD

Pre-heat the grill to high. Grill the pilchards for about 3 minutes on each side, until cooked through. Leave to cool, then break the fish into small flakes, discarding the skin and bones.

Toast the bread on both sides until golden brown. Rub one side of each piece with the peeled garlic cloves, then drizzle over some of the olive oil. Put the flaked pilchards, tomatoes, onion and parsley on top of the bread, then drizzle with the remaining oil and season well with black pepper. Serve straight away, before the bread has time to go soft.

salad of ormers with noodles, shiitake mushrooms, ginger and truffle oil

No, I don't expect you to get hold of ormers for this dish, unless you live in the Channel Islands. They are known as abalone everywhere except the Channel Islands, and fishing for them in Guernsey, Jersey and Alderney ranks extremely highly. Over about six very low spring tides in the months of January and February, the locals wade out up to their necks in ice-cold water, wearing their normal clothes, and reach under the water through the clammy brown weed that grows below the tidemark for these prized molluscs. There are not that many left now, though conservation measures are very strict, but the delight of finding a good-sized ormer outweighs all the discomfort of fishing for them. They are difficult to cook, being extremely tough. The Chinese slice them raw into incredibly thin slices and drop them into boiling stock for a few seconds, but you can also cook them very slowly in the oven for several hours, until they become very tender and full of flavour. I have adapted this recipe for abalone/ormers to suit cuttlefish as well. It comes from a friend of mine, Neil Perry, who has a wonderful restaurant in Sydney called the Rockpool. It is one of the best first courses I have ever eaten. Make it with cuttlefish and it's just as good – exotic but a tremendous experience.

SERVES 4

4 X 50 G (2 OZ) PREPARED ORMERS OR
  A 100 G (4 OZ) PIECE OF CLEANED CUTTLEFISH
120 ML (4 FL OZ) OLIVE OIL
5 CM (2 INCH) PIECE OF CINNAMON STICK
2 STAR ANISE
25 G (1 OZ) DRIED RICE VERMICELLI NOODLES
100 G (4 OZ) MIXED ENOKI AND SHIITAKE MUSHROOMS
4 THIN SLICES OF PEELED FRESH GINGER,
  CUT INTO FINE JULIENNE
2 SPRING ONIONS, HALVED AND VERY FINELY SHREDDED
2 TEASPOONS DARK SOY SAUCE
4 TEASPOONS TRUFFLE OIL

METHOD

Pre-heat the oven to 110°C/225°F/Gas Mark ¼.

Put the ormers or cuttlefish into a small casserole with the olive oil, cinnamon and star anise. Cover and bake for 4–5 hours if using ormers or just 1 hour for the cuttlefish, until tender.

Remove the casserole from the oven, lift the fish out of the oil and leave to cool. Then cut it into the thinnest possible slices and set to one side.

Drop the noodles into a pan of boiling water, then remove from the heat and leave to soak for 2 minutes. Drain and refresh under cold water. Drain well again.

Slice the enoki mushrooms away from their matted base into separate stems, leaving them as long as possible. Trim the stalks of the shiitake mushrooms and cut the caps into thin slices.

To serve, build up the salad in layers on 4 plates, using the noodles, mushrooms, ginger, spring onions and sliced ormers or cuttlefish, shaping them into small mounds about the size of a cricket ball. Drizzle with the soy sauce and truffle oil and serve.

mackerel with lightly grilled beef tomatoes and tapenade dressing

Few flavours go totally successfully with very oily fish, such as herring and mackerel, but tomato is one that does very well indeed. So that's the main flavour here, plus some nice little punchy elements such as olives, anchovies and capers. Do make sure the mackerel is very fresh – i.e. still green and blue on the fishmonger's slab.

SERVES 4

4 SMALL MACKEREL, CLEANED,
   TRIMMED AND FILLETED
2 LARGE BEEF TOMATOES, THINLY SLICED
LEAVES FROM 5-6 SPRIGS OF THYME
SALT AND FRESHLY GROUND BLACK PEPPER

FOR THE TAPENADE DRESSING:
15 G ($\frac{1}{2}$ OZ) BLACK OLIVES, STONES REMOVED
1 ANCHOVY FILLET IN OLIVE OIL, DRAINED
$1\frac{1}{2}$ TEASPOONS CAPERS IN BRINE,
   DRAINED AND RINSED
1 SMALL GARLIC CLOVE
4 TABLESPOONS EXTRA VIRGIN OLIVE OIL
1 TABLESPOON RED WINE VINEGAR

METHOD

Pre-heat the grill to high. Slash the skin of each mackerel fillet two or three times and place, skin-side up, on a lightly oiled baking tray or the rack of the grill pan.

Arrange the tomato slices in a single layer on another lightly oiled baking tray. Season lightly with some salt and pepper and sprinkle with the thyme leaves, then turn them over and season again.

For the dressing, finely chop the olives, anchovy, capers and garlic, but leave them with a little texture; they shouldn't be worked to a paste. Whisk together the oil and vinegar, then stir in the rest of the ingredients and season to taste.

Grill the mackerel for $1\frac{1}{2}$–2 minutes, until the skin is crisp and the fish is cooked through. Remove and keep warm while you grill the tomatoes for just 1 minute. Put the tomatoes on 4 warmed plates and spoon over a little of the dressing. Place the mackerel fillets on top and spoon the remaining dressing around them. Serve immediately.

black bream steamed over seaweed with fennel butter sauce

Nothing in fish cookery matches the exhilaration of lifting the lid from a casserole of fish steamed over seaweed in a nice restaurant, like mine. The aroma of the sauce that wafts past you, and the sight of a nice, plump black bream lying on its bed of bladderack, will make your glass of Bourgogne Aligoté Domaine de Bouzeron, with chilled moisture clinging to the outside of the glass and 'tasting of Flora and the country green' (to quote Keats), all the better. The accompanying hollandaise sauce flavoured with fennel and Pernod will charm you, too.

Most fishmongers should be able to get hold of bladderack seaweed, or you could collect it yourself if you live by the sea. Just wash well before use.

SERVES 4

750 G (1^1/$_2$ LB) FRESH BLADDERACK SEAWEED
4 X 225 G (8 OZ) BLACK BREAM, CLEANED
SALT AND FRESHLY GROUND BLACK PEPPER

FOR THE FENNEL BUTTER SAUCE:

1 SMALL FENNEL BULB
100 G (4 OZ) UNSALTED BUTTER
1 TABLESPOON PERNOD
2 TABLESPOONS WHITE WINE VINEGAR
^{1}/$_2$ TEASPOON SALT
1 EGG YOLK
1 TEASPOON CHOPPED FENNEL HERB OR FENNEL FRONDS

METHOD

Wash the seaweed and spread it over the base of a sauté pan large enough to hold the fish in a single layer (if you don't have a large enough pan, use two). Add 300 ml (10 fl oz) of water, put the fish on top and cover with a tight-fitting lid. Set to one side.

For the fennel butter sauce, remove and discard the outer layer of the fennel bulb. Cut the rest into thin slices. Melt 25 g (1 oz) of the butter in a pan, add the fennel and cook gently for 7–8 minutes, until soft but not browned. Add the Pernod, vinegar and salt and simmer until the liquid has almost completely evaporated. Remove the pan from the heat and leave to cool a little. Then tip the mixture into a liquidizer, add the egg yolk and blend until very smooth. Melt the remaining butter for the sauce in a small pan until it is hot and bubbling. Turn on the liquidizer, with the fennel mixture still in it, and gradually pour in the hot butter to make a smooth, hollandaise-like sauce. Transfer it to a small, warmed serving bowl and stir in the chopped fennel herb and some seasoning to taste. Keep warm.

Place the pan of fish and seaweed over a high heat and, as soon as some steam starts to leak out from underneath the lid, turn the heat down and steam gently for 5 minutes until the fish are cooked through.

Without lifting the lid, take the pan of fish to the table, together with the fennel butter sauce. Remove the lid so your guests can appreciate the aroma and serve with some plain boiled potatoes.

salmon en croûte
with currants and ginger

George Perry-Smith discovered this old English recipe, brought it up to date and made it one of his most famous restaurant dishes. George started the Hole in the Wall in Bath, then went on to open two restaurants in the West Country – the Carved Angel in Dartmouth and the Riverside at Helford in Cornwall. He cooked in the Riverside and his wife, Heather, ran the restaurant. Another cook from the Hole in the Wall cooked at the Carved Angel, Joyce Molyneux, while Tom Jaine, also from the Hole in the Wall, ran the restaurant there. I mention these people because, to me, they have been as influential in improving the standing of cooking and restaurants in Britain as cookery writers like Jane Grigson and Arabella Boxer. This dish is a hymn to a particularly British way with food.

SERVES 6

2 X 550 G (1¼ LB) PIECES OF SKINNED SALMON FILLET,
   TAKEN FROM BEHIND THE GUT CAVITY OF
   A 3-4 KG (7-9 LB) FISH
100 G (4 OZ) UNSALTED BUTTER, SOFTENED
4 PIECES OF STEM GINGER IN SYRUP,
   WELL DRAINED AND FINELY DICED
25 G (1 OZ) CURRANTS
½ TEASPOON GROUND MACE
750 G (1½ LB) CHILLED PUFF PASTRY
1 EGG, BEATEN, TO GLAZE
SALT AND FRESHLY GROUND BLACK PEPPER

METHOD

Season the salmon fillet well with salt. Mix the softened butter with the stem ginger, currants, mace, ½ teaspoon of salt and black pepper. Spread the inner face of one salmon fillet evenly with the butter mixture and then lay the second fillet on top.

Cut the pastry in half and roll one piece out on a lightly floured surface into a rectangle about 4 cm (1½ inches) bigger than the salmon all the way around – approximately 18 x 33 cm (7 x 13 inches). Roll the second piece out into a rectangle 5 cm (2 inches) larger than the first one all the way round.

Lay the smaller rectangle of pastry on a well-floured baking sheet and place the salmon in the centre. Brush a wide band of beaten egg around the salmon and lay the second piece of pastry on top, taking care not to stretch it. Press the pastry tightly around the outside of the salmon, trying to ensure that you have not trapped in too much air, and then press the edges together well. Trim the edges of the pastry neatly to leave a 2.5 cm (1 inch) band all the way around. Brush this once more with egg. Mark the edge with a fork and decorate the top with a fish scale effect by pressing an upturned teaspoon gently into the pastry, working in rows down the length of the parcel. Chill for at least an hour.

Pre-heat the oven to 200°C/400°F/Gas Mark 6 and put a large baking sheet in it to heat up.

Remove the salmon en croûte from the fridge and brush it all over with beaten egg. Take the hot baking sheet out of the oven and carefully slide the salmon parcel on to it. Return it to the oven and bake for 35–40 minutes. Leave it to rest for 5 minutes.

Transfer the salmon to a warmed serving plate and take it to the table whole. Cut it across into slices to serve.

red mullet en papillote with thyme

The Italians cook a lot of fish with water, wine, lemon juice, salt and olive oil. It's hard to think of a more effective combination for delicately bringing out flavour in fish. I've just added some thyme here. You clean the whole mullet, season it, place thyme inside and out, and bake it in foil with the *aqua pazza*, which means mad water, referring to the frenzied boiling and amalgamation of olive oil and water, which in this case happens inside the papillote.

SERVES 4

4 X 225-275 G (8-10 OZ) RED MULLET,
   CLEANED AND TRIMMED
A SMALL BUNCH OF THYME
120 ML (4 FL OZ) EXTRA VIRGIN OLIVE OIL
50 ML (2 FL OZ) DRY WHITE WINE
JUICE 1 LEMON (ABOUT 8 TEASPOONS)
SEA SALT AND FRESHLY GROUND BLACK PEPPER

FOR THE TOMATO, BLACK OLIVE AND CHILLI SALAD:

450 G (1 LB) SMALL, VINE-RIPENED TOMATOES,
   CUT INTO WEDGES
1/2 MEDIUM-HOT RED FINGER CHILLI, SEEDED AND
   FINELY CHOPPED
1 GARLIC CLOVE, FINELY CHOPPED
50 G (2 OZ) GOOD-QUALITY BLACK OLIVES, PITTED
4 TABLESPOONS EXTRA VIRGIN OLIVE OIL
1 TABLESPOON CHOPPED FLAT-LEAF PARSLEY

METHOD

Pre-heat the oven to 220°C/425°F/Gas Mark 7.

Season the fish inside and out with salt and pepper. Put 2 sprigs of thyme in the cavity of each one. Brush four 30 cm (12 inch) squares of foil with a little of the olive oil and put a fish diagonally across the centre of each piece. Bring the sides of the foil up around the fish and crimp it together tightly at each end, leaving the top open.

Mix the wine with 50 ml (2 fl oz) of water. Pour 2 tablespoons of the wine and water mixture, 2 tablespoons of olive oil and 2 teaspoons of lemon juice into each parcel, add the remaining sprigs of thyme and season with a little more salt and pepper. Seal the parcels well and place on a large baking sheet. Bake the fish for 10 minutes.

Meanwhile, prepare the salad: scatter the tomato wedges, red chilli, garlic and olives on 4 small plates and drizzle with the olive oil. Season with some salt and pepper and sprinkle with the chopped parsley.

To serve, put the unopened parcels of fish on 4 warmed plates and take them to the table with a bowl of chips cooked in olive oil and the plates of tomato salad. Allow each person to open up their own parcel.

deep-fried plaice with spring onion and chilli seasoning

The plaice from the coast of south and south-west England – Devon, Dorset and Hampshire – are the best anywhere, I think. The locals will tell you about the fishes' fondness for nestling in the lea of several long gravel banks stretching all along the coast from Start Point to Portland Bill while they feed on a diet of cockles and mussels. These plaice seem to be thicker than others, with a clean, unmuddy flavour, and are perfectly suited to this dish of tempura-coated fillets with a spiky seasoning of spring onion, chilli, garlic and Sichuan pepper.

SERVES 4

750 G (1½ LB) THICK PLAICE FILLETS, SKINNED

SUNFLOWER OIL FOR DEEP-FRYING

SALT

A SMALL BUNCH OF CORIANDER SPRIGS,
  TO GARNISH

LIME WEDGES, TO SERVE

**FOR THE SPRING ONION AND
CHILLI SEASONING:**

SUNFLOWER OIL FOR FRYING

1 SMALL ONION, FINELY CHOPPED

2 GARLIC CLOVES, FINELY CHOPPED

1 MEDIUM-HOT RED FINGER CHILLI, THINLY SLICED

3 SPRING ONIONS, THINLY SLICED

1 TEASPOON SEA SALT FLAKES

½ TEASPOON SICHUAN PEPPERCORNS, CRUSHED

FOR THE BATTER:

50 G (2 OZ) PLAIN FLOUR

50 G (2 OZ) CORNFLOUR

A PINCH OF SALT

175 ML (6 FL OZ) ICE-COLD SODA WATER
  FROM A NEW BOTTLE

METHOD

For the spring onion and chilli seasoning, pour about 1 cm (½ inch) of sunflower oil into a frying pan and leave it to get hot. Add the chopped onion and fry for about 3–4 minutes, until it is beginning to brown. Then add the garlic and cook for 1 minute. Add the chilli and fry until the onion and garlic are crisp and golden brown. Lift the mixture out with a slotted spoon on to lots of kitchen paper and leave to go cold. Then transfer it to a bowl and mix in the spring onions, salt and Sichuan pepper.

Heat some oil for deep-frying to 190°C/375°F. Meanwhile, season the plaice fillets with salt on both sides and cut them into strips about 2.5 cm (1 inch) wide.

For the batter: sift the flour, cornflour and salt into a bowl and stir in the ice-cold soda water until only just mixed; it should be a bit lumpy. Dip the strips of plaice into the batter a few pieces at a time, then drop them into the hot oil and fry for 2 minutes, until golden. Drain briefly on kitchen paper and keep hot while you cook the rest.

Pile the fried plaice on to a serving platter and sprinkle over the spring onion and chilli seasoning. Scatter over the fresh coriander sprigs and serve straight away, with the lime wedges.

warm salad of samphire,
asparagus and crab

Samphire, just blanched in fresh water, then tossed in good olive oil with a squeeze of lemon juice and served warm, is sensational. I've made it into a warm salad with some cooked but still crunchy asparagus and nice chunks of white crab meat, preferably picked yourself so you can ensure the pieces are as big as possible. Throw in a little broad-leaf parsley and finish with a few Parmesan shavings.

SERVES 4 AS A STARTER

1 X 1.25–1.5 KG ($2^3/_4$–3 LB) COOKED BROWN CRAB

350 G (12 OZ) THIN ASPARAGUS

225 G (8 OZ) SAMPHIRE, PICKED OVER AND WASHED

$^1/_4$ GARLIC CLOVE, FINELY CHOPPED

2 TABLESPOONS EXTRA VIRGIN OLIVE OIL,
   PLUS EXTRA FOR SERVING

JUICE OF $^1/_4$ LEMON (ABOUT 2 TEASPOONS)

1 TABLESPOON CHOPPED FLAT-LEAF PARSLEY

SEA SALT FLAKES

A FEW PARMESAN SHAVINGS, TO GARNISH

METHOD

Remove the meat from the crab (see page 189).

Snap off the woody ends from the asparagus where they break naturally and discard them. Cut the asparagus stalks in half. Break off and discard the woody ends of the samphire and break the rest into 2.5 cm (1 inch) pieces.

Bring a pan of water to the boil. Add the samphire and asparagus and cook for 1 minute. Drain and refresh under cold water to stop them cooking and help set the colour. Drain well once more and then tip into a bowl. Add the garlic, olive oil and lemon juice, toss together lightly and season to taste if necessary.

Divide the asparagus and samphire between 4 plates and arrange pieces of the white crab meat and a little of the brown meat over the top. Sprinkle with the chopped parsley, drizzle over a little more olive oil and season with a few sea salt flakes. Scatter over the Parmesan shavings and serve.

john dory with chargrilled leeks,
soft-boiled eggs and mustard vinaigrette

When my main course arrives in a restaurant I often think that I would have been happier having two first courses. The idea of the starter, the main course and the sweet is all a bit much when, after an amusing and delightful first course, the middle course all too often turns out to be something designed to be weighty, rich and impressive. I prefer simple and charming dishes like this – pretty on the plate and not too filling, with lots of uncomplicated flavour.

SERVES 4

16–20 BABY LEEKS, TRIMMED

4 EGGS

A THICK PIECE OF PARMESAN CHEESE

2 X 350 G (12 OZ) JOHN DORY FILLETS

25 G (1 OZ) BUTTER, MELTED

SEA SALT AND FRESHLY GROUND BLACK PEPPER

COARSELY CRUSHED BLACK PEPPER, TO SERVE

FOR THE MUSTARD VINAIGRETTE:

$1^1/_2$ TEASPOONS DIJON MUSTARD

$1^1/_2$ TEASPOONS WHITE WINE VINEGAR

8 TEASPOONS EXTRA VIRGIN OLIVE OIL

METHOD

Pre-heat the grill to high. Cook the leeks in boiling salted water for 2–3 minutes, until just tender but still *al dente*. Drain and refresh under cold water, then dry out on kitchen paper.

Cook the eggs in boiling water for just 7 minutes so that the yolks remain slightly soft. Cool, peel and cut in half. Shave some thin slices of Parmesan cheese and set aside.

For the mustard vinaigrette, mix the mustard and vinegar together in a small bowl and then gradually whisk in the olive oil. Season to taste with some salt and pepper.

Heat a ridged cast-iron griddle over a high heat. Brush with a little oil, then place the leeks diagonally across it and grill them for slightly less than 1 minute on each side, so that they get nicely marked with diagonal lines. Remove the leeks from the griddle and arrange in the centre of 4 large warm plates. Stir $1^1/_2$ teaspoons of warm water into the mustard vinaigrette and drizzle it over the leeks. Put two halves of egg on each plate.

Brush the John Dory fillets on both sides with the melted butter and season well with salt and pepper. Lay the fillets skin-side up on a lightly greased baking sheet or the rack of the grill pan and grill for 4 minutes. Remove and place on top of the leeks. Scatter over the Parmesan shavings, sprinkle over a little coarsely crushed black pepper and some sea salt flakes and serve.

RESTAURANTS SERVING GOOD SEAFOOD

Bath, B & NES
Green Street Seafood Café
6 Green Street
Bath BA1 2JY
Tel: (01225) 448707
Website: www.fishworks.co.uk

Directions
It's a good idea to park in the Waitrose car park; Green Street is just off Broad Street.

The idea of putting a restaurant selling nothing but seafood above a pretty comprehensively stocked fishmonger (see The Fish Market, page 29) appeals to me. I like being able to browse over piles of fresh fish, then nip upstairs to a laid-back restaurant and enjoy some good modern cooking at the hands of Andy Bird and Mitch Tonks. I enjoyed some sublime crab with spaghetti, garlic, chilli and parsley and some blindingly simple whole grilled red mullet with tapenade and roasted tomatoes. and a bottle of Thevenot-Le-Brun Hautes Côte de Nuit 1997 Chardonnay.

west country selection

Bristol
Quartier Vert (formerly Rocinantes)
85 Whiteladies Road
Bristol BS8 2NT
Tel: (0117) 973 4482
Fax: (0117) 974 3913

Directions
Just outside the city centre, before you get to the Downs.

Situated as it is just down the road from the BBC in Bristol, I've been to Rocinantes (as it used to be called)

lots of times. It's one of those places where you seem to end up deep in conversation and you hardly notice that the seafood coming on countless plates in tapas form is extremely good.

Bristol
River Station
The Grove
Bristol BS1 4RB
Tel: (0117) 914 4434
Fax: (0117) 934 9990
Website: www.riverstation.co.uk

Directions
On the waterfront, just off Queens Square, near St Mary Redcliffe.

I knew nothing about River Station when I was asked to turn up there for a photo shoot for *Radio Times*. I recall one of the shots was of me surrounded by a load of bread rolls. I can't quite remember why, but I do remember the restaurant and the food very well. it was one of those places right on the river with lots of chrome, stainless steel and light wood where you think, as you're sipping your first glass of Pinot Grigio, 'Bristol's coming along.' And then I had the excellent roast cod, puy lentils, fennel al forno and salsa verde.

Padstow, Cornwall
The Seafood Restaurant
Riverside
Padstow PL28 8BY
Tel: (01841) 532700
E-mail:
seafoodpadstow@cs.com
Website:
www.rickstein.com

Directions
On the harbour, with a large white conservatory at the front.

St Petroc's Bistro
4 New Street
Padstow PL28 8EA
Tel: (01841) 532700

Directions
Up the hill from the central square; an elegant white Georgian building with a front porch.

Rick Stein's Café
Middle Street
Padstow PL28 8AP
Tel: (01841) 532700

Directions
Tucked away behind the cinema, right in the heart of Padstow.

It's very difficult to write up an entry about your own restaurants without being either over-generous or too mean, so I'm not going to try. Instead, I'll name a few dishes that you might find on the menus. At the Seafood Restaurant you might find a fillet of brill with stir-fried spinach and coriander, a salad of cuttlefish with noodles, shiitake mushrooms, ceps, ginger and truffle oil, or skate with black butter and capers. At St Petroc's Bistro there might be whole lemon sole with lemongrass butter, or roast cod with onion confit, bay leaf and garlic. At Rick Stein's Café you could choose between deep-fried fish in a tortilla with tomato, chilli and red onion salsa, or mussels with linguine, parsley, garlic and olive oil.

St Ives, Cornwall
Alfresco
Harbourside
Wharf Road
St Ives TR26 1LF
Tel: (01736) 793737

Directions
Right on the harbour, overlooking Godrevy Island and Virginia Woolf's *To the Lighthouse* lighthouse.

I had hopes that this was going to be good because Grant Nethercott, the resident chef, used to work with Paul Sellars, who was my sous-chef for eight years, and now runs the courses at the Padstow Seafood School. I was not disappointed. Grant served up some monkfish cassoulet, which was hot and aromatic with garlic and paprika sausage, a serious seared-tuna Niçoise and a dish of pasta and clams.

St Ives, Cornwall
Porthminster Café
Porthminster Beach
St Ives TR26 2EB
Tel: (01736) 795352

Directions
On the beach below the railway station car park.

The Porthminster Café is an unpretentious café-style restaurant housed in an attractive art deco building, built in the 1930s. Inside, the room is simply decorated, with tiled floors and square pine tables, where you can enjoy dishes such as monkfish and aubergine curry with brown rice and spicy naan bread, or roast cod with leeks and a lightly curried butter sauce. One nice, quirky little touch is that the wine is cooled in plastic seaside buckets.

St Mawes, Cornwall
Tresanton Hotel
27 Lower Castle Road
St Mawes TR2 5DR
Tel: (01326) 270055

Directions
Half-way down the narrow road along the waterfront. They will park your car for you in their own car park, situated up the cliff behind the hotel.

I had very much wanted to put the Tresanton in the guide since reading about the hotel and the fantastic refit done by its proprietor, Olga Polizzi. I'd also heard, though, that the service was a bit slack, but reasoned that this was due to teething troubles – an early report of our restaurant had described our waitresses as 'sloppy'. I needn't have worried, the service was professional but informal and the seafood spot on. I had a crab and herb salad, which was very Italian, followed by a small pan-fried monkfish tail coated in herbs and fennel seeds, such a good idea, with pipérade. The hotel is a delight, understated and comfortable, with an upmarket British seaside feel to it.

PUBS SERVING GOOD SEAFOOD

Broadhembury, Devon
Drewe Arms
Broadhembury EX14 3NF
Tel: (01404) 841267
Fax: (01404) 841765
E-mail: drewe.arms@btinternet.com

Directions
Situated next to the church.

I had had a thin couple of days looking for good places to eat fish on the South Devon coast and so it was with a feeling of some depression that I drove the twelve miles inland to the Drewe Arms. The cook, Kerstin Burge, had impressed me with her knowledge of fish and her enthusiasm for cooking it simply when I met her at an annual bash of West Country hoteliers and restaurateurs in Bristol a couple of years ago – how my

melancholia slipped away! The menu offers lots of simply cooked fish, such as scallops with black butter and capers, half a lobster, whole grilled lemon sole, turbot hollandaise, fillet of brill with sauce rémoulade and steamed bass with pesto.

FISH AND CHIPS

St Ives, Cornwall
Beck's Fish and Chips
Longstone Hill
Carbis Bay
St Ives PR26 2LJ
Tel: (01736) 796241

Directions
On the main road into St Ives.

Queues outside this fish and chip restaurant and take-away bear testimony to the quality of the fish and chips that they sell.

Braunton, North Devon
Squire's
Exeter Road
Braunton EX33 2JR
Tel: (01271) 815533

Directions
Situated in the main high street (the A361).

I found their cod and chips great, with very light batter covering thick fillets of very fresh fish and the chips were thick, floury on the inside and beautifully crisp on the outside. I had less luck, sadly, with their poached fillet of cod with hollandaise sauce. Can we have a world moratorium on jars and packets of hollandaise sauce?

FISHMONGERS

Bath, B & NES
The Fish Market
6 Green Street
Bath BA1 2JY
Tel/Fax: (01225) 447794

Directions
It's a good idea to park in the Waitrose car park; Green Street is just off Broad Street.

This is the comprehensively stocked fishmonger's situated underneath the Green Street Seafood Café (see page 28). All the seafood is supplied by Wing of St Mawes (see page 30). On a typical day you will see a great selection of prime fish, such as red mullet, John Dory, crayfish tails, turbot, brill and sea bream, as well as the more usual cod and haddock fillets, but in really peak condition.

Falmouth, Cornwall
Arwenack Fisheries
29 Arwenack Street
Falmouth TR11 3JE
Tel: (01326) 312235

Directions
In the main street near Trago Mills.

Here you will find a good selection of fresh fish, including lemon, megrim and Dover soles, small skate wings, prepared scallops, local brown crabs, cod and haddock fillets. They also specialize in salt pollack.

Fowey, Cornwall
Fowey Fish
37 Fore Street
Fowey PL23 1AH
Tel: (01726) 832422
Fax: (01726) 832887

Directions
In the street near the Fowey Harbour Office on the quayside.

This tiny fish shop has a surprisingly good selection of fresh fish, such as turbot, brill, Dover sole, lemon sole, monkfish tails, small sea bass, red mullet, pin hake, cooked brown crabs and scallops. They will also vacuum-pack any fish for you to take away.

Indian Queens, Cornwall
Wing of St Mawes Direct
4 Warren Road
Indian Queens
St Columb Major TR9 6TF
Tel: (0800) 0523717
Website: www.Cornish-Seafood.co.uk

Directions
Just past McDonald's on the A30 from Truro.

Rob Clifford-Wing runs a trawler out of St Mawes and has a wholesale fish business in the delightfully named Indian Queens on the A30. You can buy fish from Wing's retail counter there, but there is also a mail-order service, which will deliver fish (whole or already prepared), shellfish and smoked fish to your door the next day. Orders can also be placed on the website (address above).

Port Isaac, Cornwall
Dennis Knight
1 Fore Street
Port Isaac PL29 3GB
Tel: (01208) 880498
Fax: (01208) 880934

Directions
You'll find Knight's in an old pilchard shed at the back of the main beach and harbour in this very atmospheric Cornish fishing village. Park on the beach if the tides are right.

Last time I was there a film crew was shooting a Conrad short story called 'Amy Foster'. I couldn't believe how many Cornishmen had bushy black beards. Amazing what make-up artists can do with some whiskers and glue. On the day I visited I found some very nice Dover sole, megrim sole, lemon sole, farmed sea bass, brill, turbot, hake, monkfish, cod, haddock and salmon for sale.

Porthleven, South Cornwall
Quayside Fish
The Harbourside
Porthleven TR13 9JU
Tel: (01326) 562008
Website: www.quaysidefish.co.uk

Directions
Stand looking out to sea and it's on the right-hand side of the harbour.

At this fishmonger's you will find locally caught fish, such as sea bass, red mullet, John Dory, plaice, mackerel, lobster and local crab. The kippers and smoked, undyed haddock from their own smokehouse are good too. The business is run by former fisherman John Strike. John also provides an overnight delivery service to anywhere in Britain – you either choose what you want, or stipulate a price and receive a surprise selection.

St Ives, Cornwall
Matthew Stevens & Son
Back Road East
St Ives TR26 1NW
Tel: (01736) 799392
Fax: (01736) 799441

Directions
Take the road behind the Sloop Inn car park and carry on to the top of Fish Street.

When we went to see Matthew I knew I'd found a serious seafood lover. 'Look at these codling,' he said, 'just out of the bay this morning. Did you ever see anything more beautiful?' His family have had a fish shop in the town of St Ives for the best part of fifty years. It is beautifully kept, with great displays of very fresh wet fish and shellfish. He also sells fresh and smoked fish by mail order, guaranteed to be delivered to your door the next day.

Brixham, Devon
Browse Seafoods (formerly Brixham Seafoods)
2 Paradise Place
Brixham TQ5 8JH
Tel: (01803) 852942
Fax: (01803) 850112

Directions
You'll find this right by the central multi-storey car park, up a narrow alleyway at the back of the harbour.

Although this small wet-fish shop is well stocked, it is the crabs for which Graham and Kay Browse are famous. The cock crabs, fished off nearby Start Point, are reputedly some of the largest in the world, weighing 4–8 lb, sometimes even more. Here you can buy freshly cooked whole crabs, as well as freshly picked white and brown crab meat. Nothing is ever frozen.

Torquay, Devon
Nicole's Yorkshire Fisheries
32 Fore Street
St Marychurch
Torquay TQ1 4LY
Tel: (01803) 327555
Fax: (01803) 329117

Directions
Follow signs for the model village and park in the car park there. The fish shop is next to the village.

They have a good selection of very fresh wet fish and smoked fish, bought from nearby Brixham Market.

Taunton, Somerset
Phil Bowditch
7 Bath Place
Taunton TA1 4ER
Tel: (01823) 253500

Directions
Just off the high street, down the alley beside the Woolwich Building Society.

Phil Bowditch is my friend Tamasin Day-Lewis's favourite fishmonger. On the day I went there, in addition to a display of some lovely-looking fish, he had fresh smelts. I picked one up, gave it a good sniff and yes, they do really smell of cucumbers! If you're lucky enough to get them, try cooking them as in the recipe for *Braised Trout with Mint, Parsley and Caper Sauce* on page 164. All the fish comes from either Brixham Market or one of Phil's boats.

SEAFOOD SUPPLIERS

Barrow Gurney, nr Bristol, B & NES
Heritage Fine Foods
Lakeside

Bridgewater Road
Barrow Gurney BS48 3SJ
Tel: (01275) 474707
Club Chef direct order line:
01275 475252
Website: www.clubchefdirect.co.uk

Directions
Situated on the A38, three miles
south of Bristol.

Steve Downey is an inspiring supplier
of fresh seafood. He supplies a lot of
the leading restaurants with high-
quality ingredients by overnight carrier.
Prime fish is dispatched with a
minimum of delay. Club Chef Direct
provides a mail-order service for fresh
seafood and a wide selection of high
quality ingredients that are delivered
overnight to anywhere in the country.
You can also order from the website
(address above).

The following are good suppliers
based at Padstow Quay, South Quay,
Padstow PL28 8BL, Cornwall

Padstow Fisheries
Tel: (01841) 532763 (unit 2)
Trevose Seafoods
Tel: (01841) 532973 (unit 3)
Stein's Seafood Deli
Tel: (01841) 533466 (unit 4)
Murts Shellfish
Tel: (01841) 533777 (unit 5)

Porth Navas, South Cornwall
Duchy of Cornwall Oyster Farm
Porth Navas TR11 5RJ
Tel: (01326) 40210

Directions
Drive into Porth Navas and go down
the private road at the end of the
creek. The oyster farm is on the
second quay.

We made a little film at the Duchy
Oyster Company as part of my first
series. We got through about five

dozen native oysters and a similar
number of Pacifics, or gigas, as they
are often called. We tried ten very
smart white wines, which our wine
merchant, Bill Baker, improbably
delivered by helicopter. The object
was to try and find the best match of
oyster and wine but, when David the
director came to look at the footage,
the whole thing looked so élitist it was
sickening. But it was a great day, and
if you ever get the chance, go, and
take your own wine. The oysters are
available from September through to
April, personal callers only.

Oak Farm, Kenton, nr Exeter, Devon
River Exe Shellfish Farms
Lyson
Kenton EX6 8EZ
Tel: (01626) 890133
E-mail: David@resf.freeserve.co.uk

Directions
At Starcross take the B3381 to
Newton Abbott and Mamhead. Turn
right at the crossroads towards Lyson
and Oxton until you get to Oak Farm.

Pacific oysters and cultivated mussels
can be bought from the farm (just ring
to make sure they're in before you
go). They also run oyster bars at
county shows such as Henley Royal
Regatta, the Devon County Show and
Badminton Horse Trials. Finally, they
offer a mail-order service with
overnight delivery (minimum order
one dozen oysters).

SMOKERIES AND OTHER SPECIALIST SEAFOODS

Charlestown, Cornwall
The Cornish Smoked Fish Company
Charlestown
St Austell PL25 3NY
Tel: (01726) 72356
E-mail: cornishsmokedfish@cornwall-county.com
Website:
www.cornishsmokedfish.co.uk

Directions
Follow signs for Charlestown from the
A390, skirting the southern edge of St
Austell. Take the first exit off the mini
roundabout and the smokery is on
the left, at the head of the dock.

We've been buying Martin
Pumphrey's smoked fish ever since
we opened the Seafood Restaurant in
1975. I may be wrong, but I think he
might have been the pioneer in this
country for cold-smoked mackerel,
which, I think, when thinly sliced, is as
nice as smoked salmon. His kippers

too are excellent – he uses Icelandic
herrings, which he buys when in
season. (As well as his retail shop,
Martin operates a mail-order service.)

Newlyn, South Cornwall
British Cured Pilchards Ltd
The Pilchard Works
Newlyn TR18 5QH
Tel: (01736) 332112
Fax: (01736) 332442
E-mail: pilchardco@aol.com
Museum website: www.pilchards.net
Wet-fish supply website:
www.cornishfish.com

Directions
Approaching Newlyn on the A30,
follow signs for the Pilchard Works.
The building is fifty yards upstream
from Newlyn Bridge.

Nick Howell's Pilchard Museum is a
must for any seafood lover. He sells
fresh Cornish pilchards (whole and
filleted), as well as the salt pilchards
he cures in the traditional way,
pressed into wooden barrels. The
whole process is on show, and the
pleasure of seeing those 'fair maids'
pressed into neat circles with the
smell of curing, wood and hemp
sacks is wholly worth the trip. 'Fair
maids' actually comes from the
Portuguese *fumados* (cured), but to
me it will always refer to the
shimmering beauty of those pretty
herrings falling into a net. Nick also
sells local salt cod and an interesting
range of sea salt and seaweed
products from Brittany, where his wife
comes from. He operates a mail-
order service for wet fish, too.

OTHER PLACES WHERE I'VE EATEN GOOD FISH RECENTLY

Bath, B & NES
The Olive Tree
Queensberry Hotel
Russel Street
Bath BA1 2QF
Tel: (01225) 447928
Fax: (01225) 446065
E-mail: queensberry@dial.pipex.com

Bristol
Markwicks
43 Corn Street
Bristol BS1 1HT
Tel/Fax: (0117) 926 2658

Chagford, Devon
Gidleigh Park
Chagford TQ13 8HH
Tel: (01647) 432367
E-mail: gidleighpark@gidleigh.co.uk

THERE'S A NEW BATTLE OF HASTINGS EVERY TIME THE FISHING FLEET GOES OUT. IT'S HARD PHYSICAL WORK LAUNCHING DIRECTLY OFF THE PEBBLE BEACH AND THAT'S JUST THE START...

the south c

We arrived at Hastings just before lunch and were directed to some black-tar painted net-drying sheds that stood tall and narrow in rows on the shingle beach. I felt as though I were back in Victorian England and that I might see Peggotty's house further along the beach. Or maybe

oast

Terence Stamp would emerge from a side alley between two of those rows of sheds dressed in a red and blue army uniform straight out of *Far From the Madding Crowd*. Maybe we were a bit too far east for that.

PRETTY THEY'RE NOT, BUT THESE ARE WORKING BOATS AND THE MEN WHO WORK THEM ARE STRUGGLING TO MAKE A LIVING. IT'S THE FISHING COMMUNITY THAT MAKES HASTINGS SPECIAL.

We parked the crew van amongst all the muddled, rusty equipment designed for the launching and equipping of fishing boats off the pebble beaches of the south of England. Greased and rusting giant winches wound with frayed steel, old corrugated iron sheds with a jumble of broken fish boxes, buoys and nets, a long black rubber mat extending over the pebbles down to the beach to make walking easier, and everywhere the pervasive smell of ripe fish.

It was a beautiful English summer's day, still and shimmering – a busy bank holiday, if I remember. We met fishermen Paul Joy and Tush Hamilton who told us that the local council had been trying to clear up the end of the beach for years. They wanted to get rid of the sheds, the tatty polythene sheets, the buckets of grease and the seagull-splattered anchors and to make it neat and pretty for the tourists, just like the rest of Hastings. But the fishermen had fought back. Paul discovered, after some astute research, that the fishermen had been granted working rights to this end of the beach – the 'Stade' as it is known – at the time of the Spanish Armada and that this decree was still intact. The gear stayed, the boats stayed and the atmosphere of that scruffy end of town, long held in contempt by the councillors, was preserved. Now those net-drying sheds are listed buildings and that end of town is what makes Hastings special – a seaside town with a working fishing community.

There's a fishing museum down by the black sheds or 'dieses'. The main exhibit is a clinker-built sailing lugger. Its timbers are thick and reassuring; it's broad and strong – designed to withstand being hauled up and down the shingle beach every day. In the old days these boats were pulled up the beach by a capstan turned by carthorses, now each boat has a diesel engine in a little flat-roofed shed to do the job.

One of my main reasons for going to Hastings was to meet an artist whose work I'd first seen at the art gallery in Newlyn, and who has spent 25 years painting the spare and lean scenes of fishing from Hastings beach. Laetitia Yhapp's paintings show angular fishermen in blue overalls and yellow oilskins at

WHILE TECHNOLOGY HAS TAKEN OVER MANY TEDIOUS OR DANGEROUS TASKS, SET NETTING FOR COD IN THE ENGLISH CHANNEL STILL DEMANDS STRENGTH, SKILL, STAMINA AND BRAVERY.

COD, THE FISH THAT LAUNCHED A THOUSAND CHIPS, HAS BEEN POPULAR SINCE MEDIEVAL TIMES. EVEN HERRING GULLS PESTER FOR A TASTE AS THE FISH ARE CLEANED AT SEA.

work; the reality is always quite harsh – the faces look pinched and there's often an underfed dog or two. The fishing clobber lies all around, rusty and tangled. I remember one where a drowned blue-looking fisherman has been laid on the shingle and his friends are crowding round. It looks like a cold bitter day of easterly winds, a nasty little day. There are lots of cigarettes alight between thin fingers; it's a long way from the romantic scenes by Stanhope Forbes of reassuringly bearded and dependable fishermen rowing across Newlyn harbour. Nevertheless, Laetitia's paintings are also a celebration. They are a true reflection of the human condition and somehow when you see the truth in art it lifts the spirit – even when the subject is a poor, blue-skinned dead fisherman laid out on the beach.

That hot afternoon was a long way removed from the scenes of Laetitia's paintings, however. We filmed a chat with her and then the landing of some plump grey mullet. They were the type we call bay mullet, but are correctly called golden grey mullet – they have a golden flash on their gill cover and seem to make better eating than the common grey mullet, although I'm fond of the taste of the fish anyway. Afterwards, Paul and Tush invited us to a barbecue at their houses that lie next to each other at the back of the town – the gardens have a lovely view right over the harbour. Each house had its own bar in the basement, looking out onto the garden. One was decorated in a Greek taverna style, while the other was ship-shape, like the interior of a trawler. They were such hospitable and cheerful people. It was a bit like taking part in a nautical version of *The Darling Buds of May*. We drank lots of beers and Tush showed us how he barbecues fish, cooking *a la plancha*. He'd bought an enormous old paella pan at a car boot sale and built a charcoal fire in his brick barbecue which stood at the side of the lawn with a seating area and tables for his friends. He threw in olive oil and took small slip soles, little dabs, gurnards that he expertly trimmed and skinned, patted them in seasoned flour and fried them. He cooked a whole sea bass in a concrete oven he'd modelled on clay oven he had seen in Greece. The fish was very overcooked but we sat and ate it in the shed, his 'gazebo', by an enormous rambling fishpond at the bottom of the garden and pronounced it excellent.

I came away from that afternoon thinking that these fishermen had something a bit special. The catches on the south coast are not spectacular, over-fishing has put paid to that, but these men were making a living. They'd seen off the council and stuck up for their rights – they had a hard life, as Laetitia shows, but they weren't complaining, they loved fishing, and felt strongly about their heritage and where they lived and they were enjoying themselves on that sunny, summer afternoon.

The south coast may not teem with fish any more but the fish it does deliver is some of the best quality anywhere in the country. It's only commercially viable, however, to small local boats like Paul Joy's that land their fish daily and sell it at the back of the beach. This is a scenario repeated all the way from West Bay to Whitstable. You can go down onto the beach and buy fantastic lemon and Dover sole, codling, whiting, monkfish, flounders, dabs plaice and tub gurnards and plaice. I've always considered plaice to be an also-ran fish; it can be great when it's very fresh but not really worth considering otherwise. That was until I went to Portland Bill and met Paul Saunders of Saunders & Wilson. He gave me a couple of plaice to take home of such quality and flavour, I would have sworn I was eating brill. It was firm, sweet and not a bit 'muddy' tasting.

The quality of the flavour is all to do with what the fish are feeding on, where they're feeding and the time of year. These plaice had recently spawned and migrated to a gravel bank off Portland called the Shambles. At the same time – early May – the Shambles is covered with seed mussels, which have thin shells and make very nutritious food for the plaice. Immediately after spawning, fish are in poor condition and need to get back their vitality as quickly as possible, hence the migration to the Shambles and the feasting frenzy on the thin-shelled mussels. It fattens them up in no time. It was some of these shellfish-fattened fish that Paul gave me – once tasted you never forget them.

Remembering those splendid plaice makes me think about the fillets that you often see on fish counters in our supermarket chains. The public demands a steady supply of the fish they know, like plaice, haddock, and cod and whiting, so the market supplies them, whatever their condition. No fish is worth eating immediately after spawning – some species lose up to half their weight – yet still the supermarkets offer either emaciated fillets or frozen fish, or fillets

WHITSTABLE IN KENT, FAMOUS FOR OYSTERS THANKS TO THE RIGHT MIX OF SILT AND SALT, IS HOME TO OTHER SHELLFISH TOO, INCLUDING MORE HUMBLE COCKLES AND WHELKS.

from other parts of northern Europe where the spawning season is slightly different. None of these tastes anything like the fresh fish in season straight off a beach in Brighton, Weymouth or Dover; no wonder people find so much fish bland and boring. If only we could accept seasonality in our fresh produce we'd enjoy it so much more.

Yes, the fish on the south coast is very good; it's a pity there aren't more good places to eat it. Of course, I found some fabulous restaurants, but so often when I followed a lead to somewhere I was disappointed. I suspect it's something to do with the lack of good chefs in this country and the difficulty of keeping them because more often than not the restaurant and décor and seaside outlook are fine, but the cooking appalling. I kept getting the feeling that I'd arrived just too late. You know the remark from Saki 'The cook was a good cook, as cooks go; and as good cooks go, she went'. That was written in about 1900 and nothing much has changed. Maybe I expected a better hit rate from the south coast because it's close to London; I found plenty of good restaurants in London but pathetically few outside. There are signs, however, that things are changing, I noticed one or two old beach kiosks that have been turned into the sort of relaxed beach eating venue they do so well in Australia.

Nevertheless, you can find very good seafood on the south coast if you plan ahead. Go down to Whitstable, for example, and try The Whitstable Oyster Fishery Company at the grandly named Royal Native Oyster Stores. I've always liked Whitstable from the first time I went there about 15 years ago to get advice from Seasalter Shellfish on growing my own oysters in Padstow. It's so much nicer now with a stylish restaurant to look forward to. Right at the other end of this stretch, probably more West Country than south coast, is what I always call Arthur and Janet's place, the Riverside Restaurant at West Bay. It's worth a serious detour – the red mullet's always full of shellfish flavour.

brandade and haricot
bean soup with truffle oil

I love white, frothy soups made with lots of beans, garlic and olive oil. I've had them in restaurants all over the place but never with the obvious enhancement of salted cod, made into the warm Mediterranean dip, brandade. This is an aromatic, friendly and nourishing soup, which would partner a Provençal rosé such as Bandol Domaine Tempier and some thick slices of rye bread with great aplomb.

SERVES 4

175 G (6 OZ) DRIED HARICOT BEANS

FRESH SALTED COD (SEE PAGE 186),
   MADE WITH 450 G (1 LB) UNSKINNED
   THICK COD FILLET

600 ML (1 PINT) CREAMY MILK

6 GARLIC CLOVES, SLICED

120 ML (4 FL OZ) OLIVE OIL

300 ML (10 FL OZ) DOUBLE CREAM

1 TABLESPOON TRUFFLE OIL

CHOPPED FLAT-LEAF PARSLEY,
   TO GARNISH

METHOD

Cover the haricot beans with plenty of cold water and leave them to soak overnight.

The next day, drain the beans and put them into a saucepan with 900 ml (1^1/$_2$ pints) of water. Bring to the boil, then cover and simmer for 1–2 hours, until they are soft and just starting to break apart. Drain, reserving the cooking liquor.

Put the prepared salted cod into a large saucepan with the milk. Bring to a simmer and cook for 4–5 minutes or until just done. Lift the cod out on to a plate and, when it is cool enough to handle, break it into flakes, discarding the skin and any bones. Reserve the milk.

Put the flaked fish into a liquidizer with the garlic. Heat the oil and cream together in a small pan until boiling, then add to the fish with the beans and blend together until smooth. With the machine still running, gradually add the reserved milk.

Return the soup to the pan and reheat gently but do not let it boil. Add a little of the bean cooking liquor, if necessary, to obtain a good consistency. Ladle the soup into 4 warmed soup bowls, drizzle over the truffle oil and garnish with a little chopped parsley.

stir-fried clams with garlic and ginger

In Southampton Water, quite close to the Transatlantic boat terminal, there used to be a large colony of hard, blue-shelled clams. They originally came from America, tossed out of the portholes of boats such as the *SS United States* and other large American liners, whose passengers had a passion for the chowders of New England and New York. The clams thrived in the warm mud and for 30 or 40 years fishing them was good business for the locals. They used to sell these beautiful molluscs to the Chinese community, who made fantastic stir-fries with them, amongst other dishes. Sadly their stocks have dwindled to almost nothing, either through over-fishing or through various mud-dredging operations. They can, however, sometimes be bought directly from fishermen (see note below).

SERVES 4

12 LARGE HARD-SHELLED CLAMS OR 36 SMALL CLAMS,
  CLEANED (SEE PAGE 188)
3 TABLESPOONS SUNFLOWER OIL
3 GARLIC CLOVES, FINELY CHOPPED
5 CM (2 INCH) PIECE OF PEELED FRESH GINGER,
  VERY FINELY SHREDDED
100 G (4 OZ) SHIITAKE MUSHROOMS, SLICED
1 HEAD OF PAK CHOI,
  SLICED INTO 2.5 CM (1 INCH) STRIPS
A GOOD PINCH OF DRIED CHILLI FLAKES
1 TABLESPOON DARK SOY SAUCE
1 TABLESPOON OYSTER SAUCE
FRESHLY GROUND SICHUAN PEPPER
  OR BLACK PEPPER
4-6 SPRING ONIONS, SLICED ON THE DIAGONAL

METHOD

Place the hard-shelled clams in a single layer in a large shallow pan with a little water. Cover and cook over a high heat for 2–3 minutes, until only just opened – this is just so you can remove the clams from the shells, not cook them completely. Slide a small knife into each shell and cut through the two muscles that hold the shells together. Break off the top shells, remove the clams from the bottom shells and slice them thinly. If using small clams, put them into a pan with 50 ml (2 fl oz) water. Cover and cook over a high heat for 2–3 minutes until just opened. Strain through a colander and when cool enough to handle, remove the meats from the shells and leave whole.

Heat a wok over a high heat. Add the oil, followed by the garlic and ginger and stir-fry for 30 seconds. Add the clams and stir-fry for another 30 seconds–1 minute, then add the mushrooms and stir-fry for 30 seconds. Add the pak choi and chilli flakes, stir-fry for 30 seconds, then add the soy sauce, oyster sauce, Sichuan or black pepper and finally the spring onions. Toss together briefly and serve.

N O T E : Blue-shelled clams can be purchased through Mick Carty, the fisherman that I went out with. Telephone (02380) 226716 for details.

moules farcies (stuffed grilled mussels)

This is the classic French stuffing for various types of shellfish, including mussels and clams. A plate of mussels, stuffed and grilled like this, delivered to you just after the bottle of chilled Muscadet has arrived in its bucket, will remind you what a delight it would be to be somewhere like Plougastel in Brittany, where the smells and tastes of good seafood are just as they always were.

SERVES 4 AS A STARTER

48 LARGE MUSSELS, CLEANED (SEE PAGE 188)

50 ML (2 FL OZ) WATER

1 LARGE GARLIC CLOVE, HALVED

1 LARGE SHALLOT, HALVED

A HANDFUL OF PARSLEY LEAVES

PARED ZEST OF $1/4$ LEMON

100 G (4 OZ) UNSALTED BUTTER, SOFTENED

75 G (3 OZ) FRESH WHITE BREADCRUMBS

SALT AND FRESHLY GROUND BLACK PEPPER

METHOD

Put the mussels and water into a large pan, cover and place over a high heat for 3–4 minutes, shaking the pan now and then, until the mussels have just opened. Drain the mussels through a colander, then break off and discard the empty half-shells, leaving the mussels in the other shell.

Pre-heat the grill to high. Very finely chop the garlic, shallot, parsley and lemon zest together – if you have one of those mini food processors it will do the job beautifully. Mix with the softened butter in a bowl and season to taste.

Dot each mussel with some of the garlic and parsley butter, then sprinkle with some of the breadcrumbs. Lay them on a baking tray and grill for about 3 minutes, or until they are crisp and golden brown. Serve immediately.

devilled mackerel
with mint and tomato salad

The tradition of devilling food in English cooking goes back over 150 years. To me, it seems to be a bit of a Victorian joke for describing highly spicy food, and while the idea may have come from India at some time the flavourings are essentially British: mustard, cayenne, pepper and vinegar. The coating offsets the oiliness of the mackerel most pleasingly and you'll find the simple tomato salad a perfect accompaniment.

SERVES 4

4 X 350 G (12 OZ) MACKEREL,
   CLEANED AND TRIMMED
40 G (1$^{1}/_{2}$ OZ) BUTTER
1 TEASPOON CASTER SUGAR
1 TEASPOON ENGLISH MUSTARD POWDER
1 TEASPOON CAYENNE PEPPER
1 TEASPOON PAPRIKA
1 TEASPOON GROUND CORIANDER
2 TABLESPOONS RED WINE VINEGAR
1 TEASPOON FRESHLY GROUND BLACK PEPPER
2 TEASPOONS SALT

FOR THE MINT AND TOMATO SALAD:

225 G (8 OZ) SMALL, VINE-RIPENED TOMATOES,
   SLICED
1 SMALL ONION, HALVED AND VERY THINLY SLICED
1 TABLESPOON CHOPPED MINT
1 TABLESPOON FRESH LEMON JUICE

METHOD

Pre-heat the grill to high. Slash the skin of the mackerel at 1 cm ($^{1}/_{2}$ inch) intervals on both sides, from the head all the way down to the tail, taking care not to cut too deeply into the flesh.

Melt the butter in a shallow flameproof dish or roasting tin. Remove from the heat, stir in the sugar, mustard, spices, vinegar, pepper and salt and mix together well. Add the mackerel to the butter and turn them over once or twice until well coated in the mixture, spreading some into the cavity of each fish as well. Transfer them to a lightly oiled baking sheet or the rack of the grill pan and grill for 4 minutes on each side, until cooked through.

Meanwhile, layer the sliced tomatoes, onion and mint on 4 serving plates, sprinkling the layers with the lemon juice and some seasoning. Put the cooked mackerel alongside and serve, with some fried sliced potatoes if you wish.

grey mullet and pasta
with sage, garlic and fennel

I love this dish. Throughout this book I have tried to find ideas that bring out the unique properties of each species of fish best, and I think this makes grey mullet taste better than I've ever known it taste before. The flavours of the sage, garlic and fennel with olive oil, concentrated around the small steaks of fish, make eating this plate of pasta a delight. As with so many of the recipes in this book, I have tried to keep things as simple as possible so that it's the sort of thing you will cook, rather than the sort of thing you think it would be nice to cook some day.

SERVES 4

50 ML (2 FL OZ) EXTRA VIRGIN OLIVE OIL

1 HEAD OF GARLIC, BROKEN INTO CLOVES

A HANDFUL OF SAGE LEAVES

1/2 TEASPOON FENNEL SEEDS

175 G (6 OZ) DRIED SPAGHETTI

A 900 G-1.5 KG (2-3 LB) GREY MULLET,
   CLEANED AND CUT INTO STEAKS
   4 CM (1 1/2 INCHES) THICK

50 ML (2 FL OZ) DRY WHITE WINE

SALT AND FRESHLY GROUND BLACK PEPPER

METHOD

Bring a large pan of well-salted water to the boil. Meanwhile, heat the oil in a large sauté pan, add the unpeeled garlic cloves, the sage leaves and fennel seeds and fry over a low heat for 5 minutes, until the garlic is soft and lightly browned.

Add the spaghetti to the pan of boiling water and cook for 8–9 minutes or until *al dente*. Meanwhile, season the grey mullet steaks on both sides with salt and pepper. Push the flavourings to the side of the sauté pan and add the steaks. Increase the heat and fry for 3 minutes on each side, until lightly browned. Add the wine to the pan, cover and cook for 3 minutes or until the fish is cooked through. Lift the steaks out on to a plate, cover and keep hot.

Drain the spaghetti, add it to the remaining juices in the pan and toss together well so that it picks up the garlic, sage and fennel. Adjust the seasoning if necessary. Divide the spaghetti between 4 warmed plates and top with the fish steaks. Serve with some crisp green salad leaves.

eliza acton's sole
cooked in cream

Although I've done recipes for fillets of Dover sole in the past, I can't help thinking it's far better cooked and served on the bone. In this dish the whole fish is not poached, but rather braised, in cream. It sounds as though it could be exceedingly rich but it's not. The pleasure of the dish lies in a particularly British combination of firm fillets of sole and a small amount of unctuous cream flavoured with cayenne pepper, mace and lemon juice.

SERVES 2

2 X 275–350 G (10–12 OZ) DOVER SOLES, SKINNED

BUTTER FOR GREASING

A GOOD PINCH OF CAYENNE PEPPER

A GOOD PINCH OF GROUND MACE

250 ML (8 FL OZ) DOUBLE CREAM

2 TEASPOONS FRESH LEMON JUICE

1 TABLESPOON CHOPPED PARSLEY

SALT

METHOD

Pre-heat the oven to 230°C/450°F/Gas Mark 8.

Place the skinned Dover soles side by side, slightly overlapping if necessary, in a buttered shallow baking dish and sprinkle them with some salt, the cayenne pepper and ground mace. Pour the cream over the fish and bake for 10–12 minutes, by which time the fish should be cooked through and the cream reduced and thickened.

Carefully transfer the fish to warmed serving plates. Stir the lemon juice and parsley into the sauce and adjust the seasoning if necessary. Spoon the sauce over the fish and serve with some small, boiled new potatoes.

gurnard fillets with a potato, garlic and saffron broth

Gurnard is chiefly used in this country as bait for lobster pots, and jolly good bait it is too, but that seems to me a poignant example of how little we value our seafood. In America they use chicken necks and bulls' noses for their crab pots – I wonder if anyone has thought of trying these things over here? Maybe they would if we learnt to value gurnard as highly as they do in France and Spain. It's a delight, firm and sweet, and it always makes me think of the bright pink colour of lots of seafood all around the Mediterranean. So I've come up with a dish of saffron, garlic and oregano-flavoured potatoes to echo the flavours of that part of the world. If you can't buy gurnard, bream makes a good alternative.

SERVES 4

4 TABLESPOONS EXTRA VIRGIN OLIVE OIL

4-6 SPRIGS OF OREGANO,
   PLUS 1¹/₂ TEASPOONS CHOPPED OREGANO

1 SMALL HEAD OF GARLIC, BROKEN INTO CLOVES

50 ML (2 FL OZ) DRY WHITE WINE

1 LEEK, CLEANED AND SLICED

550 G (1¹/₄ LB) POTATOES, PEELED AND
   THICKLY SLICED

600 ML (1 PINT) *FISH* OR *CHICKEN STOCK*
   (SEE PAGE 185)

A PINCH OF SAFFRON STRANDS

4 X 450 G (1 LB) GURNARD, CLEANED AND FILLETED

2 TABLESPOONS *ROUILLE* (SEE PAGE 187)

1 TEASPOON CAPERS IN BRINE, DRAINED AND RINSED

SALT AND FRESHLY GROUND BLACK PEPPER

METHOD

Heat 2 tablespoons of the oil in a medium saucepan. Add the oregano sprigs and unpeeled garlic cloves and cook for 2 minutes, until the garlic is lightly browned. Remove the pan from the heat, cool a little, then add the wine. Return to the heat and boil rapidly until it has almost completely evaporated. Add the leek to the pan and cook, stirring, for 1 minute. Add the sliced potatoes with the stock, saffron and some seasoning, then cover and leave to simmer for 15–20 minutes until the potatoes are tender.

Shortly before the potatoes are ready, heat the rest of the olive oil in a large frying pan. Add the gurnard fillets, skin-side down, and fry for 2 minutes, until lightly browned. Turn over and fry for another minute or until they have cooked through and are lightly browned on both sides.

Put the rouille into a small bowl and whisk in 50 ml (2 fl oz) of slightly cooled cooking liquor from the pan of potatoes. Stir this back into the pan and cook over a gentle heat for about 1 minute, being careful not to let it boil or it will curdle. Divide the potatoes and their liquor between 4 warmed soup plates and place the gurnard fillets on top. Sprinkle with the capers and chopped oregano and serve.

fried john dory
with rémoulade sauce

Rather a nice way of cooking fish outdoors. It doesn't always have to be a barbecue. Just get yourself a big frying pan, some flour, salt and olive oil and you may never go back to burnt bits of fish squished between the grill bars again.

SERVES 4

4 X 225-350 G (8-12 OZ) JOHN DORY,
　CLEANED
2 TEASPOONS SALT
175 ML (6 FL OZ) OLIVE OIL
50 G (2 OZ) PLAIN FLOUR
LEMON WEDGES, TO SERVE

FOR THE RÉMOULADE SAUCE:

1/2 QUANTITY OF *MUSTARD*
　MAYONNAISE (SEE PAGE 186)
25 G (1 OZ) GHERKINS, CHOPPED
15 G (1/2 OZ) CAPERS IN BRINE, DRAINED,
　RINSED AND COARSELY CHOPPED
1 TABLESPOON EACH COARSELY CHOPPED
　PARSLEY, CHERVIL AND TARRAGON
1 ANCHOVY FILLET IN OLIVE OIL,
　DRAINED AND FINELY CHOPPED
1 TEASPOON DIJON MUSTARD
SALT

METHOD

Trim away the fins of each John Dory, as close to the flesh as you can, and season each one inside and out with the salt. Set aside for 15 minutes. Meanwhile, mix together the ingredients for the rémoulade sauce.

Heat the olive oil in a large frying pan. Pat the fish dry on kitchen paper and then coat them in the flour, patting off the excess.

Shallow-fry the fish, one or two at a time, over a medium-high heat until crisp, golden and cooked through – about 3 minutes on each side for smaller fish, 4 minutes on each side for larger ones. Drain briefly on kitchen paper and keep warm in a low oven while you cook the rest of the fish. Serve with the rémoulade sauce and lemon wedges.

warm squid salad
with green beans, ceps and hazelnut oil

I wrote this to take advantage of the method of cooking large squid down in Portland Bill, the big rock that feels like an island off the coast of Dorset. We spent an amiable evening jigging for quiddles, as they call squid there, in a little rowing boat just off Chesil Beach. It was a cold, clear dusk as we sculled the boat under a harvest moon. We went back to Ken Lyneham's house and cooked the squid in a pressure cooker till they were soft and full of flavour, then sat down to high tea and ate them with butter, vinegar and lots of sliced bread. They were amazingly tender and the cooking had concentrated the flavours. I thought the steamed quiddles would be great in a warm salad but actually I think they taste better for this when sliced and seared in a hot frying pan.

SERVES 4 AS A STARTER

450 G (1 LB) MEDIUM-SIZED SQUID, CLEANED (SEE PAGE 189)

50 G (2 OZ) FRESH CEPS OR CHESTNUT MUSHROOMS

75 G (3 OZ) FRENCH BEANS, TRIMMED AND HALVED

2 TABLESPOONS OLIVE OIL

50 G (2 OZ) LAMB'S LETTUCE (CORN SALAD)

A SMALL HANDFUL OF CHERVIL SPRIGS

SALT AND FRESHLY GROUND BLACK PEPPER

FOR THE DRESSING:

1 1/2 TABLESPOONS CHAMPAGNE VINEGAR
  OR GOOD-QUALITY WHITE WINE VINEGAR

2 TABLESPOONS HAZELNUT OIL

4 TABLESPOONS OLIVE OIL

1/2 TEASPOON SALT

METHOD

Cut along one side of each squid pouch and open it out flat. Cut in half lengthways and then cut across on the diagonal into slices 1 cm (1/2 inch) thick. Separate the tentacles if large.

Wipe and trim the mushrooms, then slice them. Cook the beans in boiling salted water for 2–3 minutes, until just done but still a little crunchy. Drain and keep warm. For the dressing, whisk all the ingredients together and set aside.

Heat the olive oil in a large, heavy-based frying pan, add the squid and sear over a high heat, stirring now and then, for 2 minutes, until lightly browned in places. Tip on to a plate, season with salt and pepper and leave to cool slightly.

To serve, arrange the lamb's lettuce, French beans, sliced mushrooms, chervil sprigs and squid on 4 large plates. Spoon over the dressing, grind over a little black pepper and serve while the squid is still warm.

RESTAURANTS SERVING GOOD SEAFOOD

Burton Bradstock, Dorset
The Hive
Beach Road
Burton Bradstock DT5 3RF
Tel: (01308) 897070

Directions
Right on the beach.

Grilled fish and salad on the beach at Burton Bradstock. Jerry Page manages to lease this kiosk from the local council and has turned it into just the sort of relaxed beach-side café that you would find anywhere in Sydney.

Southbourne, Bournemouth, Dorset
Bistro on the Beach
Solent Promenade
Southbourne Coast Road
Bournemouth BH6 4BE
Tel: (01202) 431473
Fax: (01202) 252091
E-mail: bistro@ryancatering.fsuk

Directions
Park at the top of the cliff and walk down on to the beach-side path.

south coast selection

The chef, David Ryan, said they'd been full for four and a half years. I can well understand it; the largely seafood menu is lively, the cooking pretty sparkly and the prices in no way frightening. Bistro on the Beach is more on the beach than is sometimes good for it – during winter storms the waves literally smash against the windows. It's all great fun. I had a seafood salad – just scallops, squid and mussels – all freshly cooked, and tossed with curly endive and tomato in slightly sweet balsamic and olive oil

dressing; then I went for a plain grilled Dover sole, which was perfectly cooked, and lots of well-cooked vegetables – far too much of course, but that's what the British appreciate.

West Bay, Dorset
Marsh Barn Restaurant
Burton Road
Bridport DT6 4PS
Tel: (01308) 422755
(Closed Mondays – open only until 6 p.m.)

Directions
Take the B3157 out of Bridport towards Burton Bradstock. The restaurant is at the junction with the first small turning on the right.

Just out of West Bay there's a converted barn owned by David Sales, a lobster and crab fisherman. He catches and his wife, Jill, cooks. They're salt of the earth Dorset locals, and the cooking is in no way fancy, but the crab pâté and the West Bay crab and lobster salads are extremely good. The restaurant itself is a delight – stone walls embedded with ammonite fossils, high old beams with lobster pots hanging from them, stripped wood floors and red-and-white-checked tablecloths – it is what it is, no more and no less.

West Bay, Dorset
The Riverside Restaurant
West Bay DT6 4EZ
Tel: (01308) 422011
Fax: (01308) 458808

Directions
Right by the harbour in the centre of West Bay.

Arthur and Janet Watson's Riverside Restaurant has provided me with an image of the sort of place I had hoped to see everywhere around the coast of Britain and Ireland. It seems to fit naturally into a niche between a British café and a French restaurant so that nobody eating there feels anything but completely at ease. The last time I was there it was August after a hot morning's filming what they call GVs (general vision shots) where I walk past the camera, normally with Chalky, for 17 takes using different lenses. This time I walked up a hill 17 times, so I was pretty puffed, as was Chalky. I had a couple of glasses of Riverside Jurançon sec, and my companion a bowl of water. I ate John Dory fillet on salad leaves with feta, caper berries and balsamic dressing, followed by a simply grilled lobster. Arthur came out from the kitchen and did a passionate piece to the camera about over-fishing on the south coast, where he described the sea bed after a beamer trawler had been over it as just like a ploughed field.

Seaview, Isle of Wight
The Priory Oyster
Priory Bay Hotel
Priory Drive
Seaview PO34 5BU
Tel (mobile): (07974) 431352 or (01983) 613146 for the hotel
Fax (hotel): (01983) 616539
E-mail (hotel): ejb@priorybay.co.uk
Website (hotel): www.priorybay.co.uk

Directions
On the main road between Nettlestone and St Helens.

The Priory Oyster is a summer pavilion above the beach, down a long forest track from the beautiful Priory Bay Hotel. You will certainly enjoy a stay there – the rooms are fabulous, and if you're there in the summer months, you can eat some great seafood on the deck looking out over the Solent. The quality of everything I had at lunch testified to a love of only the freshest produce from the sea. I had perfect moules marinières and grilled Bembridge lobster, but there was also dressed crab salad, lobster or fish of the day from the barbecue and plateâu de fruits de mer for 1 or 2 people made up of lobster, crab, langoustines, clams, mussels, whelks, prawns, oysters and winkles. Check on their opening times as they tend to be seasonal.

Sandgate, Kent
Restaurant La Terrasse
Sandgate Hotel
The Esplanade
Sandgate
Folkestone
Kent CT20 3DY
Tel: (01303) 220444
Fax: (01303) 220496

Directions
Overlooking the sea on the coast road between Sandgate and Hythe.

I remember seeing an article about the Sandgate Hotel and thinking thank goodness someone's had the sense to take a traditional, pretty seaside hotel and do something intelligent with it. When I finally got to eat there, I was so excited just walking into the place and seeing how well they had realized my dream. It feels like being in La Rochelle: everyone is French, the menu's in French and the cooking

owes nothing to any other country, serving only to remind you of how bloody good French seafood cooking is. Just imagine this: three plump scallops with a little pocket cut into each side, the thinnest sliver of black truffle pushed in, the scallops seared in a hot pan with a lick of butter and served on some discs of new potato cooked until soft and creamy in some elusive, faintly fragrant stock, then this surrounded with a reduction of truffle juice. I need say no more.

Whitstable, Kent
The Whitstable Oyster Fishery Company
Royal Native Oyster Stores
The Horsebridge
Whitstable CT5 1BU
Tel: (01227) 276856
Fax: (01227) 770666
Website: www.oysterfishery.co.uk

Directions
Right on the pebble beach.

It would be hard to imagine a more exciting setting for a restaurant than a restored oyster store with views through the windows of the sea, pebbles and boats pulled up on the beach. It's all exposed brick and natural wood, and there's an enormous cold counter laden with oysters, mussels, wet fish, lobsters and crabs, which are cooked simply and served most unpretentiously in the restaurant. I felt quite understanding on the August bank holiday that I visited, when one of the owners admitted he'd probably rather be doing something else. The restaurant is incredibly busy and he was suffering from what I call the 'August blues' – in other words, fatigue from cooking too many meals. But as one of my friends once observed, 'You're moaning with your wheelbarrow filled with cash all the way to the bank.' As soon as it gets a

bit quieter in September, enthusiasm for cooking in restaurants comes flooding back. Anyway, the native oysters from Whitstable were all that I had hoped they would be, as was the roasted sea bass with garlic and rosemary.

Brighton, East Sussex
The Regency Restaurant
131 King's Road
Brighton
BN1 2HH
Tel: (01273) 325014
Fax: (01273) 747028
Website: www.theregencyrestaurant.com

Directions
On the seafront, opposite the west pier.

Thank God for Greek Cypriots –they can usually be relied upon to lay on simple, fresh seafood in cafés catering to local tastes. This is just an ordinary, corner-of-the-street restaurant run by two university-educated brothers, Roberto and Emilio, who decided that they wanted to get back to the more important things in life, such as cooking good food. The menu is unpretentious and includes fried calamari, grilled Dover sole, oysters au nature, grilled red mullet and John Dory, with great Greek salads and, of course, ice cold retsina.

PUBS SERVING GOOD SEAFOOD

Bembridge, Isle of Wight
Crab and Lobster Inn
Bembridge PO35 5TR
Tel: (01983) 872244
Fax: (01983) 875349

Directions
Signposted from village centre.

This is a pub with a fairly uneventful menu except, that is, when their prawns are in season. Then you can order a pint mug of huge, plump, bright orange-and-pink-striped Bembridge prawns with mayonnaise, lemon and crusty bread and butter. And it's a great location, overlooking Bembridge beach.

FISH AND CHIPS

Westbourne, Bournemouth, Dorset
Chez Fred
Seamoor Road
Westbourne
Bournemouth BH4 9AN
Tel: (01202) 761023
Fax: (01202) 764133
Website: www.chezfred.co.uk

Directions

One mile from Bournemouth town centre towards Poole.

The thing I remember most about Chez Fred is the wall covered with pictures of all the stars who have eaten fish and chips there: Cliff Richard, Max Bygraves, Bobby Davro and Jools Holland, among others. Fred's brother also has a chippy in Seabourne Road, Bournemouth (Tel: 01202 426158) called Chez Nick.

Weymouth, Dorset
Fish n Fritz
9 Market Street
Weymouth DT4 8DD
Tel: (01305) 766386

Directions

From Customs House Quay, walk up the road running by the Ship Inn and it'll be on your right.

I must admit that sometimes I have to eat two lunches and two dinners in order to try out as much as possible. When I got to Fish n Fritz's, I honestly didn't want any more food, but I tasted the fish and chips and decided that they were extremely good. As I came out of the shop, I offered the rest to two cold, shivering boys with surf boards. They looked at me like I was mad, and said, actually quite kindly, 'Thanks, but Mum and Dad own the shop.'

Lymington, Hampshire
The Spinnaker
130 High Street
Lymington SO41 9AQ
Tel: (01590) 677850

Directions

In the high street at the bottom of the hill, just near the sharp bend.

A good, busy shop in this pleasantly old-fashioned Georgian town on the Solent in Hampshire. It has both a restaurant and a take-away.

Portsmouth, Hampshire
Still & West
Bath Square
Portsmouth PO1 2JL
Tel: (023) 9282 1567
Fax: (023) 9282 6569

Directions

Follow the signs for the Isle of Wight ferry, and the brown tourist signs for Old Portsmouth Town. Head for the waterfront and the pub is hidden away around a corner.

It's very reassuring that a pub as famous as this should have been

renovated as well as this, but it's such a shame that the newspaper in which the fish and chips used to be sold has been discarded. What is it about newspaper – is it the printer's ink, are there terrible tales of people curling up and dying after a surfeit of fish and chips? It didn't seem to do me any harm as a boy, and, gosh, I used to love the smell. Anyway, the cod and chips were immaculate: a really thick piece of fresh cod straight out of the fryer, and you can't get much more nautical than having the Isle of Wight ferry pass within 30 yards of where you're sitting.

Shanklin, Isle of Wight
June's Fish Bar
87 High Street
Shanklin Old Village PO37 6NR
Tel: (01983) 868570

Directions

In the Old Village, opposite the main car park.

Big, thick pieces of very fresh cod in crisp batter. In the restaurant everything was served, reassuringly, on those rather thick, pale green plates that we are all so familiar with.

FISHMONGERS

Brighton, East Sussex
Alan and Carol Hayes
201 Kings Road Arches
Brighton BN1 1NB
Tel: (01273) 723064

Directions

Half-way between the two piers, situated in the arches that back the promenade at sea level, right next to the Brighton Fishing Museum.

This tiny fishmonger's has a small selection of fresh fish, but they have the supreme advantage of it coming straight off the boats. On the day I visited they had little more than mackerel, but who cares with mackerel of that quality.

Milford on Sea, Dorset
Monk & Son
98 High Street
Milford on Sea SO41 0QE
Tel: (01590) 642176
Fax: (01590) 643230

Directions

In the centre of the village, on the road towards Keyhaven.

Mr Monk and his staff were serving at this tiny fish shop in Milford the day I visited but, sadly, there was nothing much left to buy. The shop is so

small and the fish so good that it more or less swims out of the door, so you have to get there early. But isn't this how fishmongers should be? We've been conditioned by supermarkets to expect constant supplies of all species, even on Mondays. Wouldn't it be great to have a fishmonger like this in every town? And, by the way, they are always willing to deliver, no matter how small the order.

West Bay, Dorset
Samways
Station Road
West Bay DT6 4EN
Tel: (01308) 424496
Fax: (01308) 423903
E-mail: admin@samways-fish.co.uk

Directions

On the road running away from the back of the harbour.

You hear so many depressing stories of fishmongers going out of business and citing encroaching supermarkets as the reason that it's a real pleasure to find one fishmonger whose boss says the business is doing very nicely and who doesn't regard the supermarkets as a problem. Supermarket bosses themselves aver that good fishmongers and butchers will always thrive. That is exactly what Samways is – a good fishmonger. On the day we visited, owner David Williams had a fantastic selection. Here's a few fish to give you an idea. Turbot, both whole and filleted, halibut, John Dory, octopus, cuttlefish, gurnard fillets, whole plaice, black bream, megrim soles and brill. He was getting some nice hake in the next morning, he had all 'the oilys' – herring, mackerel, salmon and sardines, prawns, mussels, oysters – and even some bloaters. They make their own fish cakes and have a good stock of deli items to go with fish, as well as compatible vegetables, such as lemon, shallots, parsley and coriander. They do fresh lobster and crab to order. 'God's in his heaven and all's right with the world.'

Hastings, East Sussex
Rock-a-Nore Fisheries
3 Rock-a-Nore Road
Hastings TN34 3DW
Tel/Fax: (01424) 445425

Directions
Up a narrow alleyway opposite the black fishing sheds, next to the Mermaid Restaurant.

I mentioned the net-drying sheds in the introduction to this chapter. You could tie in a visit to them with a trip to Rock-a-Nore Fisheries, which is just opposite. They were unloading boxes of very fresh squid, grey mullet, sea bass, small monkfish tails, Dover soles, lemon soles and plaice on to a mountain of ice while we were there.

Hove, East Sussex
Gibson & Coe
49 George Street
Hove BN3 3YB
Tel/Fax: (01273) 731407
E-mail: alan.gibson.cwcom.net
Website: www.gibsonandcoe.co.uk

Directions
In a pedestrianized street off Church Road, opposite Boots the Chemists. This street is closed to cars between 10 a.m. and 4 p.m.

On a few occasions during my travels, I've noticed that the local butcher is also the fishmonger. Since both professions are under threat from the incursion of supermarkets, it makes quite a lot of sense. The skills of both professions are similar, and the enthusiasm for quality materials shown by shops like Gibson & Coe inspire confidence in their customers. I must say I was delighted to see some garfish the day I visited – it's all too hard to get hold of this green-boned delicacy these days, although you can catch them quite readily in early summer on the south coast.

Hove, East Sussex
Kevin's of Hove
17 Richardson Road
Hove BN3 5RB
Tel: (01273) 738779

Directions
Slightly out of the centre of town, off New Church Road in the side street alongside the church.

I have friends in Brighton who use Kevin's regularly and say the fish is excellent, always fresh and always consistent. His smoked haddock is a speciality – it's undyed and has no chemical additives.

Rye, East Sussex
Fish R Us
1 Rope Walk
Rye TN31 7NA
Tel (mobile): (07714) 696225

Directions
Just off the main road passing through the town.

The boat's called the Angelina, and whatever they catch goes straight into Fish R Us, their tiny fish shop. The display was small but select and all the fish that day – gurnard, skate, red mullet, turbot and brill – were very fresh. It's sometimes difficult to get them on the phone, but they're open six days a week, so it's definitely worth dropping in if you're in the area.

Hythe, Kent
Grigg's of Hythe
Fisherman's Landing Beach
Hythe CT21 6HG
Tel: (01303) 266410
Fax: (01303) 262943

Directions
Take the turning off the coast road, opposite the Stade Court Hotel. Follow the road along the shore, take the next on the left and you'll see the sign on the left.

'You name it and we've got it.' I had no reason to disagree with Michael Jaggar on the day I visited Grigg's. They had a large selection of fantastically fresh 'summer' fish, including dabs, Dover soles, cuttlefish, sea bass, gurnard, turbot and brill; in winter they land red mullet, conger, pollock, cod and whiting, all of it straight off the boats that pull up on to the beach outside their large shed. They also had Whitstable oysters, local cockles, a wide selection of shellfish and they smoke their own fish too.

SEAFOOD SUPPLIERS

Portland Bill, Dorset
Saunders & Wilson
17 Chiswell
Portland DT5 1AN
Tel: (01305) 822997
Fax: (01305) 861036

Directions
Drive on to 'The Bill' and at the first roundabout, instead of following the through traffic signs, go straight on. The shop will be facing you.

I met Paul Saunders in Portland when we went fishing for squid off Chesil

Beach. He's not a fisherman, but he has a fisherman's knowledge of where the best fish comes from on the south coast. I can listen to him for hours talking about fishing for sea bass in the Portland Bill race off Pulpit Rock, or why the plaice caught on the Shambles Bank are so good. He's got a thriving wholesale business supplying some pretty famous London restaurants, and his retail shop on Portland is a must if you're in the area. Don't forget to ask for those plaice – they don't taste at all 'muddy' – they're up there in quality with turbot and brill. The shop has extensive vivier tanks, and you can buy great lobsters, crabs (both spiders and browns) and hand-dived scallops.

Weymouth, Dorset
Abbotsbury Oysters
Ferryman's Way
Ferrybridge
Weymouth DT4 9YU
Tel: (01305) 788867
Fax: (01305) 760661

Directions
Take a small turning to the right after the roundabout, just before the causeway for Portland.

I hope that now they've built a brand-new shed for eating oysters that Abbotsbury Oysters don't dismantle the charming, rough wooden counter and chairs to match under an old lean-to at the side of the original oyster shed. The new café is looking good – you can eat their Pacific oysters 'au naturel' with lemon and bread and butter, or their mussels as moules marinières, and whole Portland crab. Oysters and mussels can be bought from the door or by mail-order. It would be great if there were more shacks like this all around the coast.

Whitstable, Kent
Seasalter Shellfish
East Quay
The Harbour
Whitstable CT5 1AB
Tel: (01227) 272003
Fax: (01227) 264829
E-mail: seasalter@compuserve.com
Website: www.seasaltershellfish.co.uk

Directions
Right on the harbour.

In their small retail outlet, Seasalter Shellfish, the home of Whitstable oysters, sell Pacific and native oysters and, very importantly, carpetshell clams, which are known as *palourdes* in France and *vongole* in Italy. These are farmed and, in my opinion, are the best-tasting clams in the world.

SMOKERIES

Bridport, Dorset
Bridfish
Unit 1
The Old Laundry Industrial Estate
Sea Road North
Bridport DT6 3BD
Tel: (01308) 456306
Fax: (01308) 456367
E-mail: bridsmoke@clara.co.uk

Directions
Take the A3066 out of Bridport
towards Beaminster. Bridfish is almost
immediately on the left.

Bridfish has a good selection of trout,
mackerel, kippers and salmon, plus eel,
which Dorset people jokingly refer to as
'smoked worms'. They also produce
some rather attractive presentation
boxes such as the 'Great Bridfish
Breakfast' – kippers, smoked haddock
and smoked streaky bacon, with some
marmalade, smoked cheese and a
bottle of Cox's apple juice.

OTHER PLACES WHERE I'VE EATEN GOOD FISH RECENTLY

Bray, Berkshire
Waterside Inn
Bray SL6 2AT
Tel: (01628) 620691
Fax: (01628) 784710

East Grinstead, W. Sussex
Gravetye Manor
Vowels Lane
Near East Grinstead
RH19 4LJ
Tel: (01342) 810567
Fax: (01342) 810080

Rowde, Wiltshire
The George and Dragon
High Street
Rowde SN10 2PN
Tel: (01380) 723053
Fax: (01380) 724738
E-mail: gd-rowde@lineone.net

...AND THE BEST PLACES TO EAT SEAFOOD IN THE CAPITAL

Bibendum Oyster Bar
Michelin House
81 Fulham Road
SW3 6RD
Tel: (020) 7581 5817
Fax: (020) 7823 7925
E-mail: manager@bibendum.co.uk

I'm suprised that almost no one else in
London seems to have grasped the
enormous selling potential of having
your seafood on ice almost on the
pavement, but you'd hardly see a
better display in Paris than the Michelin
Building forecourt on the Fulham Road
with the little blue Citroën van spilling
out boxes of oysters and a massive ice
display of crustacea and molluscs.
It puts you in a mood to sit down at the
elegant oyster bar inside and order
selections of oysters from all over
Great Britain and Ireland, or
langoustines, lobster or crab if you
prefer, or best of all, the plateau de
fruits de mer and the Muscadet.

Fish
Cathedral Street
SE1 9AL
Tel: (020) 7234 3333
Fax: (020) 7234 3343
E-mail: fish@bgr.plc.uk
Website: www.info@fishdiner.co.uk

Seafood lovers owe Tony Allen a debt.
About fifteen years ago, he and a fellow
chef, Ron Truss, started a small fish
wholesaling business in the Old Kent
Road. They bought straight from the
coast, gave the chefs what they
wanted, and flourished exceedingly.
They opened Bank restaurant in
Aldgate (see page 55), and have since
launched into a chain of cheaper
restaurants called Fish with the aim of
selling what is best on the market and
keeping it simple. The first Fish, at
Borough Market has been yet another
blinding success. On the evening I went
there they had halibut, sea bass, lemon
sole, monkfish, brill and fish and chips
with mushy peas. For starters there
were potted shrimps, a great prawn
cocktail, dressed crab, and mussels
with chilli and coriander. The only thing
was, being a conventional sort of
person underneath, I suppose, I prefer
the chef to decide what I'm going to
eat. You see, you have to decide how
your fish is going to be cooked, then
what sort of sauce you want to go with
it and so on. If you're a novice or a bit
pissed, it's a tricky assignment.

Mandarin Kitchen
14–16 Queensway
W2 3RX
Tel/Fax: (020) 7727 9012

You've got to hand it to the Chinese,
they know their seafood. So it's not for
no reason that on the Mandarin
Kitchen's menu, it says, 'We only serve
the finest Scottish wild lobsters simply
because they are probably the best in
the world.' The last meal I had there
was what I'd class as memorable,
mainly due to one dish – lobster with
ginger, spring onions and noodles.
What astonished me was how very
willing they were to part with the
recipe; I always thought Chinese
cooks were a bit secretive. We had a
very good chef working for us called
David Wong, who now runs the
Mandarin Hotel in Singapore. I once
asked him for a recipe for proper
sweet and sour pork – he said, 'I don't
know, I just watch my mum.'.

Sheekey's
28–32 St Martin's Court
WC2N 4AL
Tel: (020) 7240 2565
Fax: (020) 7240 8114
E-mail: reservations@j-sheekey.co.uk

This has to be one of my favourite
restaurants in the whole world.
The depth of thinking Jeremy King,
Christopher Corbin and chef Mark
Hicks put into the décor, service and
food in all their restaurants, i.e.
Sheekey, The Ivy and The Caprice,
makes most of the rest of us look like
amateurs. Eating there is such a
pleasurable experience, I would defy
even a icthyophobe not to enjoy eating
fish in this restaurant, everything is so
scrumptious. A list of my favourites
includes jellied eels, shrimps from
Yarmouth, sole belle Hélène, chargrilled
squid with chorizo, smoked cod with
poached egg and enormous grilled
Dover sole, which will set you back a
bob or two, but is the one fish I can
keep eating and never get tired of.

Zilli Fish
36–40 Brewer Street
Soho
London W1F 9TB
Tel: (020) 7734 8649

You could find the interior of Zilli Fish
either slightly irritating or very soothing
being done out, as it is, like the
bottom of the sea complete with a
corner decked out with wave-like
banquette seating and blue
downlights. Either way, you wouldn't
have anything but praise for Aldo's
Italian seafood which is vivid,
straightforward and fresh. Simple
sautés of squid with garlic and olive oil
and a winning way with lobster,
tomato and pasta. Like the robust
cooking, Aldo himself is quite larger
than life too, no question where the
buzz and bustle of this corner
restaurant in Soho emanates from.

GOOD FISH AND CHIPS

Fish Central
149–151 Kings Square
Central Street
EC1V 8AP
Tel: (020) 7253 4970

A very busy restaurant with good fish and chips and a simple, clean, Cypriot way with fish.

....AND SOME GOOD FISHMONGERS IN LONDON

Alexander & Knight
18 High St
Barnes
SW13 6TY
Tel: (020) 8876 1297

They also have another shop, Knights Fisheries, at 20 Station Parade, Virginia Water, Surrey GU25 4AE. Tel: (01344) 842634; Fax: (020) 8643 2235.

Blagden Fishmongers
65 Paddington Street
W1M 3RR
Tel/Fax: (020) 7935 8321
E-mail: blagfish@vossnet.co.uk

Chalmers & Gray
67 Notting Hill Gate
W11 3JS
Tel: (020) 7221 6177
Fax: (020) 7727 3907

Covent Garden Fishmongers
37 Turnham Green Terrace
W4 1RG
Tel: (020) 8995 9273
Fax: (020) 8742 3899
Website:
www.fishmongersagenet.com

The Good Harvest Fish & Meat Market
14 Newport Place
London WC2H 7PR
Tel: (020) 7437 0712

This is a very good fish shop in London's Chinatown which serves the large number of Chinese restaurants in this part of London. On the day I visited they had an exciting variety of live shellfish: scallops, cockles, large American-style clams, razor clams, oysters, mussels, and even Asian-blue swimming crabs from the Far East. There were washing-up bowls full of different-sized raw prawns, un-cleaned squid and cuttlefish, together with a display of grey mullet, black and pink bream, sea bass, whole scabbard fish, Dutch eels, rainbow trout, grouper, conger eel, all those things that you would expect to see on the menu of a good Chinese restaurant.

La Marée
76 Sloane Avenue
SW3 3DZ
Tel: (020) 7589 8067
Fax: (020) 7581 3360

Shop of fish restaurant La Poissonnerie de l'Avenue, 78 Sloane Avenue, SW3 3DZ. Tel: (020) 7589 2457; Fax: (020) 7581 3360.

Le Pont de la Tour Smoked Fish & Crustacea Store
The Butlers Wharf Building
36d Shad Thames
SE1 2YE
Tel: (020) 7403 4030
Fax: (020) 7403 0267
Website: www.conran.com

Steve Hatt
88–90 Essex Road
N1 8LU
Tel: (020) 7226 3963

OTHER PLACES WHERE I'VE EATEN GOOD FISH IN THE CAPITAL

Alastair Little
49 Frith Street
W1V 5TE
Tel: (020) 7734 5183

Assaggi
39 Chepstow Place
W2 4TS
Tel: (020) 7792 5501

Bank
1 Kingsway
WC2 6XF
Tel: (020) 7234 3344
Website: www.bankrestaurant.co.uk

Le Caprice
Arlington House, Arlington Street
SW1A 1RT
Tel: (020) 7629 2239
Fax: (020) 7493 9040

Clarke's
124 Kensington Church Street
W8 4BH
Tel: (020) 7221 9225
Website: www.sallyclarke.com

Coast
26b Albermarle Street
W1S 4HY
Tel: (020) 7495 5999

Fifth Floor, Harvey Nichols
Knightsbridge/corner of Sloane Street
SW1 7RJ
Tel: (020) 7235 5250
Website:
chriswilliams@harveynichols.co.uk

Fung Shing
15 Lisle Street
WC2H 7BE
Tel: (020) 7437 1539

Le Gavroche
43 Upper Brook Street
W1K 7QR
Tel: (020) 7408 0881
Website: www.le-gavroche.co.uk

Greenhouse
27a Hay's Mews
W1 7RJ
Tel: (020) 7499 3331/3314
Website:www.capitalgrp.co.uk

Kensington Place
201–209 Kensington Church Street
London W8 7LX
Tel: (020) 7727 3184
Fax: (020) 7229 2025
E-mail: kp@placerestaurant.com

Nobu
19 Old Park Lane
W1Y 4LB
Tel: (020) 7447 4747

Quaglino's
16 Bury Street
SW1Y 6AL
Tel: (020) 7930 6767
Website: www.conran.com

River Café
Thames Wharf Studios
Rainville Road
W6 9HA
Tel: (020) 7381 8824
Fax: (020) 7381 6217

Sartoria
20 Savile Row
W1X 1AE
Tel: (020) 7534 7000
Website:www.conran.com

Villandry
170 Great Portland Street
W1W 5QB
Tel: (020) 7631 3131
Website: www.villandry.com

Zafferano
15 Lowndes Street
SW1X 9EY
Tel: (020) 7235 5800

THIS COAST IS A CHAIN OF FISHING HARBOURS FROM NORTHUMBERLAND, TO ESSEX, VIA SEAHOUSES, WHITBY AND SCARBOROUGH.

BELOW: DEREK FORTUNE OF FORTUNE'S KIPPERS, WHITBY.

east anglia

I was looking for a scene from Philip Larkin's 'The Whitsun Weddings' – 'Where sky and Lincolnshire and water meet'. I drove through Hull and out through Skeffling down the sandy spit of land to Spurn Head and gazed out over the flat emptiness of the Humber estuary, 'the river's level drifting breadth'. There was a bitterly cold wind

& the east coast

from the east, not strong but biting, hardly

Whitsun weather, but I saw what Larkin saw.

It was one of those winter days on which

we used to be told at my boarding school at

Uppingham, just across the flatness of East

Anglia, that there was nothing between us and

the Ural Mountains in Siberia.

TO THE TOURIST THE LOBSTER POTS AND NETS ON THE HARBOUR-SIDE ARE A PICTURESQUE INGREDIENT OF THE SEASIDE SCENE. BUT, TO THE FISHERMEN, THEY ARE THE ESSENTIAL TOOLS OF A TRADE THAT IS FREQUENTLY FRAUGHT WITH DANGER.

The North Sea was muddy brown, waves thumping up on to the beach below the maram grass. I looked out to sea, grey and featureless, the sort of view that always recalls, for me, Robert Frost's poem 'Neither Out Far Nor in Deep':

The people along the sand
All turn and look one way.
They turn their back on the land
They look at the sea all day.

I couldn't help feeling how lucky I was to be here so deep in winter. The Sandy Beaches Caravan Site was empty, there was no one but the North Sea and me.

I often have this teasing thought about what this country in which I live would seem like if I weren't English. What features would delight me? What would depress me? What aura would this pale blue-green dune grass, this brown sea and cold, spiky wind, the built shapes of factories and pylons across the Humber at Immingham and the enormous span of the Humber Bridge leave in my mind? It's all so familiar, it's Britain, it's where I live.

I went on to Flamborough because a friend of mine had said it was a fishing community, just like Padstow, with a reassuring independence, just like Padstow. It was still early in the morning, the shops just opening, low red-brick houses, the brick smudged with grey, and chalkstone cottages all with terracotta tiled roofs and the cosy, slightly acrid smell of just-lit coal fires. I looked into the window of the Dog and Duck: it looked very homely and inviting. I saw they had draught Bass on and made a mental note to return.

I went back in early summer this year to go long-lining for cod with Richard Emerson and his crew, Keith and Dave, and Richard's girlfriend Joanne. She looked like the hero of a pantomime with a faded pink and blue flannel working shirt, blue jeans and black waders turned down in a rakish slant. She had three silver stud earrings in each ear. Fair haired and tanned, she stood proudly on the foredeck with her arm round the mast as we put to sea.

Richard has a Yorkshire coble called *Prosperity*. Cobles are blunt wide-beamed boats with massive ribs, designed to be hauled up beaches. He keeps the boat at North Landing, a beautiful round, chalk-cliffed cove etched with caves and arches populated by clouds of swirling seabirds nesting in all the ledges and fissures. They had an old International caterpillar tractor with an almost-smooth tractor tyre on the front to nose the boat down the pebble beach into the water; they use old driftwood logs and thick sections of blue alkathene water pipe as runners We put out 1,200 hooks baited with whelk. Joanne had cracked the live whelks and hooked them the day before. We caught three cod, each weighing about half a kilo, and two ling. Richard had hoped to catch a box, about 45 kg, but he wasn't surprised. He knew what had caused the lack of fish – over-fishing and a lack of control of

THE SAND AND SHINGLE SHORE OF CROMER, ON THE NORTH NORFOLK COAST, SUPPORTS HUGE POPULATIONS OF BROWN CRABS, FAMOUSLY FATTER AND SWEETER THAN ANYWHERE ELSE.

what size of boats could fish there. He said there could have been a reasonable living to be had out of the inshore waters of the South Yorkshire coast but it was too late now. There had been too many large trawlers working the area. He said that square mesh panels installed in all trawl nets years ago would have saved the fishery, though.

It is frustrating that the inclusion of a panel of net with a square mesh has never been made a legal requirement. The physics are simple. Nets are made in a diamond shape because they're stronger. However, as the net is towed through the water, the diamond closes up, trapping small fish which otherwise could have swum through. A square mesh panel in the top of the net allows small fish to escape because the square meshes stay open. I've seen a research film of a trawl net with the panel fitted and a flurry of small fish escaping. These juvenile fish currently make up much of the one-third of fish thrown back dead from trawling. They're known euphemistically as the 'by-catch'. One-third of all trawled fish is a mighty amount lost.

I don't know why but I always seem to experience some moments of great clarity about seafood whenever I go to Whitby in North Yorkshire. In the past it's been about fish and chips. This time it was just a cod. I was outside the fish market there talking to Dennis Crooks, a fish merchant, about fishing when he produced a fish weighing about 5 kg. It was green with brown-yellow speckles, its white underbelly a sheen of platinum, its gills a perfection of glistening pink, each segment clear and sharp against the shiny skin. Its eye was deep and lustrous, its barbell underneath its bottom lip like a trigger, and its body firm and stiff as if alive. I recall two emotions: a marvelling at the sheer perfection of such a creature and a fear that such beautiful fish may soon be gone.

All the great fishing ports on the east coast – Great Yarmouth, Lowestoft, Grimsby, Hull and North Shields – trail memories of former fishing glory. Grimsby, in spite of being a prosperous food-producing town, has a grim end-of-era feel about it down on the fishing docks, and evidence that it was once the largest fishing port in the world. The fishing museum there is all the more nostalgic for being set in the now-empty scene of such former prosperity. It's definitely worth a detour. You find yourself on board the heaving deck of a Grimsby trawler with all the noise, chill and even smells of life at sea off the coast of Iceland from where much of the cod and haddock came. There are scenes of the galley with floor sloping from the swell, the bridge and a stoker stripped to his wiry muscled waist shovelling coal into the boiler fire. All are populated with life-sized waxwork figures with unnerving still, glass eyes. There are scenes from the close-knit streets of 1950s Grimsby with a sad, final, sparse front room and a mother sitting in an armchair wearing carpet slippers and a message coming over the Bakelite radio about a trawler lost at sea, toppled over, having become fatally unbalanced from tons of ice on the decks, ropes, rails and winches.

I'm sure the museum's impact has to do with the underlying esteem we all have for fishermen. In spite of our safe lives of Radio 2 and lifestyle magazines, we share an identity of an island nation whose prosperity and courage has always been dominated by the sea. The image of a trawler setting out across the silver sea from the safety of a harbour to the limitless line on the horizon is deeply embedded. We know those seafarers endure lives of great hardship, but somehow they're free like we were always meant to be. No wonder we gaze

STIFFKEY MARSHES IN NORFOLK IS HOME TO LOCAL COCKLES KNOWN AS 'STEWKEY BLUES'. THEY'RE STILL GATHERED BY HAND WITH A RAKE AND NET.

TIME AND TIDE WAIT FOR NO MAN, BUT JOE JORDON MUST WAIT PATIENTLY FOR LOW TIDE ON STIFFKEY MARSHES WITH NET AND RAKE BEFORE HE CAN REAP HIS HARVEST OF COCKLES.

out to sea; it still fills us with a sense of hope and expectancy. Whenever you ask a fisherman what he feels as he's hauling his net and line, it's just that – the anticipation.

These days, with ever-diminishing stocks, the hauling is a triumph of hope over reality but the North Sea is remarkably rich in plankton. With just a modicum of control, it could recover. Some fishermen have an optimistic theory that over-fished species recover naturally once there are not enough left to make them viable to the large, ruthlessly efficient trawlers. The news is not all bad. There are still fish markets at all those once-vast fishing ports.

AS YOU STROLL PAST THE BOATS ON THE SHINGLE BEACH AT DUNWICH, LOOK OUT TO SEA. IF IT'S LOW TIDE AND YOU'RE LUCKY, YOU MAY SEE THE CHURCH SPIRE OF WHAT WAS ONCE, LONG AGO, THE SITE OF ONE OF ENGLAND'S LARGEST TOWNS.

Take North Shields. Gone are the days of the big trawlers. Today there's a small modern market selling the landings of much smaller boats. The fish has all been recently caught, a lot of it only one or two days old. The prices are good and, most heartening, most of the fish is sold locally in Northumberland, indicating that in the north east, the locals enjoy good fish. There were some lovely red mullet, wolf fish, octopus, sea trout, big, thick plaice spotted with orange and a couple of nice halibut the day I was there. The streets around the market are filled with fishmongers. I could have stocked my restaurant fridges quite happily.

Like most of the coastal areas in this book, the east coast is not richly endowed with good restaurants. It's got some of the best fish and chip shops, particularly in Whitby and Scarborough, but there seems to be a lack of initiative in celebrating the still-rich produce from the North Sea with a restaurant doing bowls of mussels and fish soup, shrimps with mayonnaise, grilled flatfish and roasted halibut or cod. There is more hope in the south of the region – Essex, Suffolk and Norfolk – than further north. I had a great time at a little seafood shack down In West Mersea called The Company Shed, just outside Colchester. You can order just-boiled lobsters and crabs and plates of oysters washed down with a bottle of wine bought in the off-licence across the road, and there's some good eating around Aldeburgh and Southwold in Suffolk. I had some nice grilled sea bass at The Hoste Arms in Norfolk on the night before a shrimp trawling trip out of King's Lynn – a memory of a vast seawater boiler on the back of the trawler with steam billowing into a pink sunrise over the Wash, the colour in the sky matching the delicate hue of the good catch of pink shrimps. I took about 10 kg home the next morning and we gave a little pile to each customer in the restaurant that night as something to 'amuse the mouth', as the French say, while drinking a glass of kir or chilled Madfish Bay Chardonnay.

poached sea bass
with beurre fondue

I'm a great fan of poaching well-flavoured fish like bass, especially when it is served with this blindingly easy but totally successful sauce, beurre fondue. It's a bit like hollandaise but you can't go wrong with it. Just think of slicing through that moist, silvery skin into white, glistening flesh, with a smell of warm butter, wine and chives wafting across the table.

SERVES 4

4 X 450 G (1 LB) SEA BASS, OR A 1.5–1.75 KG (3–4 LB)
   SEA BASS, CLEANED AND SCALED

FOR THE COURT-BOUILLON:

2 FRESH BAY LEAVES

1 TEASPOON BLACK PEPPERCORNS

1 CARROT, SLICED

1 SMALL ONION, SLICED

1 SMALL LEMON, SLICED

2 TABLESPOONS SALT

3 TABLESPOONS WHITE WINE VINEGAR

3.4 LITRES (6 PINTS) WATER

FOR THE BEURRE FONDUE:

100 G (4 OZ) CHILLED UNSALTED BUTTER,
   CUT INTO SMALL DICE

1 SHALLOT, FINELY CHOPPED

50 ML (2 FL OZ) DRY WHITE WINE

1 TABLESPOON CHOPPED CHIVES

SALT AND FRESHLY GROUND WHITE PEPPER

METHOD

Put all the ingredients for the court-bouillon into a fish kettle, bring to the boil and simmer for 5 minutes. Add the fish, bring the court bouillon back to the boil and allow it to bubble for 10 seconds. Remove from the heat, cover and leave for 5 minutes, if using small bass, or 15 minutes for the larger fish, during which time they will continue to cook very gently. Lift the sea bass out of the fish kettle, allow the excess water to drain off and then transfer it to a warmed serving plate. Cover and keep warm. Strain 50 ml (2 fl oz) of the court bouillon and set aside.

For the beurre fondue, melt 15 g (^{1}/2 oz) of the butter in a small, non-aluminium saucepan. Add the shallot and cook gently for 5 minutes, until softened but not browned. Add the wine and boil until reduced to 1 tablespoon, then add the reserved strained court bouillon and bring to a fast boil. Whisk in the rest of the chilled butter pieces, a few at a time. Add the chives, season to taste, then pour the sauce over the poached sea bass and serve.

baked cromer crabs
with berkswell cheese

I used to think that those little dressed crabs from Cromer, which sadly often appear on supermarket fish counters fresh from the deep freeze, sometimes still part frozen, were rather tasteless and insignificant. That was until I went to Cromer to see for myself. There is a ledge under the North Sea that stretches 20 miles either side of the pretty Norfolk seaside town of Cromer. The bottom is sandy and gravelly and the sea supports an incredibly populous colony of brown crabs, which seem to thrive and grow quicker and fatter and sweeter than anywhere else. The fishing of them is carefully controlled, and the fishing community fiercely guards its rights of access to the fishing grounds, so that year after year we can all benefit from the delight of these small, full-shelled crustaceans.

One of the real pleasures of the Cromer crab is that its back shell provides a helping just right for one person. I've kept this stuffed, baked crab recipe as simple and as English as I can. Use dressed Cromer crabs with pure crab meat in the back shell, not ones bulked out with biscuits, bread and lots of brown meat.

Berkswell is a nutty, hard ewe's milk cheese, like Parmesan but with its own unique flavour. Feel free to use Parmesan instead if you can't get it.

SERVES 4

4 DRESSED CROMER CRABS

25 G (1 OZ) BUTTER

JUICE OF $^1/_2$ LEMON

1 TEASPOON MADE ENGLISH MUSTARD

4 GRATINGS OF FRESH NUTMEG

A GOOD PINCH OF CAYENNE PEPPER

LEMON WEDGES, TO SERVE

FOR THE TOPPING:

15 G ($^1/_2$ OZ) FRESH WHITE BREADCRUMBS

1 TABLESPOON MELTED BUTTER

25 G (1 OZ) BERKSWELL CHEESE, FINELY GRATED

METHOD

Pre-heat the oven to 200°C/400°F/Gas Mark 6.

Remove the crab meat from the shells and put it in a large bowl. Melt the butter and then mix in the lemon juice, mustard, nutmeg and cayenne pepper. Gently fold this mixture through the crab meat, taking great care not to break up the larger chunks.

Spoon the crab mixture back into the shells and lightly level the tops. Mix the breadcrumbs with the melted butter, then stir in the grated cheese and sprinkle the mixture evenly over the crab. Place the crabs on a baking tray and bake for 10–12 minutes, until they are golden brown and the filling has heated through. Serve hot, with the lemon wedges.

ravioli of fresh crab
with warm parsley and lemon butter

Nothing much to it, just good crab meat, fresh pasta, butter, parsley and lemon juice but it's the sort of dish I long to find on my travels looking for uncomplicated seafood dishes. I remember long ago, when I was a slightly worse skier than I am now, my Austrian ski instructor told me as I leant the wrong way on a tight turn, 'You think too much.' Too many recipes, particularly from restaurants, think too much, are too complicated. This one doesn't.

SERVES 4

175 G (6 OZ) FRESH WHITE CRAB MEAT

1 TABLESPOON MELTED BUTTER

A PINCH OF CAYENNE PEPPER

SALT AND FRESHLY GROUND BLACK PEPPER

FOR THE PASTA:

225 G (8 OZ) PLAIN FLOUR

$1/4$ TEASPOON SALT

$1/2$ TEASPOON OLIVE OIL

2 MEDIUM EGGS

2 MEDIUM EGG YOLKS

FOR THE PARSLEY AND LEMON BUTTER:

100 G (4 OZ) BUTTER

2 TABLESPOONS CHOPPED FLAT-LEAF
   PARSLEY

$1/2$ TEASPOON FINELY GRATED LEMON ZEST

2 TEASPOONS FRESH LEMON JUICE

2 GARLIC CLOVES, VERY FINELY CHOPPED

METHOD

For the pasta, put all the ingredients into a food processor and blend until they come together into a dough. Tip out on to a work surface and knead for about 10 minutes, until smooth and elastic. Wrap in clingfilm and leave to rest for 10–15 minutes.

For the filling, mix the crab meat with the melted butter, cayenne pepper and a little salt to taste.

Cut the pasta dough in half and set one piece aside, wrapped in clingfilm, so that it doesn't dry out. Roll the other piece out on a floured work surface into a 38 cm (15 inch) square, making sure it doesn't stick. Then, with your fingertips, make small marks at 7.5 cm (3 inch) intervals in 3 evenly spaced rows (i.e. 3 rows of 5 indentations) over one half of the square. Place a teaspoon of the crab mixture on each mark, then brush lines of water between the piles of mixture. Fold over the other half of the square so that the edges meet, then, working from the centre of the folded edge moving outwards and towards you, press firmly around each pile of mixture with your fingers to press out any trapped air and seal in the filling. Trim off the edges of the dough and cut between the rows with a sharp knife. Lift the ravioli on to a lightly floured tray. Repeat with the second piece of pasta dough to make 30 ravioli in all.

Bring 3.5 litres (6 pints) of water to the boil in a large pan with 2 tablespoons of salt. Drop the ravioli into the pan of boiling water and cook for 4 minutes. For the parsley and lemon butter, gently melt the butter with the parsley, lemon zest, lemon juice and garlic. Season to taste with a little salt and pepper.

Drain the ravioli well and divide them between 4 warmed pasta plates. Spoon over the warm parsley and lemon butter and serve.

NOTE: If you want to make the ravioli in advance, drop them into the pan of boiling water and cook for just 20 seconds. Drain well, place in a single layer on a plastic tray and cover with clingfilm. Chill until required.

jellied eels

The best jellied eels I've ever tasted were at Estuary Seafoods at the cockle sheds in Leigh on Sea. This was because the usual bland treatment of poaching the eels in salted water with little other flavouring had been abandoned in favour of a jelly made with lemon juice, bay, cloves and peppercorns. I've included all these ingredients in my recipe, plus lots of fresh parsley. You've got to eat the eels with plenty of good malt vinegar, freshly ground white pepper, brown bread and butter and a pint of Adnam's Suffolk bitter, or Young's bitter if you're a Londoner.

SERVES 4–6

900 G (2 LB) EELS, KILLED AND SKINNED

PARED ZEST AND JUICE OF 1 LEMON

3 BAY LEAVES

4 CLOVES

8 BLACK PEPPERCORNS

4 TEASPOONS SALT

1 SMALL BUNCH OF CURLY PARSLEY, CHOPPED

METHOD

Cut the spines out from the top and bottom edge of the eels, then cut the eels into 4 cm (1 1/2 inch) pieces. Put the pieces into a large saucepan with the lemon zest, juice, bay leaves, cloves, peppercorns and salt. Add enough cold water just to cover, then bring to the boil and simmer for 20 minutes. Transfer the eels and their cooking liquor to a bowl and leave to cool.

Stir in the chopped parsley and divide the mixture between 4–6 small pots. Cover and chill until the jelly has set, then serve.

shrimp and samphire risotto

I recently went shrimping on a trawler from King's Lynn. We left at about midnight and were in place way out in the Wash as dawn came up on a perfect August morning. The memory of the pink sky and the pink shrimps, and the steam rising up out of the saltwater boiler are all encapsulated for me in this dish. David, the director, suggested including the samphire that grows all around the marshy coast of Norfolk. Samphire is available in season (May to August) from good fishmongers and, occasionally, from greengrocers. You can also use North Atlantic prawns in the shell for this recipe.

SERVES 4

750 G (1 1/2 LB) UNPEELED COOKED PINK SHRIMPS
   OR NORTH ATLANTIC PRAWNS
100 G (4 OZ) SAMPHIRE, PICKED OVER AND WASHED
75 G (3 OZ) UNSALTED BUTTER
1/2 ONION, CHOPPED
1.2 LITRES (2 PINTS) *FISH STOCK* (SEE PAGE 185)
1 PIECE OF BLADE MACE
2 SHALLOTS, FINELY CHOPPED
1 GARLIC CLOVE, FINELY CHOPPED
350 G (12 OZ) RISOTTO RICE
120 ML (4 FL OZ) DRY WHITE WINE
25 G (1 OZ) PARMESAN CHEESE, FRESHLY GRATED
SALT AND FRESHLY GROUND BLACK PEPPER

METHOD

Peel the shrimps and set them aside, reserving the shells. Break off and discard the woody ends of the samphire and break the rest into 2.5 cm (1 inch) pieces.

Melt 25 g (1 oz) of the butter in a large saucepan, add the onion and fry for 5 minutes, until soft and lightly browned. Add the shrimp shells and fry for 3–4 minutes, then add the stock and mace and bring to the boil. Cover and simmer for 20 minutes. Pass the stock through a conical sieve into a clean pan, pressing out as much liquid as you can with the back of a ladle. Bring back to a simmer and keep hot over a low heat.

Melt the rest of the butter in a large saucepan. Add the shallots and garlic and cook gently for a couple of minutes. Add the rice and turn it over until all the grains are coated in the butter. Pour in the wine and simmer, stirring constantly, until it has been absorbed. Then add a ladleful of the hot stock and stir until it has all been taken up before adding another. Continue like this for about 20 minutes, stirring constantly, until all the stock has been used and the rice is tender but still a little *al dente*.

Shortly before the risotto is ready, drop the samphire into a pan of boiling water and cook for 1 minute, then drain well. Stir the shrimps, Parmesan cheese and some seasoning into the risotto. Heat for 1 minute, then stir in all but a handful of the samphire. Divide the risotto between 4 warmed bowls and serve, garnished with the rest of the samphire.

omelette arnold bennett

This is the sort of dish, like eggs Benedict, that I would like to see reappearing on hotel breakfast menus. It's thoroughly agreeable when made using lightly poached smoked haddock, good eggs, cream and Parmesan cheese. There are many different versions of this dish, named after the novelist who made the pottery towns of Staffordshire come alive. I must confess I had only read *Anna of the Five Towns* when I filmed the cooking of omelette Arnold Bennett. Now I've read *Clayhanger* and *The Card*, and rediscovered an author who writes so understandingly about the human condition – who writes, as he says, about 'the interestingness of existence'. All that pleasure from one simple omelette from the Savoy.

SERVES 2

300 ML (10 FL OZ) MILK

3 BAY LEAVES

2 SLICES OF ONION

2 SLICES OF LEMON

6 BLACK PEPPERCORNS

275 G (10 OZ) UNDYED SMOKED HADDOCK FILLET

6 EGGS

20 G ($^3/_4$ OZ) UNSALTED BUTTER

2-3 TABLESPOONS DOUBLE CREAM

2 TABLESPOONS FRESHLY GRATED
  PARMESAN CHEESE

SALT AND FRESHLY GROUND BLACK PEPPER

METHOD

Mix the milk with 300 ml (10 fl oz) of water, pour it into a large shallow pan and bring to the boil. Add the bay leaves, onion and lemon slices, peppercorns and smoked haddock and simmer for about 3–4 minutes, until the fish is just cooked. Lift the fish out on to a plate and leave until cool enough to handle, then break it into flakes, discarding any skin and bones.

Pre-heat the grill to high. Whisk the eggs together with some seasoning. Heat a 23–25 cm (9–10 inch) non-stick frying pan over a medium heat, then add the butter and swirl it around to coat the base and sides of the pan. Pour in the eggs and, as they start to set, drag the back of a fork over the base of the pan, lifting up little folds of egg to allow the uncooked egg to run underneath.

When the omelette is set underneath but still very moist on top, sprinkle over the flaked smoked haddock. Pour the cream on top, sprinkle with the Parmesan cheese and put the omelette under the hot grill until lightly golden brown. Slide it on to a warmed plate and serve with a crisp green salad.

grilled cod with green split peas and tartare sauce

I hope you'll enjoy the way the flakes of cod, the peas and the tartare sauce complement each other. I tested this at our seafood cookery school where I've built a recipe-testing kitchen with a view over the Camel Estuary to Rock. I invited Paul Sellars, the teacher at the school, to come and try it and he said, 'This is what British cooking is all about.' I was delighted with that.

SERVES 4

4 X 225 G (8 OZ) PIECES OF THICK, UNSKINNED COD FILLET

50 G (2 OZ) BUTTER, MELTED

SALT AND FRESHLY GROUND BLACK PEPPER

FOR THE GREEN SPLIT PEAS:

450 G (1 LB) GREEN SPLIT PEAS, SOAKED OVERNIGHT

1 ONION, QUARTERED

2 GARLIC CLOVES, PEELED BUT LEFT WHOLE

1 CELERY STICK, HALVED

2 BAY LEAVES

1 SPRIG OF THYME

25 G (1 OZ) BUTTER

FOR THE TARTARE SAUCE:

150 ML (5 FL OZ) *MUSTARD MAYONNAISE* (SEE PAGE 186)

1 TEASPOON FINELY CHOPPED GHERKINS

1 TEASPOON FINELY CHOPPED CAPERS

1 TABLESPOON CHOPPED FLAT-LEAF PARSLEY

1/2 SMALL GARLIC CLOVE, CRUSHED

METHOD

Drain the split peas and put them into a pan with the onion, garlic, celery, bay leaves and thyme. Cover with 1.2 litres (2 pints) of water, bring to the boil and simmer gently for 1 hour, until the split peas are really tender and most of the liquid has evaporated but the mixture is still quite wet (the peas will continue to absorb the liquid after the cooking time is up). Mix together all the ingredients for the tartare sauce.

Lift out and discard the onion, garlic, celery, bay leaves and thyme from the peas and mash the peas briefly with a potato masher to make a coarse paste. Stir in the butter and some seasoning to taste and keep warm.

Pre-heat the grill to high. Brush the pieces of cod with the melted butter and season on both sides with salt and pepper. Place skin-side up on a greased baking tray or the rack of the grill pan and grill for 8–10 minutes, until the skin is crisp and the cod is cooked through. Meanwhile, make sure the split peas are hot and add a little water if necessary to give them a creamy texture.

Serve the cod on top of the peas with the tartare sauce.

a casserole of cockles
with smoked bacon, tomato and pasilla chilli

This dish is based on a classic Portuguese recipe cooked in a *cataplana*, the flying-saucer-shaped pan in which the dish is served. If you haven't got one hanging somewhere in your kitchen gathering dust, from some long-distant holiday in the Algarve, you'll find Le Creuset make a nicely suitable stove-enamelled shallow casserole dish for both oven and table. We use them copiously in our cookery school, where we chose the blue ones to match the maritime decor.

SERVES 4

3 TABLESPOONS EXTRA VIRGIN OLIVE OIL

175 G (6 OZ) PIECE OF RINDLESS SMOKED
   STREAKY BACON, CUT INTO SMALL STRIPS

2 GARLIC CLOVES, FINELY CHOPPED

1 DRIED PASILLA CHILLI, FINELY CHOPPED
   (OR $1/2$ TEASPOON DRIED CHILLI FLAKES)

1 ONION, FINELY CHOPPED

1 TABLESPOON PAPRIKA

150 ML (5 FL OZ) RED WINE

450 ML (15 FL OZ) TOMATO PASSATA

1.75 KG (4 LB) LARGE COCKLES, CLEANED
   (SEE PAGE 188)

A SMALL HANDFUL OF FLAT-LEAF PARSLEY,
   CHOPPED

SALT AND FRESHLY GROUND BLACK PEPPER

METHOD

Heat the oil in a large, shallow casserole, add the bacon and fry gently for 3 minutes, until lightly browned. Add the garlic, chilli, onion and paprika and fry for another 5 minutes, until the onion is soft. Add the red wine and boil until it has almost completely evaporated. Stir in the tomato passata and simmer for 8–10 minutes, until it has reduced to a thick sauce.

Add the cockles to the pan, then cover and cook over a medium heat for 8–10 minutes, giving them a good stir half way through, until they have all opened. Stir in the parsley and some seasoning to taste, then take the casserole to the table and serve with plenty of fresh crusty bread.

NOTE: You can buy pasilla chillies from The Cool Chilli Company. Call (0870) 902 1145 for details.

a fricassée of turbot
with button mushrooms and salad onions

Though the word fricassée might suggest a French dish, it has been part of British cooking for a very long time. It has been ruined by the use of bland, floury sauces but as long as you keep the flour to a minimum, use a first-class fish stock, start the dish by frying the turbot to give the sauce colour, reduce everything well, season with lemon juice and finish with some small button mushrooms and salad onions, then when you cut into that steak of turbot together with that luscious sauce, you'll see why it's such a good way of cooking such a great fish.

SERVES 4

65 G (2$^{1}/_{2}$ OZ) BUTTER

15 G ($^{1}/_{2}$ OZ) PLAIN FLOUR

4 X 225 G (8 OZ) TURBOT STEAKS, SKINNED

175 G (6 OZ) SMALL BUTTON MUSHROOMS, WIPED CLEAN AND HALVED

12 SALAD ONIONS OR LARGE SPRING ONIONS, TRIMMED AND CUT INTO 4 CM (1$^{1}/_{2}$ IN) PIECES

600 ML (1 PINT) *FISH STOCK* (SEE PAGE 185)

1 EGG YOLK

50 ML (2 FL OZ) DOUBLE CREAM

1 TEASPOON FRESH LEMON JUICE

1 TEASPOON CHOPPED PARSLEY

SALT AND FRESHLY GROUND WHITE PEPPER

METHOD

Make a beurre manié by working the flour with 15 g ($^{1}/_{2}$ oz) of the butter. Season the turbot with a little salt.

Melt the rest of the butter in a shallow oven-to-table pan, just large enough to hold the fish steaks side by side. Gently cook the mushrooms and onions for about four minutes, seasoning them with salt. Using a slotted spoon, remove them to a plate and add the turbot to the pan. Turn up the heat a little and let the steaks brown slightly on either side. Add the fish stock, cover and poach the steaks for about 6 minutes.

Lift out the turbot and pour the cooking liquid into a small pan, then return the turbot and the vegetables to the main pan. Keep warm while you complete the sauce. Rapid boil the cooking liquid until it has reduced by about half, then stir in the beurre manié and cook, stirring continuously, for about 3 minutes until the sauce has thickend. Take off the heat.

Mix the egg yolk and cream together in a small bowl, then stir into the sauce. Reheat gently, but don't let it come to the boil. Add the lemon juice and season to taste with salt and white pepper. Pour the sauce over the fish and vegetables in the pan. Sprinkle with chopped parsley and serve with some steamed new potatoes and a soft green lettuce salad.

RESTAURANTS SERVING GOOD SEAFOOD

Harwich, Essex
The Ha'Penny Bistro
The Quay
Harwich CO12 3HH
Tel: (01255) 241212
Fax: (01255) 551922

Directions
Right on the harbour front in Harwich.

The idea of the pier is to give people leaving on the ferry to Holland some good British seafood before they depart, and the Ha'Penny Bistro does this very well. You can have a drink in the cheerful, modern nautical bar beforehand and then enjoy a great dish of haddock and chips with mushy peas, or maybe a half pint of prawns with mayonnaise, or dressed local crab. What's nice about this relaxed and informal fish restaurant is the wine list from Lay and Wheeler. I had a great bottle of Quincy, a Sauvignon from the Loire which is as

east anglia & the east coast selection

good as Sancerre but at least £5 a bottle cheaper.

West Mersea, Essex
The Company Shed
129 Coast Road,
West Mersea CO5 8PA
Tel: (01206) 382700

Directions
Near the lifeboat station.

Richard and Heather Haward loved the seafood shacks on piers in New England and brought the idea back to

West Mersea. There's a wooden shed with a stone floor, rugged chairs and tables covered with bright yellow oilcloth. There's a blackboard outside saying what fresh fish they've got in and what you can order up to eat. The fish display is not extensive, but everything is of excellent quality. I had a lobster salad and a cold bottle of Chablis, which I bought from the shop across the road. It really is wonderfully laid-back – it takes real style to do something as basic as this.

Burnham Market, Norfolk
The Hoste Arms
The Green
Burnham Market PE31 8HD
Tel: (01328) 738777
Fax: (01328) 730103
Website: www.hostearms.co.uk

Directions
Right on the village green.

The Hoste Arms is a bit of a tour de force from the point of view of the buildings and the size of the operation. You think it's just a pub but it stretches right back with lots of public rooms, bars, an art gallery, a restaurant and twenty-eight well-appointed rooms. Paul Whittome is a real enthusiast – he's an ex-potato farmer from East Anglia who got bored with spuds. He taught me a great deal about potatoes, though. Important facts like why chips can be greasy (they're handled roughly). The seafood dinner was good if the service a tad brusque. I had Cromer crab with lamb's lettuce and rocket salad and sea bass with chargrilled aubergine and a nice bottle of Zind-Humbrecht Riesling.

Staithes, North Yorkshire
The Endeavour Restaurant
1 High Street
Staithes TS13 5BH
Tel: (01947) 840825

Directions
In the centre of the village, heading down towards the quay.

You'd feel awfully disappointed to come to Staithes and not get some good fish. Sadly, there are so many fishing villages like this in our country where you can get little more than a fish finger. Staithes is a delight – it's almost like a film set, it's so unspoilt and pocket-sized. Lisa Chapman's Endeavour Restaurant is a triumph of economies of labour and space. Most of the time she cooks and waits on the tables in the tiny restaurant on her own and the menu reflects this, but it all works. I had an excellent crab mousse, very light, with cherry tomatoes and slices of avocado, and then some fillets of very fresh plaice with scallops and prawns. It's not cutting-edge cooking, just what one local girl can do easily and well.

Aldeburgh, Suffolk
The Lighthouse
77 High Street
Aldeburgh IP15 5AU
Tel/Fax: (01728) 453377

Directions
In the narrow part of the High Street.

You would expect the splendid town of Aldeburgh to have a good restaurant and indeed it has – the Lighthouse. Sara Fox and Peter Hill's restaurant is lively, comfortably decorated and very friendly. The menu is full of things you want to eat. I chose potted shrimps with toast and lemon and roast cod wrapped in Parma ham with lemon oil and a puy lentil ragout. It was all jolly good and the wine list was good too. Sara is a partner in the Aldeburgh Cookery School over the road with cookery writer Thane Prince. They do some good courses on seafood, by the way, and one day I'm going to go and do a class (Thane, promise).

Southwold, Suffolk
The Crown
90 High Street
Southwold IP18 6DP
Tel: (01502) 722275

Directions
In the main street in the centre of the town.

Southwold and Aldeburgh are two of the nicest seaside towns in England, and in Southwold you have the added advantage of the Crown Hotel, owned and run by Adnams who have one of the best wine lists in the country. The restaurant at the Crown has lots of seafood with dishes like seared fillet of pink bream with a saffron and bacon risotto and light garlic broth, a grilled fillet of monkfish tail with braised chicory, roast peppers and a red wine vinaigrette and seared scallops with wild mushrooms and baby spinach. The small dining area, slightly set aside from the lovely open bar area, is laid up with white damask linen and is a study in wood and white cloth. Just the place to drink a bottle of David Wynn's unwooded Chardonnay from Eden Valley.

Sunderland, Tyne and Wear
Brasserie 21

Wylam Wharf
Sunderland SR1 2AD
Tel: (0191) 567 6594

Directions
Follow signs for the town centre and the port. Just before the port, on the fish quay, there is a new development down to the left – this is Wylam Wharf.

On the walls there are some wine labels from Bonny Doon in California, blown up to poster size, Ca' del Solo and Le Cigar Volante – Randal Gram, the owner of Bonny Doon, has made wine labels into an art form. There's a lovely wooden bar top, wooden floors, nice wood and aluminium chairs and light wood-topped tables. The whole place feels like Sydney and it's Sunderland and the food doesn't let you down. I had a fantastic fish soup, deep and pungent, and cod on a bed of stir-fried red pepper, shiitake mushrooms, spring onions, bok choi, soy and roasted sesame oil and just a lick of butter and coconut cream in the sauce. We drank a Viognier from the Pays d'Oc. What a fantastic place – it's one of Terry Laybourne's four restaurants. The main one is 21 Queen Street (see below) where I had the best piece of halibut I've ever had in my life, just grilled with a slice of lemon – now that's style in a Michelin-starred restaurant.

Newcastle upon Tyne, Tyne and Wear
21 Queen Street
19–21 Queen Street
Princes Wharf
Quayside
Newcastle NE1 3UG
Tel: (0191) 222 0755

PUBS SERVING GOOD SEAFOOD

Craster, Northumberland
The Jolly Fisherman
Haven Hill
Craster NE66 3TR
Tel/Fax: (01665) 576461

Directions
Right on the waterfront in the village.

The thing I love about Craster is the gardens around the inside edge of the harbour. They appear to be owned by the houses on the other side of the road – it's really public-spirited to look after some ground that is a delight for everyone. The pub looks out over the sea nearby and here you can enjoy some great crab soup, well-filled crab sandwiches and Craster kipper pâté.

Barnby, Suffolk
The Swan
Swan Lane
Nr Beccles
Barnby NR34 7QE
Tel/Fax: (01502) 476646

Directions
In the middle of the small village.

The Cole brothers, Donny and Michael, own J. T. Cole (see Smokeries, page 79), one of the two very good smokehouses in Lowestoft. They also have a fish wholesale business and this pub, the Swan. It's a big, brash, friendly sort of a place; you're not going to get the trendiest seafood there, but you'll certainly get the freshest. I had fried herring milts followed by grilled slip soles.

Dunwich, Suffolk
The Ship Inn
St James Street
Dunwich IP17 3DT
Tel: (01728) 648219

Directions
In the main street through the village, heading towards the beach.

It's rather fun, having had a lunch of the Ship's excellent fish and chips (deep-fried plaice or cod with homemade tartare sauce) in the bar, and a glass or two of Adnams Ale, to wander down to the shingle beach there and gaze over the North Sea and think where you're looking was once (in the twelfth century) the largest town in England apart from London.

Snape, Suffolk
The Crown Inn
Bridge Road
Snape
Nr Aldeburgh IP17 1SL
Tel: (01728) 688324

Directions
Take the road to Snape off the A1094 to Aldeburgh. The pub is shortly before The Maltings.

I thoroughly enjoyed Diane Maylott's seafood menu. I particularly remember the lunch there – oysters, then steamed halibut with samphire, a bottle of Sancerre, and rubbernecking a conversation on the next-door table. It was all about literature and white Burgundy and I remember thinking this is quite a special part of the country.

FISH AND CHIPS

Maldon, Essex
Paul's Plaice
Bentall's Shopping Centre
Heybridge
Maldon CM9 4GD
Tel: (01621) 854223

Directions
Just off the Colchester Road, heading towards Tiptree.

Great fish and chips in a shopping mall just outside this old Essex estuary town famous for its sea salt and Anglo Saxon battle.

Scarborough, North Yorkshire
Wackers
1 Vernon Road
Scarborough YO11 2NH
Tel: (01723) 353758

Directions
In the town centre, just off Westborough, near Woolworth's.

My Yorkshire friend Brian Turner told me about Wackers, so I had to go. I would call it a shrine to the art of fish and chip restaurants – no take-away, just a 250-seater restaurant with the best dripping for frying, superb chips, and firm cod in crisp, deep brown batter. I don't know where these east coast fish and chip shops get their dripping from but it's of a quality that makes the subtle difference between good and great fish and chips. I really liked the restaurant too. The turquoise banquette seating, the colour picked up on the table legs, and the orange swirly carpet... I mean, it's not exactly what I'd have in my home but there was a pleasing aptness about it. The place was busy, efficient and friendly, full of locals – a complete success.

Whitby, North Yorkshire
The Magpie Café
14 Pier Road
Whitby YO21 3PU
Tel: (01947) 602058

Directions
Near the fish market by the harbour in Whitby.

I waxed lyrical about the Magpie Café in my last TV series, *Seafood Odyssey* – it's the best fish and chip restaurant I've ever been to. Ian Robson has a

gem of a restaurant here, a shrine to Englishness, and, by the way, a fantastic wine list too, most of which comes from Bibendum Wines in north London. The fish is straight off the quay, the batter has no gimmicks, the frying is done in 100 per cent beef dripping and the chips are Maris Piper.

Aldeburgh, Suffolk
Aldeburgh Fish & Chip Shop
226 High Street
Aldeburgh IP15 5DJ

Directions
At the southern end of the high street, heading towards the marina.

I'd heard that in the summer the queues go right down the high street and when I returned this year, I found it to be true. Peter also has a second shop, called the Golden Galleon (Tel. 01728 454685) in the centre of town.

Dunwich, Suffolk
Flora Tea Rooms
Dunwich Beach
Dunwich IP17 3DR
Tel: (01728) 648433

Directions
Right on the beach.

This is an atmospheric place for fish and chips right on the beach in Dunwich. Great thick pieces of cod, chips a bit on the thin side, but well worth a trip, and you can sit outside in the summer.

FISHMONGERS

Leigh on Sea, Essex
Estuary Fish Merchants
8 Cockle Row
Leigh on Sea SS9 2AL
Tel: (01702) 470741

Directions
Situated in the Old Town – follow signs for the station. The cockle sheds are at the bottom of the hairpin bend.

There's a whole row of seafood sheds near the pub, the Crooked Billet, which overlooks the Thames Estuary and Sheerness on the Kent coast. All of them do cockles and jellied eels, prawns, shrimps etc., but the jellied eels at Estuary Fish are much nicer because they are cooked with lemon, bay leaves, cloves and black peppercorns and they do some great smoked sprats, oysters and local pink shrimps too.

Cromer, Norfolk
Richard and Julie Davies

7 Garden Street
Cromer NR27 9HN
Tel: (01263) 512727
Fax: (01263) 514789

Directions
Right in the centre of town, near the pier.

Richard Davies is one of the top crab fishermen in Cromer and his wife Julie runs a nice fish shop around the corner from their house which naturally sells above all lots of lovely dressed Cromer crabs. They had a very good selection of fish the day we filmed there, including some lovely local codling, halibut steaks, sea bass, sardines, undyed kippers, bloaters and smoked sprats.

Aldeburgh, Suffolk
Fish on the Beach

There's quite a few sheds selling fish from straight off the boats. We bought a couple of still flapping lemon soles and some codling at Dean Fryer's shed. The selection is never big but the fish is wonderful and the prices are good.

Woodbridge, Suffolk
Loaves & Fishes
52 The Thoroughfare
Woodbridge IP12 1AL
Tel: (01394) 385650

Directions
In the main pedestrianized high street in the centre of town.

My Aunt Zoe remembered weekends at Woodbridge when she was young, in a sailing boat without supports so that low tide always meant being leaned over on the mud. So when I went there and saw all the yachts on the estuary keeled over, I thought of her. It's pretty smart these days and shops like Loaves & Fishes, a modern deli and fishmonger, are thriving. The fish display in lots of crushed ice was very exciting the day I visited – lots of whole fish, sea bass, herrings, Dover and lemon sole and monkfish tails. There were scallops in the shell and a good selection of smoked fish, including some Loch Fyne kippers.

The deli was fun too, with a cartload of fresh vegetables outside.

SEAFOOD SUPPLIERS

Southend, Essex
Gilson's
8 Burdett Road
Southend SS1 2TN
Tel/Fax: (01702) 467030
E-mail: paulgilson@dial.pipex
Website: www.fresh-fish.co.uk

Directions
Follow the signs for the Sealife Centre – Gilson's is just north of it.

I must say I was surprised to find such a good fishmonger in Southend – after all, it's a bit of a touristy town. But Paul Gilson had some great fish that day, such as grey mullet, sea bass and gurnard, not on show. I just had a nose around his cold room. They do a display on Thursday and Friday, so if you're there on any other day just ask or ring in advance to be sure. Of particular interest for me were a boxful of smelts and another one of skate knobs, which is one of his specialities. These are the cheeks of skate which can be turned into a nice gratin. See the recipe on page 143.

Staithes, North Yorkshire
Tim Turnbull's Live Lobsters
2a, 2b Staithes Industrial Estate
Saltburn by the Sea
Staithes TS13 5BB
Tel: (01947) 840917

Directions
Just before the cobbled street going down into the village, turn right into the car park at the rear of the building.

Everybody swears by Tim Turnbull's lobsters. You can buy lobsters and crabs straight from his tanks or, if you prefer, Lisa Chapman sells them in her Endeavour Restaurant in the town.

SMOKERIES

Grimsby, north-east Lincolnshire
Alfred Enderby Ltd
Fish Dock Road
Grimsby DN31 3NE
Tel: (01472) 342984

Directions
On the seafront. From the M180 follow signs for the fish dock.

Another quality smoker on the east coast using traditional naturally ventilated kilns. Very good undyed kippers and haddock, though the dyed haddock uses a natural yellow colouring from the Mexican scarlet annatto seeds.

Seahouses, Northumberland
Swallow Fish Ltd
2 South Street
Seahouses NE68 7RB
Tel: (01665) 721052

Directions
Tucked away in a street running down to the harbour.

What nice people they are, the smokers at Swallow Fish. We've dealt with them for some years now at the Seafood Restaurant. The smokery is situated in a street of old stone fish warehouses – I swear that smoked fish tastes better done in lovely old buildings like this. Seahouses and the whole of that part of the Northumbrian coast is grandly beautiful.

Whitby, North Yorkshire
Fortune's
22 Henrietta Street
Whitby YO22 4DW
Tel: (01947) 601659

Directions
From Church Street, go past the steps leading to Whitby Abbey and Henrietta Street is on your right.

The Fortune brothers had to make an important choice when faced with EU health regulations about bringing their shop up to spec. They could either move their premises and clad everything in white 'Altro' plastic and be able to sell all over the country, or stay where they were and sell at the door of the smoker. They chose the latter – good on them – and if you want their kippers, which are probably the best in the country, you'll have to go to Whitby.

Lowestoft, Suffolk
J. T. Cole
Unit 2
Ness Point House
Newcombe Road
Lowestoft
Tel: (01502) 574446

Directions
On an industrial estate, near the old gas works.

We spent half a day filming at J. T. Cole's smokehouse just near the water in Lowestoft. Colin Burgess was a real smoke artist – there's a world of difference between the product of the modern computer-controlled kiln and the traditional, tall, tar-encrusted chimneys where the quality of the finished goods depends on constantly monitoring the heat and smoke. In addition to smoking herrings and haddock, Colin also does bloaters, buckling and red herrings, the latter being a heavily salted herring, smoked for up to six weeks and originally destined for Africa where it could be stored without refrigeration.

Lowestoft, Suffolk
The Old Smokehouse
37 Raglan Street
Lowestoft NR32 2JP
Tel: (01502) 581929

Directions
A couple of hundred yards from the railway station, near the government buildings.

All the smoked fish at this very old smokehouse is done on the premises. You walk through the blue and white archway on the street into a small courtyard and on into the fish shop housed right in the old smokehouse. The fresh fish is good too and everything is displayed rather endearingly in washing-up bowls. Pride of the smoked fish for me were the bloaters (ungutted, salted and lightly smoked herrings).

OTHER PLACES WHERE I'VE EATEN GOOD FISH RECENTLY

Harrogate, North Yorkshire
The Drum & Monkey
5 Montpellier Gardens
Harrogate HG1 2TF
Tel: (01423) 502650

Northallerton, North Yorkshire
McCoy's Bistro
The Cleveland Tontine
Staddlebridge
Northallerton DL6 3JB
Tel: (01609) 882671
Fax: (01609) 882660

Hambleton, Rutland
Hambleton Hall
Hambleton
Nr Oakham
Rutland LE15 8TH
Tel: (01572) 756991
Fax: (01572) 724721
E-mail: hotel@hambletonhall.com

HADDOCK IS PRESERVED
BY SALTING AND SMOKING.
IN THE PAST A FAMILY
WOULD HAVE ITS OWN
SMOKE PIT, NOW SMOKING
IS A SPECIALIST SKILL.

BELOW AND INSET RIGHT:
ORKNEY SCALLOPS AND
VELVET CRABS.

the east co
& the orkne

I have a recurring image of the East Coast of
Scotland. There's Bill Spink at the open window of
his corrugated iron shed. I'm on the other side of
the Brothock Burn that flows out at Arbroath.
It's low tide, rather a grey day and there's only a
stream with mud and leaned-over boats. Bill is
almost spectre-like from the clouds of dense oak
smoke swirling around him from the smouldering
pit below as he lifts out the tarry poles of pale

ast of scotland

ys

golden haddock smokies that are hooked by their gills. Later, I taste the mild, reassuring wood-fire chimney taste of them, the elemental comfort of the hearthside. I enjoy the way the cured flesh parts from the bone in opal white, waxy fillets and feel a jolt of realization that I'm tasting a world-class delicacy like caviar, buffalo mozzarella or the hams made from acorn-fed pigs on the Iberian peninsula.

ARBROATH SMOKIES ARE HOT SMOKED OVER HARDWOOD CHIPS IN A KILN. THE COPPERY-GOLD FISH IS THEN READY TO EAT. COLD SMOKED HADDOCK OR KIPPERS NEED FURTHER COOKING.

In Auchmithie, where Arbroath smokies originated, the whole village used to be shrouded in smoke from a myriad of smoking pits. I walked down a steep zigzag path to the quay, little more than boulders piled to form a breakwater. Before it was built in the 1900s, the fishermen's wives of Auchmithie would carry the fishermen on their shoulders through the freezing sea to keep them dry through the lengthy day of long-lining in an open boat. Having done that, these women would bait a thousand hook lines with raw mussels, smoke the brined haddock over the pits dug in the turf, and walk 20 miles barefoot into Dundee to sell the catch. There are photographs of some of them in a book in the Auchmithie Inn up in the village – where we repair for some pints of bewilderingly awful Scottish ale. They're mostly young, not swarthy. They're fit with clear, intelligent eyes. One of them is beautiful. They look as though they'd be driving Golfs, running kids to school, or writing books or software, or presenting programmes on television today. Not many fishermen look back with a sense of loss to times when their lives were harder but simpler. How could they? To an outsider their life often seems irredeemably tough.

This severe manual way of life is rapidly disappearing. Many of the fishing villages on this coast are now just postcard-pretty with all the life that made them gone. But they still have an immensely nostalgic impact. I'm thinking of places like Sandend out on the Moray Firth. I arrived there last summer on a Sunday when the hot August weather, that we know more often in Cornwall, had spread far north. One of the rewarding results of having been on television is that people know you and come up to talk about much more interesting things than just the weather. So there, in Sandend, I fell in with a family from Aberdeen, the young

ABOVE: SMALL
HADDOCK, HEADS
REMOVED, ARE TIED IN
PAIRS OVER POLES FOR
ARBROATH SMOKIES.

RIGHT: THE FRAGRANT
WOODSMOKE FROM THE
SHEDS CAN BE SMELT
AROUND ARBROATH
HARBOUR ON A CLEAR,
SUNNY DAY.

THE MAJESTIC SANDSTONE
CLIFFS OF YESNABY HEAD
ON ORKNEY MAINLAND ARE
CONTINUALLY BATTERED BY
THE RAGING SEAS BENEATH.
THE DISTINCTIVE ROCK
STRATA AND THEIR RUGGED
OUTLINE MAKE THEM A
MAGNIFICENT SIGHT TO
BEHOLD.

mother had been born and brought up there. I think her mother still lived in the village, but there's nothing for young people to do there now. It was another pretty village with no fishing fleet left. She told me about being a child there and the fishing. She pointed out rock pools where they'd look for shrimps and fish for gobies – those inedible prehistoric-looking little black fish, so willing to be caught by children on a tiny hook baited with a little limpet prised from a rock nearby.

With her relaxed affection for the village on that shimmering summer's day, I thought how, in our haste to get off to hotter southern climates, these mild northern beaches are left empty – a charming reminder of a time before package holidays when life on the beach was pastel with innocent pleasure. It reminded me of one of those 1950s' seaside postcards, faded faint colours, but actually no less alluring than the expected bright blues and yellows of Majorca, Portofino or southern California.

Coastal villages, like Sandend, don't really function any more as fishing communities. Most of the fish is landed at the main fishing ports of Eyemouth,

A FISHING BOAT RETURNS
TO STROMNESS, SECOND
LARGEST TOWN IN ORKNEY.
IN THIS SEA-FARING
COMMUNITY, MANY OF THE
HOUSES ON MAIN STREET
HAVE THEIR OWN JETTIES.

Pittenweem, Aberdeen, Peterhead, Fraserburgh and Scrabster. I went to Fraserburgh with the television crew to film on board a massive purse-seine trawler heading for the herring spawning grounds off the Shetland Islands. The wheelhouse was like a conference room, the mess like the staff quarters on an oil rig with a menu of steaks and avocado salads, bowls of mini chocolate bars on the tables and a fridge stuffed with cola, beers mineral water and fresh orange juice. The crew were well educated, articulate and professional, but we re-named the boat The Fish Killer.

They catch up to 400 tons in one haul. Can you imagine what the 200 tons of fish, caught the day that we were there, looked like in a net? It was a great tube of silver encased in a filigree of beige net, undulating in the oily swell with seagulls diving at it to peck the fish away. In each undulation a wash of fish would shake and twitter helplessly. Then they were pumped aboard.

You stand, looking down at a stream of silver flowing into the tanks and you can't help wondering if we really need it all. Is the computerized efficiency of that fishing system the way to catch fish? Will the future bring a minute number of enormous boats fishing for a couple of months a year, while everyone else connected with the industry offers holiday lets, or re-trains in computers? The price of herrings is pitifully low. No one wants to eat them any more, but those herrings smelt like fresh wheat pouring into the holding bin on a combine harvester.

THE BEST SCALLOPS ARE CAUGHT BY DIVERS, THEN HAND SORTED AND GRADED. KING SCALLOPS ARE LARGE, WITH ONE FLAT AND ONE CURVED SHELL. 'QUEENIES' HAVE TWO CURVED SHELLS.

When we arrived back on the quay at Peterhead, we saw a Japanese buyer checking the egg quantity of the female herrings. He split open a dozen, removed the eggs and weighed them. He didn't want the males, just the roes for sashimi, and he wasn't interested in the fish themselves. What happens to all that silver perfection, I wondered? I heard dark tales of Dutch boats going after the lucrative Japanese trade equipped with machinery that can sex fish at sea and divide them so that all the males get dumped, dead, back into the water – so worthless are they in comparison with those roes in the females. We ate some fresh herrings on the boat; they were just landed, dusted with oatmeal and fried with bacon – cooked by one of the crew who had been washed overboard last winter and spent 45 minutes treading water and praying. I hope I've done justice to that memory with my recipe for *Herrings in Oatmeal with Bacon* on page 180, or the recipe for *Split Herrings with a Caper and Fresh Tomato Salsa* on page 92.

Maybe it's just being romantic to wish for a return to a time of local boats and thriving small fishing communities. The fish market at Peterhead lifted my spirits – there's so much good-quality fish in the North Atlantic. The fish auctions of Peterhead, Fraserburgh, Scrabster and Kinlochbervie are bustling and successful, with good landings of fish from the north all the way to Norway. At the market in Peterhead there were a dozen halibut all over 20 kg. I marvelled at

UNLIKE MUSSELS, SCALLOPS DON'T ATTACH THEMSELVES TO ROCKS, BUT MOVE ABOUT ON THE SEABED. HERE, AT ORKNEY SEAFAYRE, THEY ARE BOUGHT DIRECTLY FROM THE FISHERMEN AND KEPT IN TANKS OF SEA WATER UNTIL THEY'RE SOLD ALIVE.

the beauty of these immense flat fish all from the Norwegian side, but I recalled a picture I'd seen of Aberdeen market in the 1930s that showed at least 600 fish, all of this size.

I was also surrounded by boxes of the freshest brown cod I'd ever seen, speckled with yellow and tinged with green; lustrous black monkfish with heads on for the Continental market; lots of coley or 'saith', as it also known, with charcoal backs, and unusual species like wolf fish, known locally as rock turbot. In Scrabster in March this year there were a surprising number of John Dory for such northerly waters; maybe it had something to do with global warming. There were more haddock than anything, though. It's the most popular fish on the east coast. Most of it, sadly, was small, but the hake was a good size and of excellent quality. Haddock is the species favoured by the fish and chip shops of eastern Scotland: the Anstruther Fish Bar; Peppo's at Arbroath; the Bervie Chipper at Inverbervie and Zanres in Peterhead. All of these are busy and successful fish and chip shops that have borrowed the rather over-bright but modern and hygienic ideas of the fast food chains and produce a quick meal, to my mind considerably more agreeable than hamburgers.

The east coast is not over-endowed with good seafood restaurants any more than anywhere else in Great Britain. However, The Tolbooth at Stonehaven,

the Creel Restaurant at St Margaret's Hope on Orkney and The Cellar in Anstruther are all places where you do feel you are celebrating the good quality of the fish in the sea outside the door. There are some excellent fishmongers too. I think Eddie's Seafood Market in Edinburgh should be a tourist attraction; there's so much going on there. Ken Watmough's fish shop in Aberdeen supplies fish of the sort of quality that makes me feel happy to cook with it. In fact, of all the regions of Great Britain, the east coast of Scotland is the one where the fishing industry is very much alive and well, thanks to the munificence of the fishing grounds off the north coast.

I loved the seascapes of the east coast and the solid towns with stone buildings built by men who believed in permanence. Edinburgh is a beautiful city, of course, but I'm thinking of places like Dunbar, with its old town houses, and Montrose, with its curious alignment of old stone houses at right angles to the main street, and St Andrews, the university town that is so conscientiously preserved. There's a school of thought that holds that the British Empire was much more the vision of the men and women from this part of Great Britain than those from the south. These places would encourage belief in that.

I enjoyed visiting the whole of the east coast of Scotland, but it was the area north of Lybster and Wick that lingers in my memory most, that utterly captivating stretch of northern coastline to Cape Wrath. Unbelievably, my journey along that stretch was on a day of calm, but the absence of atrocious weather merely emphasized its continual presence along the cliffs and headlands. The complete lack of trees, the spiky grass cut off by the salt spray to form a sward of almost bowling-green smoothness, the oily flow of the swell in all the little inlets around the lighthouse at Strathy Point where I walked, seemed menacing rather than mellow. There were other tell-tale signs too: pieces of plastic hanging on fence wires, motionless then, and a certain languor about the exteriors of the single-storey houses. Cars and farm implements lay abandoned around the crofts – a surround of rusting hulks – one upside-down with fibreglass falling out of the holes in the dashboard where the instruments had been, a sign that gardens and suburban order have no meaning on that wind-torn coast.

But in between those fearsome headlands were the lochs, placid and far away that day, Eriboll and Hope and the Kyles of Durness and Tongue, and beautiful white sandy storm beaches, such as Torrisdale, Sango and Sandwood, with always the backdrop of the brown, heather-clad Highlands. What a beautiful country we live in and how varied. To think that that far-away place was only a couple of hours' drive from Inverness.

A TRANQUIL SCENE THAT BELIES THE BUSTLE OF KIRKWALL HARBOUR, ORKNEY. FISHING BOATS AWAIT THE TIDE, THEN THEY'LL BE GONE, SETTING THEIR BAITED POTS IN THE TIME-HONOURED WAY.

cullen skink

The highlights of my journey around Britain and Ireland for this book have been visiting places made famous by food, and nowhere more so than the town of Cullen on the east coast of Scotland. It was exactly as I expected it to be: a slightly dour, granite-built fishing village with a lovely harbour. This soup is a celebration of all the good food that comes from this fertile part of Scotland – great potatoes and sweet, mild onions, good butter and creamy milk, parsley from the garden and haddock from the North Sea. I stood on the quay trying to remember the recipe in front of the camera and whether I got it exactly right I don't know, but it doesn't really matter because it is its simple flavours that matter most.

SERVES 4

50 G (2 OZ) BUTTER

1 ONION, FINELY CHOPPED

1.2 LITRES (2 PINTS) CREAMY MILK

750 G (1 1/2 LB) FLOURY POTATOES,
   SUCH AS MARIS PIPER OR
   KING EDWARD, PEELED AND DICED

450 G (1 LB) UNDYED SMOKED
   HADDOCK FILLET

2 TABLESPOONS CHOPPED PARSLEY,
   PLUS A LITTLE EXTRA
   TO GARNISH

SALT AND FRESHLY GROUND
   BLACK PEPPER

METHOD

Melt the butter in a pan, add the onion and cook gently for 7–8 minutes, until it is soft but not browned. Pour in the milk and bring to the boil. Add the diced potatoes and simmer for 20 minutes, until they are very soft. Add the smoked haddock and simmer for 3–4 minutes, until it is cooked and will flake easily. Carefully lift the fish out on to a plate and leave to cool slightly. Meanwhile, crush some of the cooked potatoes against the side of the pan with a wooden spoon to thicken the soup a little.

When the smoked haddock is cool enough to handle, break it into flakes, discarding the skin and any bones. Return it to the pan and stir in the parsley and some seasoning to taste. Serve garnished with a little more chopped parsley.

braised ling with lettuce and peas and crisp smoked pancetta

This dish was inspired by a visit to a very good restaurant in Orkney called The Creel, in the intriguingly named fishing village of St Margaret's Hope on the island of South Ronaldsay. If ever a restaurant could be said to stick to what's good and local, this is it. The ling I had there was caught in a creel pot out in Scapa Flow. It was served grilled at the last minute and its firm texture, almost like monkfish, and freshness were astounding. I had to come up with something to do justice to that ling and the mild, grey, utterly silent spring evening by the harbour when I ate it. Orkney is a magical place. This is my memory of it in a dish.

SERVES 4

4 X 175-225 G (6-8 OZ) PIECES OF THICK LING FILLET,
   SKINNED
100 ML (3$\frac{1}{2}$ FL OZ) *CHICKEN STOCK* (SEE PAGE 185)
100 G (4 OZ) BUTTER
12 LARGE SALAD ONIONS, TRIMMED AND CUT INTO
   2.5 CM (1 INCH) PIECES
4 LITTLE GEM LETTUCE HEARTS, CUT INTO QUARTERS
350 G (12 OZ) FRESH PEAS OR FROZEN PETITS POIS
8 VERY THIN SLICES OF SMOKED PANCETTA OR
   RINDLESS SMOKED STREAKY BACON
1 TABLESPOON CHOPPED CHERVIL OR PARSLEY
SALT AND FRESHLY GROUND WHITE PEPPER

METHOD

Season the pieces of ling with some salt. Bring the chicken stock to the boil in a small pan and keep hot.

Melt half the butter in a wide, shallow casserole dish, add the onions and cook gently for 2–3 minutes, until tender but not browned. Add the quartered lettuce hearts and turn them over once or twice in the butter. Add the peas, hot chicken stock and some salt and pepper and simmer rapidly for 3–4 minutes, turning the lettuce hearts now and then, until the vegetables have started to soften and about three-quarters of the liquid has evaporated. Put the pieces of ling on top of the vegetables, then cover and simmer for 7–8 minutes, until the fish is cooked through.

Shortly before the fish is cooked, heat a ridged cast-iron griddle over a high heat and grill the pancetta or bacon for about 1 minute on each side, until crisp and golden. Keep warm.

Uncover the casserole dish, dot the remaining butter around the pan and sprinkle the chopped chervil or parsley over the vegetables. Shake the pan over the heat until the butter has melted and amalgamated with the cooking juices to make a sauce. Garnish the fish with the grilled pancetta, take the dish to the table and serve with some small new potatoes.

split herrings
with a caper and fresh tomato salsa

Herrings slipped out of popularity in the mid Seventies, when a total ban was imposed due to over-fishing. People just lost the taste for them and they are now regarded as smelly, oily and bony. I remember standing by one of the giant hoppers on the fishing boat *Chris Anna*, watching a great silver stream of herring flowing into the holds, and the smell was of fresh wheat. We scooped up a few, took them into the galley and got the cook to fry them with some fat bacon. They were neither smelly nor oily but tasted of fresh hazelnuts straight from the tree. I've been trying to come up with a dish that would rekindle everyone's enthusiasm for these wonderful fish, and this does it for me. As ever, though, they've got to be dead fresh, and then there is no better taste from the sea. This simple way of splitting open the fish also allows you to pull all the bones out before you cook them.

SERVES 4

4 X 225 G (8 OZ) HERRINGS,
   FINS TRIMMED
225 G (8 OZ) VINE-RIPENED TOMATOES,
   ROUGHLY DICED
1 GARLIC CLOVE,
   VERY FINELY CHOPPED
25 G (1 OZ) CAPERS IN BRINE,
   DRAINED AND RINSED
1 TABLESPOON COARSELY CHOPPED
   FLAT-LEAF PARSLEY
SALT AND FRESHLY GROUND
   BLACK PEPPER

METHOD

Pre-heat the grill to high. Cut the heads off the herrings and slit them open along the belly right down to the tail. Remove the guts, then open the fish out flat and place, belly-side down, on a chopping board. Now bone the fish: press firmly all along the backbone with the palm of your hand until it is completely flat, then turn the fish over and pull away the backbone, snipping it off at the tail end with scissors. Remove any small bones left behind in the fish with a pair of tweezers.

Sprinkle the herrings with a little salt and pepper on both sides, then lift them off the board and push them gently back into shape. Place them on a lightly oiled baking tray and grill for 2 minutes on each side.

For the salsa, mix together the diced tomatoes, chopped garlic, capers, parsley and some seasoning. Serve the herrings with the salsa.

arbroath smokies
and potato dauphinois

Don't get me wrong, there's no better way to eat smokies than warm from the smoke with some wheaten bread and salted butter. But this supper dish will cheer you up on a cold winter's night. I'm completely inflexible as to what you should accompany this with: a salad of sliced romaine lettuce hearts with a sunflower oil and mustard vinaigrette, and bottles of ice-chilled Budvar beer.

SERVES 4

2 X 225 G (8 OZ) ARBROATH SMOKIES

1 GARLIC CLOVE, CRUSHED

50 G (2 OZ) BUTTER, AT ROOM TEMPERATURE

900 G (2 LB) FLOURY POTATOES, SUCH AS MARIS PIPER
  OR KING EDWARD, PEELED AND THINLY SLICED

300 ML (10 FL OZ) DOUBLE CREAM

300 ML (10 FL OZ) CREAMY MILK

SALT AND FRESHLY GROUND BLACK PEPPER

METHOD

Pre-heat the oven to 200°C/400°F/Gas Mark 6.

Remove the skin and bones from the Arbroath smokies and break the flesh into large flakes. Mix the garlic with 40 g (1½ oz) of the butter. Spread it over the base and sides of a 2.25 litre (4 pint) shallow ovenproof dish. Layer the potatoes and flaked smokies in the dish, seasoning each layer lightly with salt and pepper. Finish with a neat layer of potatoes.

Mix the cream with the milk, pour it into the dish and dot the top with the remaining butter. Bake for 10 minutes, then reduce the oven temperature to 180°C/350°F/Gas Mark 4 and continue to cook for 1 hour, until the potatoes are tender and the top is golden brown.

poached haddock
with mussels, spinach and chervil

This recipe was a bit of fun for me, summing up my memories and enthusiasm for the east coast of Scotland, where we went out at 3 o'clock one cold morning, long-lining for haddock using mussels as bait. It was a pretty uncomfortable experience, on a rough day in a small open boat on the cold North Sea, talking to two fishermen from Gourdon, Peter and Steven Morrison, who had accents so broad that I could only understand one word in every five. We came back with no haddock, just codling and dabs, and retired to a small bar in Inverbervie to drink Macallan and thaw out from our icy encounter in increasing warmth and good humour. In this dish, you've got the hoped-for haddock, the mussels and the whisky.

SERVES 4

150 G (5 OZ) BUTTER

1 SHALLOT, FINELY CHOPPED

600 ML (1 PINT) MUSSELS, CLEANED (SEE PAGE 188)

4 X 175 G (6 OZ) PIECES OF UNSKINNED HADDOCK FILLET

900 G (2 LB) FRESH SPINACH, WASHED, LARGE STALKS REMOVED

1 TABLESPOON MALT WHISKY

1 TEASPOON FRESH LEMON JUICE

1 TEASPOON CHOPPED CHERVIL

SALT AND FRESHLY GROUND BLACK PEPPER

METHOD

Heat 25 g (1 oz) of the butter in a medium pan, add the shallot and cook gently for 3 minutes, until soft. Add the mussels and 150 ml (5 fl oz) of water, then cover and cook over a high heat for 3–4 minutes, until the mussels have opened. Tip them into a colander set over a bowl to collect the cooking liquor. When they are cool enough to handle, remove the mussels from all but 8 of the nicest shells. Cover and set aside.

Pour all the mussel liquor except the last tablespoon or two (which will be gritty) into a 30 cm (12 inch) sauté pan, bring to a simmer and then add the haddock, skin-side up. Cover and simmer gently for 3 minutes. Remove from the heat (leaving the lid in place) and set aside for about 4 minutes to continue cooking.

Meanwhile, melt another 25 g (1 oz) of the butter in a large pan. Add the spinach and stir over a high heat until it has wilted. Cook, stirring briskly, until all the excess liquid has evaporated, then season to taste with some salt and pepper.

Divide the spinach between 4 warmed plates and put the haddock on top. Keep warm. Return the sauté pan to the heat, add the remaining butter and boil rapidly for 3–4 minutes, until the liquor has reduced and emulsified into a sauce. Stir in the whisky and lemon juice and boil for 30 seconds. Add the chervil and mussels and stir for a few seconds, until they have heated through.

Spoon the mussels around the spinach and haddock, dividing the unshelled mussels equally between the plates, then pour over the sauce and serve.

a plate of sweet cured herrings
served in the swedish style

I think the secret of a good dressing to go with herrings is lots of flavour and a strong contrast of vinegar and sugar. You need to balance the overpowering fishiness of salt herrings. You could argue that the whole purpose is to hide the flavour, like pouring tomato ketchup over cheap meat pies. This is not so, however. There's alchemy at work here. The final taste is much greater than the sum of its parts. No wonder the Scandinavians love their *sill*.

SERVES 4 AS A STARTER

4 X 350 G (12 OZ) HERRINGS, CLEANED

50 G (2 OZ) SALT

40 G (1½ OZ) GRANULATED OR CASTER SUGAR

SALT AND FRESHLY GROUND BLACK PEPPER

FOR THE SOURED CREAM AND CHIVE SAUCE:

2 SMALL SHALLOTS, VERY THINLY SLICED

1 TABLESPOON WHITE WINE VINEGAR

1 TEASPOON CASTER SUGAR

3 TABLESPOONS SOURED CREAM

1 TABLESPOON CHOPPED CHIVES

FOR THE CELERIAC AND HORSERADISH SAUCE:

1 TEASPOON MINCED HORSERADISH

25 G (1 OZ) SHALLOT, THINLY SLICED

25 G (1 OZ) PEELED CELERIAC, CUT INTO SMALL DICE

1 SMALL GARLIC CLOVE, CRUSHED

2 TABLESPOONS SUNFLOWER OIL

1 TEASPOON WHITE WINE VINEGAR

1 TEASPOON CASTER SUGAR

FOR THE CURRY AND YOGURT SAUCE WITH POTATOES AND CORIANDER:

1 TEASPOON CUMIN SEEDS

1 TEASPOON CORIANDER SEEDS

2 TEASPOONS BLACK PEPPERCORNS

1 TEASPOON GROUND TURMERIC

2 MEDIUM-HOT RED FINGER CHILLIES, SEEDED AND ROUGHLY CHOPPED

2 GARLIC CLOVES, PEELED

1 TABLESPOON CASTER SUGAR

$1^1/2$ TABLESPOONS FRESH LEMON JUICE

1 TABLESPOON SUNFLOWER OIL

75 G (3 OZ) PEELED WAXY POTATOES, CUT INTO VERY SMALL DICE

150 ML (5 FL OZ) WHOLE-MILK NATURAL YOGURT

25 G (1 OZ) PEELED GREEN DESSERT APPLE, CUT INTO VERY SMALL DICE

2 TEASPOONS WHITE WINE VINEGAR

1 TABLESPOON CHOPPED CORIANDER

METHOD

Fillet the herrings (see page 188) and put them in a small, shallow dish in a single layer. Mix the salt and sugar together and sprinkle them over both sides of the herrings. Cover tightly with clingfilm and refrigerate for 24 hours.

The next day, make the sauces to serve with the herring. For the soured cream and chive sauce and the celeriac and horseradish sauce, simply mix the ingredients together and season each one to taste with a little salt and pepper.

For the curry and yogurt sauce with potatoes and coriander, heat a small, heavy-based frying pan over a high heat, add the cumin and coriander seeds and black peppercorns and dry-roast them for a few seconds, shaking the pan now and then, until they darken slightly and become aromatic. Tip them into a spice grinder or mortar, add the turmeric and grind to a fine powder. Put the red chillies, garlic, 1 teaspoon of salt, 1 teaspoon of the sugar, the lemon juice and the ground spices into a mini food processor and blend to a smooth paste. Heat the oil in a small pan, add 1 teaspoon of the curry paste and fry for 1–2 minutes. Scrape it into a small bowl and leave to go cold. Meanwhile, cook the diced potatoes in boiling salted water for 3–4 minutes, until just tender, then drain and leave to cool. Mix the yogurt, diced potatoes, diced apple, the remaining sugar, the vinegar and coriander with the curry paste. Season with a little more salt if necessary.

To serve, lift the herring fillets out of the marinade and cut them on the diagonal into slices 2.5 cm (1 inch) wide. Arrange in 3 little piles in the centre of 4 large plates. Spoon a little of each sauce on to each pile of herring and serve with some thinly sliced rye bread.

halibut poached in olive oil
with cucumber and dill

You really do need fresh halibut for this dish because all the other flavours are light and delicate, so it will only work if the quality of the fish astonishes you. What I wanted was to cook the fish so gently that its tendency to dryness would be alleviated, and that's why I've taken so much trouble to describe this gentle cooking procedure.

SERVES 4

600 ML (1 PINT) OLIVE OIL

4 X 175 G (6 OZ) PIECES OF THICK HALIBUT FILLET,
  SKINNED

1 TABLESPOON EXTRA VIRGIN OLIVE OIL

1 LARGE CUCUMBER, PEELED AND THINLY SLICED

1 TABLESPOON CHOPPED DILL,
  PLUS A FEW SPRIGS TO GARNISH

2 TEASPOONS WHITE WINE VINEGAR

SEA SALT

METHOD

Pour a thin layer of the olive oil into a pan just large enough to hold the pieces of halibut side by side. Season the fish on both sides with a little salt, put it in the pan and pour over the rest of the oil – it should just cover the fish. Very slowly heat the oil to 55–60°C (130–140°F), agitating it with a fish slice now and then so that it heats evenly. If you don't have a thermometer, the oil should just feel unpleasantly hot to your little finger. Now take the pan off the heat and leave it somewhere warm on top of the stove for 15 minutes to poach gently in the oil. The temperature should remain at 55–60°C (130–140°F); if necessary, keep taking the pan on and off a low heat to maintain this temperature.

Shortly before the fish is ready, heat the extra virgin olive oil in a large frying pan. Add the cucumber slices and toss over a medium heat for 1 minute. Add the dill, vinegar and a little salt.

To serve, divide the cucumber between 4 serving plates. Carefully lift the fish out of the oil, allowing the excess to drain off, and put it on top of the cucumber. Pour the oil off into a jug, leaving behind the juices from the fish, which will have settled at the bottom of the pan. Spoon these juices around the edge of each plate, sprinkle the fish with a few sea-salt flakes and garnish with a sprig of fresh dill. Serve with some boiled new potatoes.

shallow-fried herring milt with a
sherry vinegar, parsley and butter sauce

Following my discovery that the Japanese have a predilection for the roes of the female herring but care little for the milt of the male, I thought I would write a recipe to celebrate one of the most delicious parts of the herring. I've passed them through flour, egg and breadcrumbs and made them into a main course with a rather nice sauce sharpened with reduced sherry vinegar. Incidentally, if you can get it, I think the vinegar from Domecq has the nuttiest flavour.

SERVES 4

25 G (1 OZ) PLAIN FLOUR, SEASONED WITH
  SALT AND PEPPER
1 LARGE EGG, BEATEN
75 G (3 OZ) FRESH WHITE BREADCRUMBS
450 G (1 LB) FRESH HERRING MILT
1 TABLESPOON SUNFLOWER OIL
25 G (1 OZ) UNSALTED BUTTER
SALT AND FRESHLY GROUND BLACK PEPPER

**FOR THE SHERRY VINEGAR, PARSLEY
AND BUTTER SAUCE:**
85 ML (3 FL OZ) SHERRY VINEGAR
85 ML (3 FL OZ) *CHICKEN STOCK* (SEE PAGE 185)
40 G (1$^{1}/_{2}$ OZ) UNSALTED BUTTER
1 TABLESPOON CHOPPED PARSLEY
1 SHALLOT, FINELY CHOPPED
$^{1}/_{2}$ TEASPOON DIJON MUSTARD

METHOD

For the sauce, put the sherry vinegar, chicken stock and butter in a small pan and bring to the boil, then boil for about 2 minutes, until reduced and slightly syrupy. Stir in the chopped parsley, shallot, mustard and a little salt and keep warm.

Put the flour, beaten egg and breadcrumbs into 3 separate shallow dishes. Season the herring milt with salt and pepper and coat half of them in flour, then in egg and finally in the breadcrumbs. Heat half the oil and half the butter in a large frying pan, add the coated milt and fry for about 2 minutes on each side, until crisp and golden. Lift out and keep warm while you repeat with the rest of the milt. Serve with mashed potatoes.

steamed wolf fish
with mild greens, soy and sesame oil

If, through the publication of this book, I could introduce a mere 50 people to the splendour of wolf fish, I would be very happy. It's totally unknown in the south of England, and in the north it is more commonly referred to as rock turbot, or sometimes catfish. Rock turbot; isn't that so typical of us as a nation, that we won't buy something called 'wolf'? Its firm, white fillets are, to my mind, superior in flavour to monkfish. I cooked it in Scotland and kept it very simple, with a little Chinese influence but not much – only six ingredients – and it's one of the most satisfactory recipes in the book. If you can't get wolf fish, still do the dish but use monkfish instead.

SERVES 4

4 X 175 G (6 OZ) PIECES OF THICK WOLF FISH
    OR MONKFISH FILLET, SKINNED

2 THIN SLICES OF PEELED FRESH GINGER
    CUT INTO FINE JULIENNE

8 SMALL HEADS OF PAK CHOI

4 TEASPOONS ROASTED SESAME OIL

6-8 TEASPOONS KIKKOMAN DARK SOY SAUCE

2 SPRING ONIONS,
    HALVED AND VERY FINELY SHREDDED

SALT

METHOD

Season the fish on both sides with a little salt, then place the pieces side by side in a steamer over about 1 cm (1/2 inch) of water and sprinkle the ginger on top. Cut the heads of pak choi lengthways into quarters and put them in a second steamer. Cover and steam the fish for 2–3 minutes or until just cooked through, and the pak choi for 3–4 minutes, until tender.

Put the pak choi on 4 warmed plates and sprinkle over the sesame oil and soy sauce. Put the fish on top, spoon a tablespoon of the fish-steaming liquor over each piece of fish and garnish with the shredded spring onions.

RESTAURANTS SERVING GOOD SEAFOOD

Stonehaven, Aberdeenshire
The Tolbooth
The Old Pier
Stonehaven AB39 2JU
Tel/Fax: (01569) 762287

Directions
Head for the waterfront in Stonehaven and the restaurant is on the left-hand side of the harbour.

The word that keeps cropping up about these old stone-built fishing villages on the coast, south of Aberdeen, is 'substantial', and Stonehaven is no exception. The Tolbooth is right on the harbourside on the first floor of a rugged old building in what was probably a net loft. It's interesting, or perhaps obvious, that there were no big windows in the restaurant with views over the pretty harbour. I was surprised to hear a smattering of

The main course of a casserole of North Sea fish in tomato, saffron and Pernod broth was almost a bouillabaisse from Scotland, with a powerful concentration of flavour in the broth. My colleague Debbie had a main course of papillote of monkfish and king prawns with a Thai coconut curry sauce, which I know was great because I tried it, but it could have done with some rice. Now, wouldn't it be nice if there was a restaurant like this on the south coast of England?

Edinburgh
The Shore
3–4 The Shore
Leith
Edinburgh EH6 6QW
Tel/Fax: (0131) 553 5080

Directions
On the waterfront at Leith, just round the corner from the Malmaison Hotel, before you get to Tower Street.

Unusually for Britain, one's a bit spoilt for choice looking for places to eat seafood in Leith, the port of Edinburgh. Faced with the choice of four – Skippers, Fishers, the Vintners Rooms and The Shore – we plumped for the last. It's a bistro in an old pub and, rather charmingly, they haven't done much to smarten it up, and I don't think it needs it. The main restaurant is in a high-ceilinged room overlooking the water and has a timeless feel about it, with lots of dark wood and crisp white tablecloths. I was much taken with my first course, which was sautéed squid with red onions and smoked paprika. It was a bit like eating squid and chorizo but without the sausage. The mussels with tarragon, cream, garlic and white wine were also good. We were being very good that day – only half a bottle of Sancerre, Domaine de Montigny 1998.

Anstruther, Fife
The Cellar
24 East Green
Anstruther KY10 3AA
Tel: (01333) 310378
Fax: (01333) 312544

east coast of scotland & the orkneys selection

American accents on the busy night I was there, but then Stonehaven is within striking distance of Aberdeen and oil. The food was spectacular: cullen skink, so special because the smoked haddock was lustrous in its freshness, some salmon fish cakes with real texture with a yogurt dressing and some salad leaves. Normally I'm a bit lukewarm about yogurt, except for cooling fiery Indian food, but fish cakes are actually quite rich, and the acidity in the yogurt made them taste even better.

Directions

Located in the street one back from the harbour.

I just managed to fit in a trip to perhaps the one fish restaurant in the whole country I needed to see last summer when we were filming in Scotland. The Cellar is held by a friend of mine, who knows more about restaurants than I do, to be the only other decent fish restaurant in the whole country apart from us, and decent it certainly was. It's a very nice old granite building just back from the harbour in Anstruther next door to the Scottish Fisheries Museum, which is well worth a visit anyway. In fact this whole coast, called the East Neuk, is lovely. Every one of the fishing villages in this eastern corner of Fife is pretty, none more so than Crail. Now back to the restaurant: the fish was outstanding – both the crab salad and the grilled cod, which I and my companion, Debbie, thoroughly enjoyed, and also the halibut which David, the director for the TV series, had. It was so perfectly cooked and so fresh that he now claims that halibut is better than turbot. He's wrong of course but I can well understand it. We went with my restaurant buff and chum, who happened to be staying up the road at the Peat Inn (see page 105), and he ordered three bottles of white fish wine, one at least of which I can remember, an Alsace Riesling Cuvée Ste Catherine, Theo Fuller 1988. It was one of those evenings you will look back upon in ten years' time and say, 'Gosh, we had some fun in those days.'

St Margaret's Hope, Orkney
The Creel Restaurant with Rooms
Front Road
St Margaret's Hope
Orkney KW17 2SL
Tel: (01856) 831311

Directions

Right on the harbour front in St Margaret's Hope.

I think Orkney is the quietest place I've ever been to in the British Isles. Standing on the quayside outside the Creel at St Margaret's Hope, I was initially puzzled by the silence. I suddenly realized how unused to it I am. It was one of those early spring evenings when it's getting lighter at night and there was a scent of change in the air. Unusually, I was told, the sea was dead calm and there

was not a puff of wind. Orkney's a pretty spiritual sort of place anyway – the whole experience was a reminder of how absurdly frenetic most of our lives are. I was set up in the right mood to enjoy some simple and honest local seafood, and so it turned out. Alan Craigie cooked for us that night a lobster broth into which he'd put some perfectly cooked ling, caught that morning in a creel pot, followed by a fillet each of fried cod and organic Orkney salmon with a lentil and tomato relish and mashed potatoes. I've often said this, but I'll never go back to a place that hasn't got at least one good restaurant. To me there's something lacking in people who can't turn out some good food. I'll be going back to Orkney.

FISH AND CHIPS

Inverbervie, Aberdeenshire
The Bervie Chipper
Cowgate
King Street
Inverbervie DD10 0HQ
Tel: (01561) 361310

Directions

Right on the main street.

You've got to admit it's a great name for a fish and chip shop, 'The Bervie Chipper'. It's one of those new-look fish and chip shops, tiles everywhere, bright lights, an environmental health officer's dream kitchen, very busy, good chips, and haddock, of course, being on the east coast. There's a bit of a problem generally with haddock – it's getting quite small these days due to over-fishing – and I think the best fish for deep frying for fish and chips must be about an inch thick, but it

was very good nevertheless. And they use lard here rather than dripping. They've now got another chippy in the main street in Stonehaven.

Peterhead, Aberdeenshire
Zanres
35 Queen Street
Peterhead AB42 1TP
Tel: (01779) 477128

Directions

Near the centre of town.

National winner of the 1998 Seafish fish and chip shop of the year. There are two branches in Peterhead in the same street but not quite opposite – one's a take-away, the other's the restaurant. Very good haddock, again, sadly, a little on the small side, and like so many of these very popular east coast chippers, very efficiently and hygienically run. Interestingly, the manageress at the restaurant, Morag Adams, said she thought the future of the fish and chip shop of the year award was in doubt because fish and chip shops had become so quality-conscious and efficient that it was becoming increasingly difficult to choose a winner. This is testimony to the success of the fish and chip trade on the east coast of Scotland. Maybe they'd like to come and open a few branches in the West Country.

Arbroath, Angus
Peppo's
51 Ladybridge Street
Arbroath
Tel: (01241) 872373

Directions
On the harbour.

My mother used to say that the only food the Italians incarcerated in Britain during the Second World War cared for was fish and chips. Peppo's has been in Arbroath since 1951 – maybe they stayed on? And they certainly know how to turn out a good portion of F & C. The place is small and friendly, and, like all the best Italian food outlets, family-run.

Anstruther, Fife
The Anstruther Fish Bar
The Shore
Anstruther KY10 3AQ
Tel: (01333) 310518

Directions
Situated right on the seafront at Anstruther.

Reputed to be the best in Fife, this shop was a finalist in the Seafish fish and chip shop awards in 1998.

FISHMONGERS

Aberdeen
Ken Watmough
29 Thistle Street
Aberdeen AB10 1UY
Tel: (01224) 640321
Fax: (01224) 315983

Directions
Last turning on the right-hand side of the main street, travelling west, then first turning on the left.

One of my sources of information for checking on fishmongers around the country has been the demos I do on book tours. We book a small theatre or conference room, or, in the case of Aberdeen, the Beach Ballroom, then I cook three or four dishes and I always comment on the quality of the local fish that has been supplied. The fish from Ken Watmough was sensational. He always has a very good selection of wet fish daily from Aberdeen fish market: farmed sea bass and sometimes wild bass when they swim that way, red fish, gurnard, occasionally red mullet, sea trout and wild salmon when in season and some interesting shellfish, razor clams and sand gapers from the Orkneys, crabs and lobsters from the Moray Firth, hand-dived scallops and huge langoustines. He also salts and dries his own cod and sells a range of smoked fish, including monkfish, Arbroath smokies, Finnan Haddies, kippers from Fraserburgh and only undyed smoked haddock. He will also prepare cold shellfish platters and cook and dress salmon and crabs to order.

Edinburgh
Eddie's Seafood Market
7 Roseneath Street
Edinburgh EH9 1JH
Tel: (0131) 229 4207
Fax: (0131) 229 9339

Directions
Close to the Sick Children's Hospital.

I've done a couple of cooking demos at Valvona and Crolla recently and, on both occasions, I was very impressed with the quality of the seafood that came from a place called Eddie's Seafood Market – so I had to go and have a look. I quickly discovered the most important thing about Eddie is that he's Chinese. That usually means there'll be a great selection. Tricky, though, trying to get directions from him but we found an unusually helpful taxi driver, Stevie, who not only got us there (giving us a guided tour of Edinburgh *en route*, with an accent not dissimilar to Rab. C. Nesbitt's) but also agreed to take pictures of Eddie with his digital camera and e-mail them to me. So we got there to find an absolute cornucopia of seafood – white fish boxes laid out all across the floor, iced up and ready to go – some giant raw prawns, the largest I've ever seen in the UK, some very nice small whelks – and very much better flavoured than the larger ones – porbeagle shark, octopus, some lovely little thread fin bream much

favoured by the Japanese, langoustines and excellent squid (that's what I cooked with last time I was there). The shop was completely filled with enthusiastic Japanese and Chinese customers.

Crail, Fife
Wilma Reilly
34 Shoregate
Crail KY10 3SU
Tel: (01333) 450476

Directions
Right down on the harbour.

On the tiny harbour at Crail there's a little shack that just says 'Lobster cooked while you wait and also dressed crab'. Next to the shack is a concrete tank and a sign that says 'Warning. Do not touch the lobsters'. That's all they sell, but Peter Jukes and his wife Susan from The Cellar restaurant in Anstruther say they're brilliant. You'll have to go to Crail anyway – it's what they sometimes say is impossibly beautiful. Check out the crabs and lobsters around the little round dormer window on a house nearby while you're there.

Perth, Perthshire
Andrew Keracher
5–8 Whitefriars Street
Perth PH1 1PP
Tel: (01738) 638454
E-mail: fish@keracher.co.uk
Website: www.keracher.co.uk

Directions
Situated on an industrial estate – at the roundabout off the motorway, follow the signs for Perth. The estate is opposite the ice rink and the swimming pool. Just follow the signs for Keracher's.

We were given the tip-off about Keracher's from the chef at Airds Hotel in Port Appin, Graeme Allen. On a normal day Peter Keracher, whose great-great-grandfather Andrew started the business in 1925, will have on sale a wide selection of fish, such as John Dory, wild and farmed sea bass, red snapper, red mullet, halibut, squid and swordfish, and marlin from France. He also has holding tanks for live lobsters and Pacific oysters, and he stocks shellfish such as razor clams and soft-shell clams weekly when they are in season. He also has another shop at 73 South Street, St Andrews (Tel: 01334 472 541) and a fish counter in the Penny Lane Supermarket in Crieff (Tel: 01764 655 759). Two years ago they opened an Oyster Bar and Keracher's Restaurant, a seafood restaurant on the site of one of their old shops at 168 South Street in Perth (Tel: 01738 449777), where you can enjoy dishes such as seafood chowder, fillet of sea bass on a spring onion and tomato couscous with orange oil, hand-dived scallops with crispy leeks and a tomato and basil sauce, or six oysters served very simply on a bed of ice.

SEAFOOD SUPPLIERS

Firth, Orkney
Orkney Seafayre
Marsdene
Grimbister
Firth KW15 1TU
Tel: (01856) 761544

Directions
On the seaward side of the road half-way between Kirkwall and Stromness, at the village of Finstown.

Duncan Geddes is a man who is passionate about shellfish. He farms his own Pacific oysters and the rest of his shellfish is supplied by local gatherers: hand-picked cockles and winkles, razor clams, hand-dived scallops, green shore crabs, velvet crabs, brown crabs and lobsters. Nothing is processed – everything is kept in tanks of fresh seawater and is sold alive.

Stromness, Orkney
Kintorran Fish Ltd
Lobster Ponds
Stromness

Directions
Drive off the ferry from Scrabster and it's the first building you see.

A small shellfish supplier with lobsters and crabs in tanks, who will sell them to you at the vivier door. He also has frozen raw lobster at a good price.

SMOKERIES

Arbroath, Angus
M. & M. Spink
10 Marketgate
Arbroath DD11 1AY
Tel: (01241) 875287

Directions
The shop is situated in a road that runs between the main street and the harbour.

Spink is a very common name in Arbroath. The family originally came from Auchmithie along with the smokies. Bill Spink's smokery and wet-fish shop is pretty atmospheric, as you will discover by reading the introduction to this chapter and watching the programme. It's the Arbroath smokies for which he's renowned. There's nothing to beat smokies straight out of the smoking pit – it's well worth calling in late morning to see whether a batch has just been completed. Spink's also have a small but quality wet-fish counter in a little shop just off the yard.

OTHER PLACES WHERE I'VE EATEN GOOD FISH RECENTLY

Gullane, East Lothian
La Potinière
Main Street
Gullane EH31 2AA
Tel/Fax: (01620) 843214

Edinburgh
Atrium
10 Cambridge Street
Edinburgh EH1 2ED
Tel: (0131) 228 8882
Fax: (0131) 228 8808

Peat Inn, Fife
The Peat Inn
Peat Inn KY15 5LH
Tel: (01334) 840206
Fax: (01334) 840536

Walls, Shetland
Burrastow House
Walls ZE2 9PD
Tel: (01595) 809307

the west co
the islands

'Our fishmonger's suicidal, he can't get any fish.'

I'd just met Lesley Crosfield at the Albannach hotel and I was standing in her well-equipped kitchen looking at the evening menu and relishing the thought of the roast monkfish. Her remark seemed a little surprising since I couldn't help noticing Lochinver harbour through the kitchen window where lots of trawlers were tied up along the fishing pier on rather a watery late afternoon. I'd arrived at the Albannach after a spectacular drive from Kinlochbervie, just below Cape Wrath.

ast of scotland &

I'd taken the narrow, winding coast road that passes Loch Nedd, Drumbeg and Clashnessie and offers unbelievably spectacular views of lochs, the Sutherland mountain peaks and the sea with islands ranged into the distance. Lochinver is tiny, just a few houses round the harbour at the head of the loch, but if anywhere felt like a safe haven it was there. Safe not only from the sea, but also from the wild rocky mountain scenery of the Highlands, a friendly sight of small houses and twinkling early evening lights with a definite tang of peat smoke in the air.

Lesley explained why David MacKay, the fishmonger, was depressed.
The fishing on the west coast of Scotland had always been so rich that the daily
supply of turbot, scallops, lobster, Dover sole and brill was expected and
unquestioned – everything was cheap and plentiful. Fish came from small boats
fishing the inshore waters and was the best fish in the world. Even as recently as
three years ago, there were lots of small boats going out from fishing ports up
and down the coast: Campbeltown, Oban, Mallaig, Ullapool, and Portree on the
Isle of Skye. But stocks of fish close to the coast have since declined. The
economics of fishing these days run the same as for most other businesses:
the bigger the outfit the better the profit. Big boats require relatively less fuel and
fewer crew and catch more fish. Large trawlers go further afield and land their
catch to a few of the bigger European fishing ports from where the fish is
transported overland.

The price for a catch from a big trawler is usually negotiated at sea before it
is landed. These boats store their fish in 400 kg (882 lb) white plastic bins which
are fork-lifted straight into the back of an articulated truck and whisked off to the
giant fish markets of Vigo and La Coruña. So how does a local fishmonger buy
his couple of stone of turbot to supply a few small hotels and restaurants like the

Albannach? Three years ago in Lochinver there was a fish auction five days a week selling small boxes of perfect fish from day boats. There have been two markets this year, and David has resorted to supplementing his income by collecting winkles.

I listened to Prince Charles talking about the demise of small abattoirs on the radio the other day. It struck a chord with my thoughts about fishing. He said it was vital for small rural communities to have a local slaughterer to process their carefully nurtured produce in order for them to sell local organic beef in Somerset, marsh lamb in Kent and old spot pork from pigs fed in apple orchards in Gloucestershire. There's a comparison here with what I want for my restaurant and what Lesley wants to buy for hers. We thrive on the excellence of the produce of local boats that go out by day and anchor at little ports like Lochinver in the evening, the fishermen getting up in time to sell their produce at the fish market at five o'clock the following morning.

This may seem romantic but I wonder: I can't help feeling we've got it all wrong. We should be looking after our inshore fish better. The Japanese have managed it. They have an incredibly sophisticated system in Japan for conserving the stocks of local fish, which is in line with their reputation for democratic collaboration in industry. Each coastal area has a fisheries cooperative that has rights of ownership to the sea in its area – similar to ownership of land. There's no such thing as the sea being open to all, and fishermen must abide by a stringent set of regulations designed to protect the resource. The result is that there are plenty of fish, about three million tons are fished from around the coastline of Japan each year – more than the entire quantity fished from the North Sea. These landings have remained stable since

MUSSELS PRODUCE A FIBROUS 'BEARD' WITH WHICH THEY ANCHOR THEMSELVES TO UNDERWATER OBSTACLES. ON LOCH ETIVE THEY ARE FARMED FROM ROPES TRAILED BENEATH RAFTS.

1925 and all the fish fetches very good prices because it's seen to be the best quality. The processes that have been put in place to ensure healthy stocks put us to shame: salmon fry have been hatched and put into the water to migrate naturally for over a hundred years, and artificial reefs and wrecks have been constructed – it's known that providing such shelter radically increases the fish population in the surrounding area. If only we could adopt some of their principles, maybe we wouldn't have a depressed fishmonger in Lochinver collecting winkles.

I feel I shouldn't be writing this gloomy stuff but it's because the waters off the west coast of Scotland are so rich that it makes me sad. There's nowhere else in the British Isles that fills me with such happy anticipation of tasting some fabulous seafood. Everywhere you look there are vistas of natural splendour, of mountain, sea and sky. I love the feeling of almost perpetual daylight in the summer in northern Scotland. I remember, one summer morning, waking on the Island of Arran at about 4.30 a.m. at a guesthouse in Lochranza called the Fyneview. I got up and looked out of my window away across to Loch Fyne and the Mull of Kintyre and there was a seal asleep on the jetty in the sparkling early morning.

That's what the west coast is like: it's another country, another world, under-populated and wild with fantastic fish. It has the same water conditions as Cornwall, the warm, plankton-rich Gulf Stream and a wide continental shelf. I've quoted this elsewhere in the book but at the Mandarin Kitchen, a Chinese seafood restaurant in London, there's a quote on the menu: 'We only serve the finest Scottish wild lobsters from the west coast, simply because they are probably the best in the world.' That says it all, turbot, sole, diver-caught scallops, brill, monkfish, everything that comes from these island-studded seas seems to have a special quality about it.

This is particularly the case with the local prawns and langoustines. Order a plate of prawns with mayonnaise, or hot with garlic butter anywhere on this coast and you get a serious pile which, more often than not, has just been boiled

in seawater. If you ask for prawns down south, you'll get a defrosted product that was cooked and frozen at sea long ago – off the coast of Greenland as like as not. In western Scotland they will probably have been landed the evening before, claws still waving.

Langoustines are something that every self-respecting fish restaurant must offer. They are everybody's ideal seafood. At least, so far, there is no shortage of them. They live in muddy holes on the seabed and crawl into creel pots after bait with the same enthusiasm as the little green shore crabs that attach themselves to a net containing a fish head dangled over the side of the quays by boys and girls in Padstow. A very knowledgeable prawn merchant called David Crystal, whom I met in Appin, just north of Oban in Argyllshire says that langoustines are a bit like the locusts of the sea. That image and the muddy holes they live in might put you off – until you taste them, that is. Needless to say the bulk of the catch goes to France and Spain, but you can get them in good fishmongers in Britain too. I haven't written a recipe for them in this chapter, mainly because there's little you need to do with them. Just boil them for 4 minutes and serve them with garlic butter or the mayonnaise on page 186. The recipe for *Grilled Dublin Bay Prawns with a Pernod and Olive Oil Dressing* in chapter seven is pretty excellent too.

A rather less well-known speciality of the west coast is the squat lobster which inhabits the boulder-strewn bed of Scottish sea lochs. It has immensely long, rather gangly claws which it uses to probe crevices and sift through sediment for food. It has a sweet flavour similar to langoustines but is cheaper to buy and often sold in fishmongers in a tail-only form they call squatties. We try to get them for our *plateau de fruits de mer* in the restaurant whenever possible. I know you can buy them from Fencebay Fisheries in Fairlie near Largs down in Ayrshire and they are to be found amidst a cornucopia of good seafood in MacCallum's in Argyle Street, Glasgow. I've also occasionally seen them in supermarkets. There's a nice recipe for squat lobster tails on page 121, *Potted Squat Lobsters with Ginger and Basil.*

THE SHALLOW INTER-TIDAL WATERS BETWEEN THE ISLES OF COLONSAY AND ORONSAY ARE PERFECT FOR GROWING OYSTERS IN SPECIAL BEDS. IT TAKES SEVERAL YEARS FOR THEM TO DEVELOP SUFFICIENTLY.

**ULLAPOOL WAS PURPOSE-
BUILT TO FISH FOR HERRING
IN LOCH BROOM. WITH
HERRING DEPLETED (AND
OUT OF FASHION), LOBSTER
AND LANGOUSTINES ARE
'CATCH OF THE DAY'.**

I had a great dinner at the Albannach. Last time I spoke to Lesley she had just picked up a box of brown crabs from her partner Colin Craig's store pot in the loch in front of the hotel. She was a little concerned while talking to me because the crabs hadn't been 'nicked' to make their claws harmless. Another place to find an abundance of good shellfish is Airds Hotel at Port Appin. You can wander over the road to the bay at low tide and pick up any number of mussels and clappydoos (giant mussels), each one weighing up to 300 g (10½ oz). I took one back to Graeme Allen's kitchen at the hotel and steamed it open with a little white wine and some chopped shallots. It was quite strongly flavoured and a bit chewy, but would make the most monumental clappydoo chowder.

I would also recommend a quick ferry trip to the island of Lismore in Loch Linnhe, just across from Port Appin, where you can pick up some clear-tasting Lismore oysters. While you're there, go over to Port Ramsay, where you can see a row of single-storey, stone fishermen's cottages that will take you back about 60 years.

Airds is a pretty idyllic place for eating seafood, as is MacCallum's Oyster Bar far down on the Ayrshire Coast at Troon, right by the seacat ferry to Belfast. Nairns in Glasgow is good too. Okay, I went there first because Nick Nairn is a friend, but eating there you are made aware that a few people really know how good the local seafood is. They want the world to come and try it where it came from, not to eat it in Galicia in northern Spain where it's sold, rather contemptuously, as foreign seafood and where spider and brown crabs usually fetch a lower price than their own.

prawn cocktail

I've noticed recently a fashion for smartening up the prawn cocktail in hotel restaurants in an attempt to move things along a bit. It often comes on a plate with a little pile of prawns, some mixed 'baby' lettuce leaves and a 'puddle' of pink Mary-Rose sauce. There'll usually be a lot of superfluous garnish, including a leaf or two of basil. Surely the whole point of the cocktail is that it should be served in some sort of glass used for cocktails? It was the chef and cookery writer Simon Hopkinson who forced us all to re-evaluate the prawn cocktail and made it okay to love it again – good for him.

The prawn cocktail has memories of the Sixties for me. I used to frequent the Half Way House restaurant between Wadebridge and St Columb in Cornwall. We'd go there in a crowd of 10 or 12, and Stuart Charles, who ran a surfing school from an old hangar on the disused airfield at St Merryn and a slightly dodgy go-kart track, would order two for pudding – in addition, that is, to the one he'd had as a starter. He was a big chap with black hair, a black beard and brawny arms, and an enthusiasm for hurling tractor tyres in front of go-karters who had had too many trips round the track.

Prawn cocktails made from small Dublin Bay prawns are just the best. You can enjoy them in many of the restaurants along the west coast of Scotland.

SERVES 4 AS A STARTER

450 G (1 LB) SMALL DUBLIN BAY PRAWNS
  OR UNPEELED COOKED NORTH
  ATLANTIC PRAWNS

2 LARGE LITTLE GEM LETTUCES,
  FINELY SHREDDED

2 SPRING ONIONS

5 CM (2 INCH) PIECE OF CUCUMBER, PEELED,
  SEEDED AND CUT INTO SMALL DICE

8-10 TABLESPOONS *MAYONNAISE* (SEE PAGE 186)

2 TABLESPOONS TOMATO KETCHUP

4-6 SHAKES OF TABASCO SAUCE

2 TEASPOONS COGNAC

1-2 TEASPOONS FRESH LEMON JUICE

PAPRIKA

THIN LEMON WEDGES, TO SERVE

METHOD

Peel the prawns and discard the shells (or save them to make stock or soup). Divide the lettuce between 4 cocktail glasses or dishes. Remove and discard the green tops of the spring onions and very finely slice the white part. Sprinkle over the lettuce with the cucumber and then pile the peeled prawns on top.

Mix the mayonnaise with the tomato ketchup, Tabasco, cognac and lemon juice. Spoon the sauce over the prawns and sprinkle with a little paprika. Garnish with the lemon wedges and serve with some crusty brown bread.

grilled scallops in the shell
with toasted hazelnut and coriander butter

It's a real delight that you can now buy scallops in the shell. These should have been cleaned, with the meat still attached to the shell. To me, it's a sign that they are genuinely fresh from the sea, and the simplest treatment is called for. Here they are grilled with one of my favourite butters, made with toasted hazelnuts and coriander, with a little chopped shallot and lemon juice.

SERVES 4

16 PREPARED SCALLOPS IN THE SHELL

25 G (1 OZ) UNSALTED BUTTER, MELTED

SALT AND FRESHLY GROUND BLACK PEPPER

FOR THE TOASTED HAZELNUT AND CORIANDER BUTTER:

20 G ($^3/_4$ OZ) UNBLANCHED HAZELNUTS

75 G (3 OZ) UNSALTED BUTTER, SOFTENED

7 G ($^1/_4$ OZ) CORIANDER LEAVES

2 TABLESPOONS FLAT-LEAF PARSLEY LEAVES

7 G ($^1/_4$ OZ) ROUGHLY CHOPPED SHALLOT

1 TEASPOON FRESH LEMON JUICE

METHOD

Spread the hazelnuts over a baking tray and toast under the grill for 4–5 minutes, shaking the tray now and then, until they are golden brown. Tip them into a clean tea towel and rub off the skins. Leave to cool, then chop them roughly and tip them into a food processor. Add the softened butter with the coriander, parsley, shallot, lemon juice, a good pinch of salt and some pepper and blend together until well mixed.

Pre-heat the grill to high. Place the scallop shells on a large baking tray (or do them in batches if necessary). Brush the scallops with the melted butter and season with a little salt and pepper, then grill for $1^1/2$ minutes. Drop a generous teaspoonful of the hazelnut and coriander butter on to each scallop and return to the grill for $1^1/2$ minutes, until cooked through. Serve immediately.

seafood and white bean stew
(cassoulet) with salt cod, garlic and toulouse sausage

This is a seafood version of cassoulet using salt cod and monkfish, which seem to give it the right robust note. It sells very well in our deli and is to be one of the star attractions of a new seafood deli we are planning to open on the quay at Padstow below our cookery school this summer.

SERVES 6

550 G (1^1/$_4$ LB) DRIED HARICOT BEANS

175 ML (6 FL OZ) OLIVE OIL

225 G (8 OZ) TOULOUSE SAUSAGE,
    CUT INTO 2.5 CM (1 INCH) PIECES

A PINCH OF DRIED CHILLI FLAKES

6 GARLIC CLOVES, FINELY CHOPPED

2 FRESH BAY LEAVES

2 SPRIGS OF THYME

900 ML (1^1/$_2$ PINTS) *CHICKEN STOCK* (SEE PAGE 185)

FRESH SALTED COD (SEE PAGE 186), MADE WITH
    225 G (8 OZ) THICK, UNSKINNED COD FILLET

350 G (12 OZ) SQUID, CLEANED AND CUT INTO
    THIN SLICES

225 G (8 OZ) MONKFISH FILLET,
    CUT INTO 2.5 CM (1 INCH) PIECES

100 G (4 OZ) ROUGH, FRESH WHITE BREADCRUMBS

1 TABLESPOON CHOPPED PARSLEY

FRESHLY GROUND BLACK PEPPER

METHOD

Cover the haricot beans with plenty of cold water and leave to soak overnight.

The next day, pre-heat the oven to 150°C/300°F/Gas Mark 2. Heat 120 ml (4 fl oz) of the olive oil in a large casserole, add the sausage pieces and chilli flakes and fry for 4 minutes, until the sausage is lightly browned. Drain the beans and add them to the casserole with 4 of the chopped garlic cloves, the bay leaves, thyme sprigs, 600 ml (1 pint) of the chicken stock and some freshly ground black pepper. Cover with foil or a well-fitting lid and bake for 1^1/$_2$ hours, until the beans are tender and most of the liquid has been absorbed.

Skin the prepared salt cod and cut it into 2.5 cm (1 inch) pieces. Heat a little of the remaining oil in a frying pan over a high heat and sear the squid and monkfish in it, in batches if necessary, until nicely browned. Stir them into the cooked beans with the salt cod, the rest of the chicken stock and a little more seasoning to taste. Increase the oven temperature to 200°C/400°F/Gas Mark 6.

For the crust, put the breadcrumbs into a bowl and rub in the remaining oil. Stir in the remaining garlic, the chopped parsley and a little salt and pepper. Spread this over the top of the beans and cook, uncovered, for 30 minutes, until crisp and golden.

octopus, pea and red wine stew
from la vela in naples

The only places I've seen octopus on sale in the UK are the markets in Blackpool, Swansea and Cork, where they are all sold to the Chinese. There are plenty of them in the sea, particularly off the west coast of Scotland, but we don't seem to go for them. Here's a recipe I got from Italy to try and tempt you. It came from an extremely *al fresco* restaurant right on a rocky beach between Naples and Pozzuoli. We filmed there during my television series, *The Seafood Odyssey*, and I went back with my wife, Jill, to enjoy it without the pressures of filming. There were only us and three old boys, who came in on a little rowing boat with a bucket of mussels they'd picked off the rocks. The mussels were cooked and they ate them with white wine, plenty of bread and lots of gusto and gesticulation.

In fact, this isn't quite the dish I ate there, my wife says I've got it wrong. But it's right in spirit, and in memory.

SERVES 4

1 X 750 G (1^1/$_2$ LB) OCTOPUS

135 ML (4^1/$_2$ FL OZ) EXTRA VIRGIN OLIVE OIL

2 GARLIC CLOVES, THINLY SLICED

4 SHALLOTS, SLICED

600 ML (1 PINT) ITALIAN RED WINE

1 TEASPOON CASTER SUGAR

2 PLUM TOMATOES, HALVED

100 G (4 OZ) FRESH PEAS OR FROZEN PETIT POIS

1 TABLESPOON FINELY CHOPPED FLAT-LEAF PARSLEY

SALT AND FRESHLY GROUND BLACK PEPPER

METHOD

Pre-heat the oven to 150°C/300°F/Gas Mark 2.

Clean the octopus by turning the body inside out and pulling away the entrails and bone-like strips sticking to the sides. Locate the stomach sac, which is about the size of an avocado stone, and cut it away. Wash the octopus well inside and out and then turn the body right side out again. Press the beak and the soft surround out from the centre of the tentacles, cut out and discard. Put the octopus into a small casserole dish with 85 ml (3 fl oz) of the olive oil. Cover and cook in the oven for 2 hours, until very tender.

Heat the rest of the olive oil in a large, shallow pan with the garlic until it begins to sizzle. Add the shallots and cook gently until they are soft and lightly coloured. Add the red wine, sugar and tomatoes, bring to the boil and then leave to simmer until almost all the wine has evaporated. Lift out the tomato skins and discard them.

Lift the octopus out of its cooking juices and cut it across into smaller pieces. Add to the red wine reduction with the cooking juices and 120 ml (4 fl oz) of water. Bring to a simmer and cook for 15–20 minutes, until the liquid has reduced by about three-quarters. Add the peas and simmer for 5 minutes. Season to taste, stir in the parsley and serve hot or cold in large soup plates, with plenty of crusty Italian bread.

lobster with ginger,
spring onions and soft egg noodles

I've referred to this dish in some detail when writing about the Mandarin Kitchen restaurant in London (see page 54). The reason that the recipe is included in the West Coast of Scotland is that the Chinese owners of the Mandarin Kitchen feel that the lobsters from this area are the best in the world and use only them. One of the pleasures of this dish to me is that it allows a reasonable-sized lobster of, say, 750 g (1½ lb) to serve 2 or 3 people, which it otherwise wouldn't. It's worth seeking out some good, fresh, fine egg noodles for this dish: the ubiquitous dried egg noodles, whose name I won't record, just won't do.

SERVES 2-3

1 X 750 G (1½ LB) LIVE LOBSTER OR SPINY LOBSTER

SUNFLOWER OIL FOR DEEP-FRYING, PLUS 1 TABLESPOON

1 TEASPOON SALT

½ TEASPOON SUGAR

1 TABLESPOON DARK SOY SAUCE

1 TABLESPOON OYSTER SAUCE

A PINCH OF FRESHLY GROUND WHITE PEPPER

1 TEASPOON ROASTED SESAME OIL

2 TABLESPOONS CHINESE RICE WINE OR DRY SHERRY

2 TABLESPOONS CORNFLOUR

2 GARLIC CLOVES, CRUSHED

120 G (4½ OZ) FRESH GINGER, PEELED AND THINLY SLICED ON A MANDOLIN

90 G (3½ OZ) SPRING ONIONS, CUT INTO 2.5 CM (1 INCH) PIECES

250 ML (8 FL OZ) *CHICKEN STOCK* (SEE PAGE 185)

175 G (6 OZ) FRESH EGG THREAD NOODLES

METHOD

To prepare the lobster, wrap one hand in a tea towel and hold the lobster firmly in the other. Cut the lobster in half from the head down to the tail. Separate the tail from the head and cut each tail half into 3 pieces. Remove the stomach sac. Chop off the claws and crack the shells with a large knife. Cut off and discard the antennae and the legs.

Heat some oil for deep-frying to 190°C/375°F. Mix the salt, sugar, dark soy sauce, oyster sauce, white pepper, sesame oil and Chinese rice wine or sherry together in a small bowl and set aside. Bring a large pan of water to the boil for the noodles.

Sprinkle the lobster pieces with 1½ tablespoons of the cornflour and deep-fry, in 2 or 3 batches if necessary, for 2 minutes. The larger claw might take a bit longer – about 3 minutes. Lift out and drain on kitchen paper.

Heat the tablespoon of sunflower oil in a wok. Add the garlic, ginger and spring onions and stir-fry for a few seconds. Add the lobster to the wok with the soy sauce mixture and stir-fry for 1 minute. Add the chicken stock, then cover and cook over a medium heat for 2 minutes. Meanwhile, drop the noodles into the pan of boiling water, cover and remove from the heat. Leave them to soak

for 2 minutes, loosening them now and then with some chopsticks or a fork.

Mix the rest of the cornflour with 2 tablespoons of cold water, add to the wok and stir for 1 minute, until the sauce thickens.

Drain the noodles and put them on a large, oval serving plate. Spoon the lobster mixture on top and serve straight away.

baked codling pie
with red wine, shallots and mushrooms

I bought a dozen rather unusual Le Creuset dishes at a sale a couple of years ago. They're stove-enamelled in orange on the outside and a great shape – long, oval, deep and narrow – which fits one fish admirably. So the baked codling came into being as something rather special to serve in those dishes.

SERVES 4

1 X 1.25 KG (2^1/$_2$ LB) CODLING, CLEANED AND FILLETED

A SMALL BUNCH OF THYME

150 G (5 OZ) BUTTER

1 SMALL ONION, CHOPPED

1 CARROT, CHOPPED

2 STAR ANISE

2 TEASPOONS PLAIN FLOUR

600 ML (1 PINT) INEXPENSIVE RED WINE, SUCH AS CABERNET SAUVIGNON

1 TEASPOON TOMATO PURÉE

1 TEASPOON SUGAR

450 ML (15 FL OZ) *CHICKEN STOCK* (SEE PAGE 185)

12 SMALL SHALLOTS, PEELED

4 RASHERS OF RINDLESS STREAKY BACON,
   CUT INTO LARDONS (SHORT STRIPS)

225 G (8 OZ) SMALL BUTTON MUSHROOMS, WIPED CLEAN

1.25 KG (2^1/$_2$ LB) FLOURY POTATOES, SUCH AS MARIS PIPER OR
   KING EDWARD, PEELED AND CHOPPED

1 EGG YOLK

SALT AND FRESHLY GROUND BLACK PEPPER

METHOD

Remove any pin bones from the fish with tweezers. Pick the leaves from half the thyme sprigs and sprinkle half of them over the cut side of the fish with some seasoning. Lay one fillet on top of the other, cut sides together.

Melt 25 g (1 oz) of the butter in a large pan, add the onion and carrot and fry over a medium heat, stirring now and then, until they are nicely browned. Add the remaining thyme sprigs and the star anise and fry for another 2 minutes. Stir in the flour, cook for 1 minute and then gradually stir in the wine. Add the tomato purée and sugar, bring to the boil, then lower the heat and simmer vigorously until reduced by half. Add 375 ml (13 fl oz) of the chicken stock and simmer once more until reduced by three-quarters to about 200 ml (7 fl oz). Pass through a sieve into a clean pan, pressing out as much flavour as you can with the back of a ladle, and season to taste with some salt. Leave to cool.

Melt 25 g (1 oz) of the remaining butter in a pan, add the whole shallots and fry them gently until browned all over. Add the remaining 50 ml (2 fl oz) of chicken stock, cover and cook over a low heat for 5 minutes, until soft.

Melt another 25 g (1 oz) of butter in a second pan, add the lardons and fry until golden. Add the mushrooms and cook over a high heat for 1–2 minutes. Season both the shallots and the mushrooms with a little salt and pepper.

Pre-heat the oven to 200°C/400°F/Gas Mark 6. Pour the red wine sauce into a shallow, narrow 1.75 litre (3 pint) ovenproof dish – the longer and thinner the dish the better, so that the sauce comes half-way up the sides of the fish. Put the prepared codling in the dish and then scatter over the shallots, bacon, mushrooms and remaining thyme leaves.

Cook the potatoes in boiling salted water until tender, then drain well and mash until smooth. Beat in the remaining butter, the egg yolk and some seasoning to taste. Spoon the potatoes over the fish and rough up the surface a little with a fork. Bake for about 35 minutes, until crisp and golden brown.

potted squat lobsters
with ginger and basil

Where on earth are you going to get squat lobsters or, perhaps more importantly, what are squat lobsters? They're a small, prawn-like crustacean with immensely long, gangly claws. They look, therefore, rather ungainly but they taste delicious, sweet and succulent. They are very common on the west coast of Scotland. I've seen them on sale in the south of England from time to time but if you can't find them, you could equally well use prawns, crab or lobster instead.

SERVES 4 AS A STARTER

60 COOKED SQUAT LOBSTERS, ABOUT 2 KG (4$^1/_2$ LB)
    OR 175-225 G (6-8 OZ) COOKED SQUAT LOBSTER MEATS,
    PRAWNS OR LOBSTER MEAT
100 G (4 OZ) UNSALTED BUTTER
$^1/_2$ TEASPOON FINELY GRATED FRESH GINGER
$^1/_2$ TEASPOON SALT
$^1/_2$ TEASPOON FINELY GRATED LEMON ZEST
1 TABLESPOON FINELY SHREDDED BASIL

METHOD

Remove the squat lobster meats from the shells – there should be about 175 g (6 oz). Melt the butter in a pan, add the ginger, salt and lemon zest, then the squat lobster meats, and stir together over a low heat for a couple of minutes until the lobster meats have heated through. Take the pan off the heat and stir in the basil. Divide the lobster meats between four 6 cm (2$^1/_2$ inch) ramekins; try to arrange them neatly in the ramekins so that they will look attractive when you turn them out. Pour any remaining butter into the ramekins and leave them somewhere cool to set for at least 2 hours – if you can avoid doing this in the fridge, they will have a softer, smoother texture.

To serve, dip the ramekins briefly into hot water, unmould them on to 4 plates and accompany with plenty of warm brown toast.

NOTE: An alternative way to serve this is to divide 50 g (2 oz) mixed baby salad leaves between the plates. Spoon over the warmed mixture, sprinkle with a little extra salt and serve while the squats are still warm.

stir-fried salt and pepper squid
with red chilli and spring onion

I wanted a dish of squid that would be quite dry when I served it. I'm not that fond of squid in a wet sauce, since as soon as the squid is introduced to it, and certainly if it is boiled, it loses its lovely caramelized flavour and gets a bit chewy. Here I've just stir-fried the squid with salt and Sichuan pepper, then tossed it with some sliced chilli and spring onions. The dressing for the watercress and beansprout salad – sesame oil with soy and a pinch of sugar – makes an apt accompaniment to this Chinese-influenced dish.

SERVES 4 AS A STARTER

750 G (1^1/$_2$ LB) SQUID, CLEANED
   (SEE PAGE 189)
^{1}/$_2$ TEASPOON BLACK PEPPERCORNS
^{1}/$_2$ TEASPOON SICHUAN PEPPERCORNS
1 TEASPOON SEA SALT FLAKES
1-2 TABLESPOONS SUNFLOWER OIL
1 MEDIUM-HOT RED FINGER CHILLI,
   THINLY SLICED (SEEDS REMOVED,
   IF YOU PREFER)
3 SPRING ONIONS, SLICED

FOR THE SALAD:

^{1}/$_4$ CUCUMBER, PEELED,
   HALVED AND SEEDED
50 G (2 OZ) BEANSPROUTS
25 G (1 OZ) WATERCRESS,
   LARGE STALKS REMOVED
2 TEASPOONS DARK SOY SAUCE
2 TEASPOONS ROASTED SESAME OIL
^{1}/$_4$ TEASPOON CASTER SUGAR
A PINCH OF SALT

METHOD

For the salad, cut the cucumber lengthways into short strips. Toss with the beansprouts and watercress and set aside in the fridge until needed.
Whisk together the soy sauce, sesame oil, sugar and salt.

Cut along one side of each squid pouch and open it out flat. Score the inner side in a diamond pattern with the tip of a small, sharp knife and then cut into 5 cm (2 inch) squares. Separate the tentacles if large.

Heat a small, heavy-based frying pan over a high heat. Add the black peppercorns and Sichuan peppercorns and dry-roast them for a few seconds, shaking the pan now and then, until they darken slightly and become aromatic. Tip into a mortar and crush coarsely with the pestle, then stir in the sea salt flakes.

Heat a wok over a high heat until smoking. Add half the oil and half the squid and stir-fry it for 2 minutes, until lightly coloured. Tip on to a plate, then

cook the remaining squid in the same way. Return the first batch of squid to the wok and add 1 teaspoon of the salt and pepper mixture (the rest can be used in other stir-fries). Toss together for about 10 seconds, then add the red chilli and spring onions and toss together very briefly. Divide the squid between 4 serving plates. Toss the salad with the dressing and pile alongside the squid, then serve immediately.

RESTAURANTS SERVING GOOD SEAFOOD

Cairndow, Argyll and Bute
Loch Fyne Oyster Bar and Smokehouse
Clachan Farm
Cairndow PA26 6BH
Tel: (01499) 600236

Directions
On the A83 at the head of Loch Fyne.

I first started doing business with Johnny Noble and Andrew Lane at Loch Fyne about 16 years ago. Their products, from that remarkably fecund stretch of water, introduced me to the glory of west coast seafood: prawns, oysters, superb little queen scallops and top-quality farmed salmon, as well as mussels, and everything they do is the best. After managing to speak to Johnny only on the phone, I finally met him last May, when he invited me and the

could almost have held two of me laid out lengthways. Johnny had a curious reluctance to replace any light-bulbs in the beautiful chandeliers that hung everywhere. Many of the corridors are lit by one 25-watt bulb. The whole place was utterly wonderful and we dined on oysters, prawns and lobsters straight out of the loch, washed down with copious amounts of Gros Plant. Would that the world contained more people like Johnny Noble: his enthusiasm for shellfish reveals itself in the simple, relaxed oyster bar just up the road and the seafood products from his smokery next door. Most memorable for me out of the meals we had at the oyster bar was a steak of perfectly fresh halibut, lightly char-grilled. He sells the Gros Plant at the restaurant too – and I had forgotten how good a seafood wine it is.

Port Appin, Argyll and Bute
Airds Hotel
Port Appin, PA38 4DF
Tel: (01631) 730236
Fax: (01631) 730535
E-mail: airds@airds-hotel.com
Website: www.airds-hotel.com

Directions
At Appin take the road to Port Appin.

west coast of scotland & the islands selection

For my first course I had three to four small pieces of red mullet and the same number of plump langoustine tails all set on a very well-flavoured aubergine caviar and a little relish of red pepper, finely diced carrot, capers, olives and lime juice. The red mullet was delicately pan-fried on the skin-side – I love red mullet skin cooked like this – and the prawn tails were the most plumptious, juicy prawn tails I've ever eaten. The whole dish was a reminder of how

whole television crew to stay at his castle overlooking the loch. I was amazed that he could accommodate us all, but there were half a dozen other people staying at the same time and it became clear that Johnny doesn't quite know how many rooms he's got. The castle was built at the end of the nineteenth century and hasn't been altered much since. I thanked my lucky stars that it was May as there was no heating whatsoever in my room. The bath

successful this Michelin style of cooking can be when it's not playing safe. I just have to record the wine too; it's called Wild Boy Chardonnay and comes from a zippy Californian wine-maker called Jim Clendenen. If you saw the label, which has a very wild-looking hippy on it, you probably wouldn't buy it. Once you'd tasted it you would, though, and then you'd think, 'How clever.' Airds Hotel is incredibly comfortable and luxurious in a remarkably understated way, and the view from the dining room across to Lismore Island is the west coast of Scotland in one glance.

Troon, South Ayrshire
MacCallum's Oyster Bar
The Harbour
Troon KA10 6DH
Tel/Fax: (01292) 319339

Directions
Follow signs in Troon for the seacat ferry. The restaurant is a red-brick building with two square towers just by the passenger terminal.

This is the restaurant opened by one of the MacCallum brothers whose shop I was so impressed with in Glasgow (see page 127). It's quite illuminating to run back in your mind how you expected a place to be against how it turns out. I expected a little fish café on the quayside doing a few grilled fish and some plates of oysters, perhaps with the odd bowl of cullen skink and some not particularly satisfactory French dry white wine. What I found astonished me. An amazingly well-turned-out modern dining room in an old stone-built fish warehouse with lots of light from high, big windows, warm, cheerful and friendly. There were a couple of remarkably attractive local girls, always a good sign in a restaurant, I think, and a menu that had lots of lovely things on it. Prawns, avocado and pine nut salad; split grilled langoustines with garlic butter, salsa verde and roasted red pepper relish; seared salmon, tomato and balsamic onion; sole with crisp batter and tomato and avocado salsa, and fish cakes with creamed leeks. I ordered the special of the day, grilled black bream with wild mushrooms, bacon, peas and fondant potato – and gosh, was that good. It's really exciting when you realize that there is a very gifted chef cooking and you've almost discovered it on your own. Debbie Major, who I work with on all my books, was with me at the time and said that she wondered whether MacCallum's really realized how good he was. We met him afterwards – Douglas Smith – and I asked him where he'd cooked before. Mostly locally, he said, but he'd worked at the Puppet Theatre in Glasgow and said that the really good team he'd been with had now split up. He was young, looked like he could have been in a rock and roll band, but was cooking instead. It's been one of the most exciting parts of my tour of these islands to find one or two really talented young people cooking up a storm.

Glasgow
Nairns
13 Woodside Crescent
Glasgow G3 7UP
Tel: (0141) 3530707
Fax: (0141) 3311684
E-mail: info@nairns.co.uk
Website: www.nairns.co.uk

Directions
Off Sauchiehall Street, near Charing Cross.

Although I've known Nick Nairn for about ten years, I'd never eaten at either of his restaurants – Braeval, which he has now sold, or Nairns – but I very much like his recipes and indeed have, shall I say, 'acquired' a couple of his ideas! So I was really looking forward to Nairns and... I was not disappointed one tiny bit. Cities like Glasgow, need restaurants like Nairns as much as cooks like Nick need nice lively cities like Glasgow to strut their stuff in. The great thing about Nairns is that it's a really cosmopolitan sort of a restaurant. The menu is biased towards seafood and I've got to tell you about the pan-seared cod with new potatoes, spinach, asparagus hollandaise and poached egg. No, first I'll tell you about the fish cakes with mushy peas that I had as a first course. The mushy peas actually came as a sort of dressing with chives, chervil, spring onions and a little white wine vinegar. It was so clever and dealt with the richness of the fish cakes in an entirely balanced way. But back to the cod – I suppose my enduring memory of that dish was its generosity, and I don't mean enormous portions – I hate that. Just that everything seemed so nice to eat. I have to record a thoroughly agreeable piece of moaning with the head chef, Derek Blair, the next morning along the usual lines of, 'You can't teach these young

chefs anything these days – they all want to run before they can walk...'

Colbost, Highlands
The Three Chimneys
Colbost
Dunvegan
Isle of Skye IV55 8ZT
Tel: (01470) 511258
Fax: (01470) 511358
E-mail:
eatandstay@threechimneys.co.uk
Website: www.threechimneys.co.uk

Directions
At Dunvegan follow signposts to Glendale. Colbost is on the way.

This charming old crofter's cottage has been converted into a singularly unpretentious restaurant, and Shirley and Eddie Spear have built six light and spacious rooms in a modern cottage next door called the House Over-By, which blends in very well. Sorry if I'm going off the point a bit but the night I was there, and ate a lovely meal of a hot mussel tart and grilled lobster and langoustines with vanilla, there was a family with two young sons aged about five and seven who tucked into their seafood with evident enjoyment, then went on to play pontoon with their mum and dad, and not once did they leave the table and charge around the dining room. Their conversation was delightful and I told their dad what very nice boys he'd got. But it's that sort of place. Oh, and I forgot to mention that the lobster bisque, which was the soup course, was a delight too.

Lochinver, Highlands
The Albannach
Baddidarrach
Lochinver IV27 4LP
Tel: (01571) 844407
Fax: (01571) 844285

On the seafront next to the Seaforth Bar.

I particularly liked the haddock I had here, and also the sweet taste of the potatoes used for the thick chips. I suppose it's quite common, but I was rather impressed with the red, white and blue cardboard box that the fish and chips came in – rather easier to eat out of than the normal paper wrapping.

FISHMONGERS

Glasgow
Alan Beveridge
188 Byres Road
Glasgow G12 8SN
Tel: (0141) 3572766

Directions
Byres Road is off Great Western Road, heading north. The shop is opposite the Burger King.

A very sound local fishmonger. Their display was exceptionally tidy and fresh-looking and the variety was exemplary. Some of the more interesting fish for sale were line-caught haddock, some really nice-looking steaks of halibut, large, unpeeled raw prawns, langoustines, whole squid and grey sole, which we know as witch in the south-west. They had a couple of peat-smoked fish too – haddock and salmon. Apparently fish smoked wholly over peat becomes too strongly imbued with the flavour; the secret is to smoke the fish over oak but add some peat part way through the process.

Directions
Take the turning for Baddidarrach over a narrow bridge, just north of Lochinver on the A837, and follow the signs to the house.

Lesley Crosfield, who cooks at this characterful old house, wrote to me about five years ago when she saw my first TV series, *Taste of the Sea*, to thank me for inspiring her to cook with some of the more unusual types of fish landed at nearby Lochinver, like John Dory and monkfish. She explained that the fish she used to cook – turbot, sole and scallops – was all being whisked off to Spain. It's a depressing scenario that's being repeated all over the west coast of Scotland and from Cork around to Donegal. All our best fish is going abroad. But, as they say, necessity is the mother of invention, and the roasted monkfish wrapped in Parma ham with a roasted red pepper dressing was a blinder. Lesley is a natural cook and Colin Craig – who looks as good as you can get in a kilt, which he wears for serving dinner – is the sort of host you always want to be served by. As Lesley said about when she first met him, 'I fell in love with his knees.' By the way, the rooms are lovely too.

PUBS SERVING GOOD SEAFOOD

Ullapool, Highlands
Morefield Motel
North Road
Ullapool IV26 2TQ
Tel: (01854) 612161

Directions
Coming into the town from Inverness, turn right at the Shell garage and follow the road until you see the sign for the pub.

The fish and chips in this pub's restaurant are excellent. The more ambitious fish cookery is less successful.

FISH AND CHIPS

Glasgow
The Unique Restaurant
223 Allison Street
Glasgow G42 8RU
Tel: (0141) 4233366

Directions
South of the river. From Victoria Road heading towards Queens Park, turn left into Allison Street. The shop is situated in the third block on the left.

You've got to admire a fish and chip shop with the name 'Unique'. This family-run fish and chip shop and restaurant was started by an Italian called Mr Fichi fifty-five years ago and is still run today by his sons, Sy and Roni, one of whom is always on duty. They are renowned for their lemon sole and haddock coated in a beautifully crisp batter served with excellent floury chips.

Ullapool, Highlands
Seafresh Foods
West Shore Street
Ullapool IV26 2TX
Tel: (01854) 612141

Glasgow
MacCallum's of Troon
944 Argyle Street
Glasgow G3 8YJ
Tel: (0141) 2044456
Fax: (0141) 2044466

Directions
Argyle Street has been chopped up by new roads, so it's essential to ring them for directions before you go. We went around in circles for ages.

James MacCallum explained that in order to have a really interesting retail shop, a fishmonger needs to have a thriving wholesale business, selling particularly to hotels and restaurants and more particularly Chinese and Japanese restaurants. I doubt if half the astonishing variety of seafood that was on display the day I went would have been there if not for them – red- and yellow-tail snapper, salmon heads, mahi mahi, red sea bream, tilapia and cuttlefish. But just to give you an idea of the range available, here is a list of the fish and shellfish they had on sale that day in addition to the above: langoustines of all sizes, razor clams, live lobsters, winkles, whelks, large cockles, oysters, mussels, brown crabs, scallops and queenies, large raw prawns, turbot, small halibut, brill, brown trout, sea bass, mackerel, megrim sole, Dover sole, lemon sole, monkfish tails and skate wings.

Portree, Highlands
Anchor Seafoods
The Harbour
Portree
Isle of Skye IV51 9DE
Tel: (01478) 612414

Directions
At the end of the pier on the harbour next to the lifeboat office.

Shirley Spear from the Three Chimneys in Colbost recommended this tiny fish shop on the quayside in Portree to us. We got there only to find out, sadly, that it was shut but, with Shirley's recommendation and the following note which we saw through the window, we were pretty confident that we'd hit on a good one: 'If our seafood were any fresher, it'd swim right off your plate.'

SEAFOOD SUPPLIERS

Duror, Argyll and Bute
D. & K. Crystal
The Old Manse
Duror of Appin PA38 4BW
Tel/Fax: (01631) 740327

Directions
South on the A82 from Fort William, then on the A828. Past Duror Hotel, take the lane on the left by the church.

I was so impressed by the quality of David Crystal's shellfish that I decided there and then to start buying from him for my restaurants. Need I say more? He specializes in langoustines and scallops.

Tarbert, Argyll and Bute
Seacroft Oysters
Baravalla
Tarbert PA29 6YD
Tel: (01880) 820583 (office);
(01880) 740686 (shore base)

Directions
Ask in the village of Tarbert for directions to the farm.

I first tasted Neil and Ileene Duncan's oysters from West Loch Tarbert at James Murphy's studio in King's Cross when we were doing the food photography for this book. James knows them well and asked them to send down a few dozen, which we polished off with a glass or two of Côtes de Saint Mont – James's house wine at the studio. They're Pacific oysters, which don't fetch the same prices as natives. I think the flavour of oysters depends less on the species than on where and how they're grown.

Fairlie, north Ayrshire
Fencebay Fisheries
Fencefoot Farm
Fairlie
Nr Largs KA29 0EG
Tel: (01475) 568918
Fax: (01475) 568921

E-mail: fencebay@aol.com
Website: www.fencebay.co.uk

Directions
On the A78, south of Fairlie.

Just down the coast from the rather attractive holiday town of Largs, the Fencebay Fisheries is, unusually for most seafood outlets, housed in the very attractive outbuildings of a north Ayrshire farm. I'm sure this makes a difference to the public's perception of quality. You sort of expect the smoked fish, shellfish and wet fish to be good, with a smart, pine-clad deli and a neat cookware and wine shop across the yard with some very nice bottles on sale, and you're not disappointed. The choice of wet fish on the day I visited was small but incredibly fresh, all landed from a local boat and fished in the Firth of Clyde. It's the smoked fish, however, that Bernard Thain and his chief smoker, Tom Campbell, are renowned for. They smoke over cords of well-dried beechwood. Try that against the average supermarket stuff. They also have a little fish restaurant next door called Fins, which makes a point of keeping everything simple and centres on their own products – cullen skink, cumbrae oysters, grilled langoustines with garlic butter and poached lobster with mayonnaise.

OTHER PLACES WHERE I'VE EATEN GOOD FISH RECENTLY

Achiltibuie, Highlands
Summer Isles Hotel
Achiltibuie IV26 2YG
Tel: (01854) 622282

A GLIMPSE OF NORTH
WALES ACROSS THE DEE
ESTUARY FROM
THURSTASTON BEACH.
TRAVEL NORTH TO
MORECAMBE BAY FOR
SHRIMPS, OR SOUTH FOR A
TASTE OF GOWER
PENINSULA COCKLES.

wales & the

The town of Morecambe seems on first encounter
to be one of those places you'd leave, never to
return – the sort of place Tom Courtenay would
have been promising to escape from with Julie
Christie in *Billy Liar* to a brilliant life in the south. It's
rather run-down, lots of charity shops and second-
hand places selling a black-and-white television,
a bright blue paddling pool, a beige vinyl holdall, and
an upright vacuum cleaner. There are still lots of

north-west coast

amusement arcades on the front, which runs along a beach largely made of mud. I had arrived there in the evening in drizzle. I stayed in a hotel that had no fish on the menu but which did have the saving grace of potted shrimps, albeit served with what I have come to think of as the Lancashire garnish since it crops up all along this coast with fish, steak and potted shrimps – a slice of orange topped with a slice of kiwi fruit and a strawberry.

The next morning, though, was different. The sun was out and the point of Morecambe was unveiled out of the mist – the view. You look across those vast, flat, famous sands to Grange-over-Sands and Flookburgh to the mountains of Cumbria. It's spectacular. Now when you notice some of the houses along that front you see a very different Morecambe, quite substantial, owned by people who want to go to their bedroom window on an early sunny morning and be uplifted by that expanse of sand and distant land of the imagination. I could think of Tolkien writing in the middle of a run-down Birmingham thinking of a view like this and of *Lord of the Rings*.

I went out shrimp fishing with an ex-fitter for ICI at Warrington called Raymond Edmondson, who had used his plant maintenance skills to build a concrete boat for trawling. We trawled up and down just outside the harbour and caught a surprising number, as it was out of season, which he boiled in seawater in a stainless steel pan on top of a hand-drilled copper burner. The ship's wheel was made out of a valve handle from the chemical works, but the boat had a cheerful charm, painted in yellow and blue. We brought the shrimps back to his

FISHERMEN TRAVEL MILES
OUT INTO MORECAMBE BAY,
ON SOMETIMES
TREACHEROUS SANDS,
ABOARD ANCIENT,
CUSTOMIZED TRACTORS TO
RAKE FOR COCKLES. THEN
THEY RACE THE TIDE HOME.

potted shrimp shop in York Street. His wife Pat peeled them so quickly that it looked like a conjuring trick. I asked her to slow down and got the sleight of hand, finally, after all these years. Crab picking, cod filleting, cutting raw mussels out of the shell for bait – I could watch people preparing seafood with the skill of years forever. The potted shrimps were superb.

That evening I had dinner at a hotel in Grange-over-Sands. The menu had one fish dish Grilled Fillet of Queen Fish. I asked what it was; the chef brought it out to show me – he was very pleased with it. It looked nice, almost as nice as the flounder we had been catching on Morecambe sands in front of the hotel earlier that day. There was no local fish on the menu. This is not unusual in Britain, yet how odd. What, I wonder, would a similar hotel restaurant in Normandy have on the menu if situated on a bay teeming with mullet, flounders, mussels and shrimps?

The flounders in the bay are known locally as flukes. They're caught out on the sands in nets fixed to stakes hammered into the sand at low tide. The fishermen travel out seven miles or more over the sand to tend their nets and pick up the fish. They work in groups, raking cockles at the same time, and travel out on some of the oldest, rustiest tractors I've seen still working. They've adapted the mudguards to fit fish and tackle boxes. It's an exhilarating feeling riding high on a tractor looking across the shimmering haze of the flat white sand and blue horizon and seeing other high black shapes of tractors, like camels in the distance crossing the desert. When you approach a low net strung across the sand, you can see the fish flapping from a distance. There's normally some good-sized mullet too and the occasional bass. The flukes are the things, though, plump and thick in the early summer, fed sweetly on a diet of young thin-shelled cockles and pretty little pale blue and pink clams called hen pennies, which I tried raw and pronounced most excellent.

Out here on the sand, miles from the shore, you can sense the inherent danger of work so dependent on the tides, which sweep across at a raging pace. There's a fisherman called Cedric who's the official guide through the sands: they're not all flat – there are gullies, rifts and quicksand. He tells stories of carts being cut off and horses and men drowning. I gaze a bit anxiously at the rheuminess of the tractor that's taking me back to the safety of Flookburgh. You can see a single stalk on the horizon over towards the coast at Heysham. It's Blackpool Tower where resides a solitary oyster bar on the front called Robert's, lost in all the garish energy.

What a contrast with these sands is Blackpool. The fishermen are tough, rugged and friendly. They work in a group and rib each other in their homely Lancashire accents, and just at that moment I was lost to think of a more rewarding way to live. Except for the money. They get 80 pence a pound for those thick, shining flounders.

SHRIMPS DETERIORATE
QUICKLY, SO HERE, AT
FLOOKBURGH, THEY ARE
COOKED BY THE SHEDS
WITHIN HALF AN HOUR OF
BEING CAUGHT.
EXPERIENCED 'PICKERS'
CAN SHELL SIXTY A MINUTE.

Their life reminds me of a visit last year to the Gower Peninsula, just by Swansea, to the village of Penclawdd. I went there to see some cockle gatherers too and to try the combination of laverbread and cockles so much part of the culture of South Wales. Again, it was a long trip out over the flats at low tide, this time walking. I had to interview two cockle gatherers called Maureen and Elwyn Murley. There's something about this life raking shells out of the mud in the wind, hail, sun and rain that suits us as human beings. They were so healthy and happy and at ease. Elwyn looked like Max von Sydow in *The Seventh Seal* – tall, angular, fit and rugged; both he and Maureen were well into their sixties. Their

appearance and the remoteness of those low hills and expanse of weed-covered stones and an old black iron lighthouse down near the water seemed like one of those moody Bergman films. At any moment I expected to see a dark, shrouded figure with a scythe glide across the mussels and seaweed.

The appeal of boiled cockles and laverbread, the red weed known in Japan as nori, was hitherto lost on me, but straight out of the boiler, eaten with a plate of equally freshly boiled cockles was a different matter altogether, and when I subsequently went to the excellent covered market in Swansea, I had to have a tub of laverbread. It grows on you, it really does. I've tried to do justice to the combination in my recipe on page 137 for *Cockle and Laverbread Vol-au-vents*. I think the enrichment of the hollandaise makes for a dish that's quite special.

The other strong feature of the market in Swansea is the number of fishmongers there, particularly Coakley-Greene. The same, as you'll see at the end of this chapter, is true of Cardiff; these markets add so much value to a city. I can't say too often how important I think food is as part of civilized life. The fact that a rather scruffy city like Swansea has such a good market in the middle makes it a place to think of fondly. Of course, supermarkets are where we now want to shop. One has just opened outside Padstow, and it's a real pleasure to go there on Sundays, my day off, to shop and, funnily enough, meet people you don't see often in the town. But there's also a place for a good food market in any town, full of small specialist stalls selling good fish and meat.

AT PENCLAWDD, ON THE LOUGHOR ESTUARY, LICENSED PICKERS RAKE COCKLES FROM THE MUD FLATS.

But back to Wales. It is different. I have an old schoolfriend called Ian Scott who's now an architect in Melbourne. During our schooldays I lived in Oxfordshire and he lived somewhere in the North West. I used to go on holiday every summer, for the whole summer, to Padstow, and he used to go to Abersoch. It sounded very similar out there on the Lleyn Peninsula overlooking Cardigan Bay, Harlech and Barmouth and the coast near Snowdon. I went there last spring for the first time and it was similar. An old fishing village with lots of evidence of summer holidays, such as a high street with two blonde Sloaney girls getting into a Range Rover, and plenty of Discoveries and Volvos up and down the street. The Lonely Planet guide describes it as having a 'haughty opinion of itself, which isn't really justified'. That sounds a bit like Rock over the Camel Estuary from Padstow. I went into the post office to buy a stamp to send a post card to Ian and waited while the postmaster and a couple finished their conversation in Welsh. It didn't seem very haughty in the way the guide meant, but I got the impression that their Welshness was a source of some pride to them and I was definitely not part of their world. Hearing those people speak in their own tongue was the best way possible to drive home the difference of Wales. I confess to having been a little bored to hear the efforts made to preserve Welsh, Cornish or Gaelic, but hearing Welsh being used as a natural language in that post office filled me with the strangeness of another language being used in a country with which I thought I was familiar. It fitted the far west feel of the place, the wild country on the way to Caernarfon, with always the mountains of Snowdonia in the background.

My four trips to the Welsh coast haven't revealed a plethora of good seafood restaurants. These visits were all made outside the summer season and I had to miss a few places which where closed whose menus looked good: Plas Bodegroes at Pwllheli, Morgan's Brasserie in Pembroke and The Harbour Lights at Porthgain.

In Newquay, I recall going up to the Mariners Café overlooking the sturdy old black slate quay with a sort of hope, but finding no fish at all on the menu. It's much the same wherever you go in Britain. A café on a beach rarely sells anything from the sea. Hope springs eternal, but I will not forget a remark from the particularly convivial owners of Oneida Viviers Ltd at Milford Haven, who described their business of transporting tons of Welsh lobsters and crabs to Spain and said, 'The Spanish laugh at us. They're happy to take it all off us but wonder why we don't eat it ourselves.'

GATHERING LAVERBREAD FROM THE ROCKS AROUND WHITFORD LIGHTHOUSE, NEAR PENCLAWDD. THE LIGHTHOUSE AT WHITFORD IS ONE OF THE LAST CAST-IRON LIGHTHOUSES IN THE COUNTRY.

mussels en croustade
with leeks and white wine

When my wife, Jill, first saw this she said it seemed a bit old-fashioned, the type of thing restaurants served in the Seventies. Or the sort of dish that might have appeared in the magazine I used to write for in the early Eighties, *Woman's Realm*. All this is true but it's also true that it's lovely, the sort of dish you'd be grateful for a restaurant to have on its menu.

SERVES 4

4 LARGE, ROUND CRUSTY BREAD ROLLS

175 G (6 OZ) BUTTER

900 G (2 LB) MUSSELS, CLEANED (SEE PAGE 188)

50 ML (2 FL OZ) DRY WHITE WINE

2 LARGE OR 4 SMALL LEEKS, CLEANED AND FINELY CHOPPED

2 TABLESPOONS DOUBLE CREAM

1 TEASPOON *BEURRE MANIÉ* (SEE PAGE 186)

1 TABLESPOON CHOPPED CHIVES

SALT AND FRESHLY GROUND WHITE PEPPER

METHOD

Pre-heat the oven to 200°C/400°F/Gas Mark 6.

Cut a thin slice off the top of each bread roll and set aside. Scoop out all the soft bread from inside each roll with a teaspoon, leaving a wall about 5 mm (¼ inch) thick. Melt 50 g (2 oz) of the butter and use to brush the inside of each roll and the lids. Place them on a baking sheet and bake for 5–7 minutes, until crisp and golden. Keep warm.

Put the mussels into a large pan with the wine, then cover and cook over a high heat for about 3 minutes, shaking the pan now and then, until they have just opened. Tip them into a colander set over a bowl to collect all the cooking liquor. Remove the mussels from their shells, cover and set aside.

Melt another 25 g (1 oz) of the butter in a pan. Add the leeks, cover and cook for 4–5 minutes, until soft. Add all the mussel cooking liquor except the last tablespoon or two (which might contain some grit), then bring to the boil and simmer until reduced by half. Stir in the remaining butter, the double cream and the beurre manié. Simmer for 1 minute until slightly thickened.

Stir the mussels, chives and some seasoning into the sauce. Spoon the mixture into the warm rolls, partly cover with the lids and serve.

buttered sea trout with red wine, star anise and prawn sauce

One of Marco Pierre White's recipes first introduced me to the idea of putting star anise with a red wine and stock reduction. It gives the finished sauce a warm spiciness, which tastes much more European than Oriental. A few warm prawns scattered over make a big difference, too.

SERVES 4

50 G (2 OZ) BUTTER

2 STAR ANISE

4 X 175 G (6 OZ) SEA TROUT FILLETS (TAKEN FROM 2 X 550 G (1^1/$_4$ LB) FISH)

1 TABLESPOON CHOPPED PARSLEY

SALT

FOR THE SAUCE:

225 G (8 OZ) UNPEELED COOKED NORTH ATLANTIC PRAWNS

75 G (3 OZ) UNSALTED BUTTER

1 SMALL ONION, FINELY CHOPPED

1 CARROT, FINELY CHOPPED

1 CELERY STICK, FINELY CHOPPED

7 G (^{1}/$_4$ OZ) DRIED PORCINI MUSHROOMS

A PINCH OF DRIED CHILLI FLAKES

1 TABLESPOON BALSAMIC VINEGAR

600 ML (1 PINT) RED WINE, SUCH AS A CHILEAN CABERNET SAUVIGNON

300 ML (10 FL OZ) *CHICKEN STOCK* (SEE PAGE 185)

1 STAR ANISE

1 TEASPOON *BEURRE MANIÉ* (SEE PAGE 186)

1 TEASPOON FRESH LEMON JUICE

METHOD

For the sauce, peel the prawns and set aside, reserving the shells. Melt 25 g (1 oz) of the butter in a medium-sized pan, add the prawn shells, onion, carrot, celery, dried porcini and chilli flakes and fry, stirring now and then, until the vegetables are lightly browned. Cut the rest of the butter into small pieces and chill. Add the balsamic vinegar to the pan, cook for a few seconds and then add the red wine, chicken stock, star anise and a small pinch of salt. Leave to simmer rapidly until reduced to about 175 ml (6 fl oz). Remove from the heat.

For the sea trout, pre-heat the oven to 200°C/400°F/Gas Mark 6. Melt the butter in a small pan with the star anise and leave in a warm place for 5 minutes, until the butter is lightly infused with the star anise. Brush the cut face of each sea trout fillet with some of the melted butter, season with a little salt and then fold them in half, skin-side outwards. Place them in a shallow oven-to-table dish and brush with the remaining melted butter. Cover with foil and bake for 20 minutes.

Strain the wine and stock reduction through a fine sieve into a clean pan. Uncover the trout and carefully pour the juices from the dish into the same pan. Sprinkle the peeled prawns over the sea trout, cover and keep in a warm place. Bring the pan containing the wine and stock reduction and the trout cooking juices back to the boil and reduce to about 100 ml (3^1/$_2$ fl oz), stirring in the beurre manié at the same time.

Whisk the pieces of chilled unsalted butter into the sauce a few at a time, until it has emulsified. Add the lemon juice and adjust the seasoning to taste. Uncover the fish and prawns and pour the sauce over. Scatter with the chopped parsley and serve. Mashed potatoes are a nice accompaniment to this dish.

cockle and laverbread vol-au-vents with hollandaise sauce

I have to be honest, the first time I tasted laverbread, a type of cooked seaweed, I thought it was something to do with the Welsh sense of humour – slimy, black and clammy. I tried and tried to like it. Then, when we were filming on the Gower peninsula, I tasted some straight out of the boiler and was suddenly converted. It hadn't been minced, it was ozone fresh and iodiney, and you could imagine it as a subtle fragrance in a sauce. I had some on crusty bread in Swansea market about a month later and it was like greeting an old friend.

In Wales, wherever there's laverbread there's cockles, but I couldn't help feeling that something was lacking when the two were brought together. For me, it's got to be hollandaise sauce. Here, the cockles and laverbread are folded into the sauce, which is then dropped into warm, featherlight vol-au-vents or bouchées of puff pastry – just perfect with a glass of champagne.

Unless you live somewhere like Swansea or Bideford you are unlikely to be able to buy fresh laverbread but it is readily available in most delicatessens in tins.

MAKES 12

350 G (12 OZ) CHILLED FRESH PUFF PASTRY

1 EGG, BEATEN, TO GLAZE

100 G (4 OZ) *CLARIFIED BUTTER* (SEE PAGE 186)

900 G (2 LB) COCKLES, CLEANED (SEE PAGE 188)

1 EGG YOLK

1 TEASPOON FRESH LEMON JUICE

4 TEASPOONS PREPARED LAVERBREAD

SALT

METHOD

Pre-heat the oven to 200°C/400°F/Gas Mark 6.

Roll out the pastry on a lightly floured surface until it is 5 mm ($^1/_4$ inch) thick. Cut out twelve 6.5 cm (2 $^1/_2$ inch) discs using a plain pastry cutter, then press a 5 cm (2 inch) plain cutter into the centre of each one, only half way down into the pastry. Take care not to cut all the way through. Put the vol-au-vents on a lightly buttered baking sheet and brush the tips with a little beaten egg. Bake for about 10–12 minutes, until crisp and richly golden, then remove from the oven. While they are still warm, carefully remove the centres with a teaspoon, making sure you scoop out all the partly cooked pastry from inside. Cover and keep warm in a low oven.

Pour the clarified butter into a small pan and leave it over a low heat. Put the cockles into a large pan with 120 ml (4 fl oz) of water. Cover and cook over a high heat for 4–5 minutes, shaking the pan well every now and then, until they have all opened. Tip them into a colander and, when they are cool enough to handle, remove them from their shells. Keep warm.

Put the egg yolk, lemon juice and 1 tablespoon of water into a liquidizer. Heat the clarified butter until it begins to bubble. Turn on the liquidizer and slowly pour in the butter through the hole in the lid to make a smooth, creamy hollandaise sauce. Scrape the mixture into a bowl and stir in the laverbread and a little salt to taste. Fold in the cooked cockles, leaving behind any liquid that might have collected at the bottom of the bowl. Spoon the mixture into the warm vol-au-vents and serve immediately.

steamed fish pudding
with leeks and saffron

I once made a fish pudding from a book of my mother's called *Good Things in England*. Good it wasn't. It came from Warwickshire and the introduction said, 'To be quite honest, this is a wartime [1914–18] emergency dish for a meatless day, but it's too good to lose.' It consisted of boiled pollack, anchovy essence, pepper and salt in suet paste. Nevertheless, the idea of putting some good seafood and aromatic accompaniments in a light, gently steamed crust appealed to me. It's extremely good. I've used cod, prawns, scallops and mussels with leeks and saffron here.

SERVES 8

750 G (1$^1/_2$ LB) MUSSELS, CLEANED (SEE PAGE 188)

50 ML (2 FL OZ) DRY WHITE WINE

50 G (2 OZ) BUTTER

1 ONION, FINELY CHOPPED

2 SMALL LEEKS OR 1 LARGE ONE, CLEANED AND SLICED

20 G ($^3/_4$ OZ) PLAIN FLOUR

300 ML (10 FL OZ) *CHICKEN STOCK* (SEE PAGE 185)

A GOOD PINCH OF SAFFRON

50 ML (2 FL OZ) DOUBLE CREAM

350 G (12 OZ) COD OR HADDOCK FILLET,
  SKINNED AND CUT INTO SLICES 2.5 CM (1 INCH) THICK

5 SCALLOPS, CUT IN HALF HORIZONTALLY

150 G (6 OZ) PEELED COOKED NORTH ATLANTIC PRAWNS

150 G (5 OZ) BUTTON MUSHROOMS, SLICED

2 TABLESPOONS CHOPPED PARSLEY

SALT AND FRESHLY GROUND BLACK PEPPER

FOR THE SUET PASTRY:

350 G (12 OZ) PLAIN FLOUR

$^1/_2$ TEASPOON SALT

175 G (6 OZ) SHREDDED SUET

METHOD

Put the mussels and wine into a large pan, cover and cook over a high heat for about 3 minutes, shaking the pan now and then, until the mussels are just open. Tip into a colander set over a bowl to collect the liquor. Leave to cool slightly, then remove the mussels from their shells.

Melt the butter in a large pan, add the onion and leeks and cook for 3 minutes, until soft but not browned. Stir in the flour and cook for 1 minute. Gradually add all the mussel cooking liquor except the last tablespoon (which might contain some grit), plus the chicken stock, saffron and double cream. Simmer for 15 minutes, stirring now and then, until slightly reduced and thickened. Leave to cool and then stir in the prepared fish and shellfish, mushrooms, chopped parsley and some salt and pepper to taste.

For the pastry, sift the flour and salt into a bowl and stir in the shredded suet. Gradually stir in about 200 ml (7 fl oz) of cold water to make a soft but not sticky dough – you might not need all the water. Bring together into a ball and roll out on a lightly floured surface into a 30 cm (12 inch) disc. Cut out one quarter and set it aside for the lid. Press the larger piece of pastry into a lightly buttered 1.75 litre (3 pint) pudding basin, sealing the join well with a little water and leaving a little of the pastry overhanging the edge of the bowl.

Spoon the filling into the bowl and moisten the edge of the pastry with a little water. Roll the remaining pastry out into a circle for the lid. Lay it over the bowl, press the edges together well to seal and neatly trim away any excess.

Cover the bowl with a sheet of lightly buttered greaseproof paper with a pleat in the centre, then a pleated sheet of foil, tying each one securely in place with string. Bring 5–7.5 cm (2–3 inches) of water to the boil in a large pan. Place a trivet in the pan and rest the pudding basin on top. Cover and steam for 2 hours.

Lift the basin out of the steamer and remove the foil and paper. Serve the pudding straight from the dish.

sashimi of sea trout, brill and scallops

I'm inordinately fond of sashimi. I love the way the fish is cut, neat and not too thinly. I applaud the near-fanatical lengths the Japanese will go to in order to get the best, freshest fish, particularly tuna. I marvel at the simple perfection of tastes – the raw fish, horseradish, soy, and pickled radish, or daikon. No wonder it's caught on so well over here. As a way of testing freshness in fish, next time you approach a fish counter ask yourself, 'Would I buy that for sashimi?' If the answer is no, don't buy the fish at all.

SERVES 4 AS A STARTER

100 G (4 OZ) SKINNED SEA TROUT FILLET, TAKEN FROM A SMALL FISH

100 G (4 OZ) SKINNED BRILL FILLET, TAKEN FROM A SMALL FISH

4 PREPARED SCALLOPS, WEIGHING ABOUT 25 G (1 OZ) EACH

1 TABLESPOON WASABI PASTE

LONG CHIVES, TO GARNISH

FOR THE SOY DIPPING SAUCE:

1 CM ($^1/_2$ INCH) PIECE OF PEELED FRESH GINGER, VERY FINELY DICED

2 SPRING ONIONS, FINELY CHOPPED

JUICE AND FINELY GRATED ZEST OF $^1/_2$ LIME

40 ML ($1^1/_2$ FL OZ) DARK SOY SAUCE

40 ML ($1^1/_2$ FL OZ) WATER

METHOD

Cut each piece of sea trout and brill across into slices 5 mm ($^1/_4$ inch) thick, angling the knife blade at 45 degrees as you do so and keeping the fish fillets in shape. Remove the corals, if any, from the scallops and slice each scallop horizontally into 2 or 3 discs. Divide the fish between 4 plates and place a small amount of wasabi paste alongside.

Mix all the ingredients for the dipping sauce together and pour into 4 small bowls or ramekins. Place on each plate next to the fish, garnish with the chives and serve.

deep-fried flounder in breadcrumbs
with costelloise sauce and basil

Flounders, or flooks as they are also known, are not considered amongst the best-tasting flat fish but the thick ones caught off Flookburgh in Cumbria are the exception. Actually, large flounders or plaice are much better eating than small ones, particularly when filleted, dredged with breadcrumbs and deep-fried. I love deep-fried fish with mayonnaise-based sauces, and sauce costelloise is what you might call hot mayonnaise. It's made like hollandaise but uses olive oil instead of butter. This version is flavoured with lemon juice, cayenne pepper and basil, stirred in at the last minute. It's the sort of dish that you just can't get enough of.

SERVES 4

SUNFLOWER OIL FOR DEEP-FRYING

12 X 75 G (3 OZ) SKINNED FLOUNDER FILLETS

50 G (2 OZ) PLAIN FLOUR

2 LARGE EGGS, BEATEN

175 G (6 OZ) FRESH WHITE BREADCRUMBS

SALT AND FRESHLY GROUND BLACK PEPPER

FOR THE COSTELLOISE SAUCE:

120 ML (4 FL OZ) SUNFLOWER OIL

50 ML (2 FL OZ) EXTRA VIRGIN OLIVE OIL

2 LARGE EGG YOLKS

JUICE OF $1/2$ LEMON

A PINCH OF CAYENNE PEPPER

4 LARGE BASIL LEAVES, VERY FINELY SHREDDED

METHOD

To make the sauce, put the sunflower oil and olive oil into a small pan and leave it over a very gentle heat until just warm. Put the egg yolks, lemon juice and 2 tablespoons of cold water into a heatproof bowl. Place the bowl over a pan of simmering water, making sure the water isn't touching the base of the bowl, and whisk vigorously until the mixture becomes thick and frothy. Then gradually whisk in the warmed oils and season to taste with the cayenne pepper and some salt. Take the pan and bowl off the heat and set aside to keep warm while you cook the fish.

Heat some oil for deep-frying to 190°C/375°F. Season the flounder fillets on both sides with some salt and pepper, then coat them in the flour, followed by the beaten egg, and finally the breadcrumbs. Deep-fry the fish, 2 or 3 pieces at a time, for 2 minutes, until crisp and golden. Drain on kitchen paper and keep warm while you fry the remaining fish.

Stir the basil into the sauce. Pile the fish on to a serving platter and serve the costelloise sauce separately.

gratin of skate cheeks
with cheddar cheese and breadcrumbs

Here some nuggets of skate are coated in a bechamel sauce nicely flavoured with nutmeg, then sprinkled with cheese and breadcrumbs and given a pleasing brown crust under the grill. I would call it pub food, or at least the sort of food I'd serve if I had a pub. An Australian chef I was working with the other day said how much he liked British pub food. I was surprised. After all, a lot of it is pretty dire. But he pointed out that when it was good it was precisely what he wanted to eat in Britain, not some ghastly rendition of Pacific Rim fusion cooking done by a pub cook with Antipodean aspirations.

These skate cheeks, or knobs, as they're called in the trade, are a couple of small nuggets of fish cut from the body section of skate or ray after the wings have been removed. I've only seen them on sale, oddly, in the similarly brash and lively resorts of Southend and Blackpool. Ask for them; normally they just get thrown away. If you can't get knobs, try cheeks from cod or monkfish – again these are usually thrown away, which is a real shame. You could, of course, use chunks of monkfish or ling fillet instead.

SERVES 4

600 ML (1 PINT) CREAMY MILK

1 SMALL ONION, PEELED AND HALVED

6 CLOVES

4 BAY LEAVES

4 GRATINGS OF FRESH NUTMEG

2 SMALL SPRIGS OF THYME

1 TEASPOON BLACK PEPPERCORNS

75 G (3 OZ) UNSALTED BUTTER

40 G (1^1/$_2$ OZ) PLAIN FLOUR

120 ML (4 FL OZ) DOUBLE CREAM

550 G (1^1/$_4$ LB) SKATE CHEEKS OR LARGE CHUNKS
   OF SKINNED WHITE FISH FILLETS, SUCH AS COD,
   HADDOCK OR MONKFISH

75 G (3 OZ) MATURE FARMHOUSE CHEDDAR,
   COARSELY GRATED

25 G (1 OZ) COARSE WHITE BREADCRUMBS,
   MADE FROM DAY-OLD BREAD

^{1}/$_4$ TEASPOON CAYENNE PEPPER

10 TURNS OF THE BLACK PEPPER MILL

SALT AND FRESHLY GROUND WHITE PEPPER

METHOD

Put the milk into a pan with the onion, cloves, bay leaves, nutmeg, thyme and black peppercorns. Bring to the boil and simmer for 5 minutes, then remove from the heat and set aside for 1 hour to allow the flavours to infuse.

Bring the milk back to the boil, then strain through a sieve into a clean pan. Melt 50 g (2 oz) of the butter in a pan, add the flour and cook gently for

2–3 minutes without letting it colour. Gradually stir in the hot milk, then bring to the boil and leave to simmer gently over a very low heat for 10 minutes, giving it a stir every now and then, until slightly reduced and thickened. Stir in the cream and season with some salt and freshly ground white pepper to taste.

Heat the remaining butter in a large frying pan until foaming. Season the skate cheeks with salt and pepper, add to the pan and fry briskly for 4 minutes, turning them now and then, until lightly browned and just cooked through. Divide the cheeks between 4 individual gratin dishes and pour over the sauce.

Pre-heat the grill to high. Mix the grated cheese with the breadcrumbs, cayenne pepper and black pepper and sprinkle them over each dish. Grill for 2–3 minutes, until crisp and golden. Serve with hot brown toast.

fish masala

I used not to be particularly fond of dogfish, or huss as it's euphemistically known, until I started to go to India and saw the way they cooked shark curry there – dogfish, after all, is a small shark. It is slightly sweet and very well flavoured, and suits spice and chilli admirably well. This is a dead easy way of cooking it. You just cut it into small steaks, grill it, then spoon over a sauce made with a chilli, coriander and aniseed paste sweetened with coconut and serve with lime wedges and sprigs of coriander.

SERVES 4

1 TEASPOON ANISEED

4 CLOVES

8 BLACK PEPPERCORNS

1 TEASPOON CORIANDER SEEDS

1 CM ($^1/_2$ INCH) PIECE OF CINNAMON STICK

$^1/_2$ TEASPOON CAYENNE PEPPER

$^1/_2$ TEASPOON GROUND TURMERIC

1 SMALL ONION, CHOPPED

4 GARLIC CLOVES, CHOPPED

5 CM (2 INCH) PIECE OF PEELED FRESH GINGER,
    ROUGHLY CHOPPED

50 G (2 OZ) MEDIUM-HOT RED FINGER CHILLIES,
    SEEDED

2 TEASPOONS LIGHT SOFT BROWN SUGAR

2 TABLESPOONS WHITE WINE VINEGAR

2 TABLESPOONS SUNFLOWER OIL

4 TABLESPOONS COCONUT CREAM

6 FRESH CURRY LEAVES (OPTIONAL)

900 G (2 LB) PREPARED DOGFISH

50 G (2 OZ) BUTTER, MELTED

SALT AND FRESHLY GROUND BLACK PEPPER

LIME WEDGES AND SPRIGS OF CORIANDER,
    TO GARNISH

METHOD

Heat a small, heavy-based frying pan over a high heat. Add the aniseed, cloves, black peppercorns, coriander seeds and cinnamon stick and dry-roast them for a few seconds, shaking the pan now and then, until they darken slightly and become aromatic. Tip them into a spice grinder or mortar, add the cayenne pepper and turmeric and grind to a fine powder.

Put the onion, garlic, ginger, red chillies, sugar, vinegar, 1 tablespoon of the sunflower oil, the ground spices and 1 teaspoon of salt into a food processor and blend to a smooth paste. Heat the remaining oil in a small pan, add 6 tablespoons of the curry paste (about half) and fry for 2–3 minutes, until it starts to separate from the oil. Add the coconut cream, 85 ml (3 fl oz) of water and the curry leaves, if using, and simmer gently for 10 minutes, stirring now and then, until reduced and thickened to a good sauce consistency. Taste and season with a little more salt and vinegar if necessary. Keep warm.

Pre-heat the grill to high. Cut the dogfish across into 12 steaks, 2.5 cm (1 inch) thick. Brush with the melted butter and season on both sides with salt and coarsely ground black pepper. Place on a lightly buttered baking tray or the rack of the grill pan and grill for 4–5 minutes on one side only, until cooked through. Transfer to 4 warmed plates and spoon over the sauce. Garnish with the lime wedges and coriander sprigs and serve with some pilau rice.

RESTAURANTS SERVING GOOD SEAFOOD

Cardiff
La Brasserie
61 St Mary Street
Cardiff CF1 1FE
Tel: (029) 2037 2164

Directions
Opposite the Philharmonic pub.

One of the ways I've evolved of finding good seafood restaurants is to ask another good seafood restaurant. Mitchell Tonks at the Green Street Seafood Café in Bath (see West Country selection page 28) told us to head for La Brasserie in Cardiff. He explained it was owned by a Spaniard called Benigno Martinez and, typically, he kept his fish cooking simple and turned it out fast. We arrived there to find it heaving, mainly, it appeared, with students from the university. Mitchell had said don't bother to go to

wales & the north-west coast selection

the more upmarket Le Monde upstairs because you get the same fish downstairs and that's where it all happens. There's an enormous chilled display of fish such as sea bass, meluza (hake) of course, Dover sole, monkfish, skate, prawns, lobster, crab, mussels and oysters. You queue up, choose your fish, tell them how you want it cooked (baked, fried or chargrilled), choose your wine at the same time, sit down and wait not very long for it all to turn up. The prices are

very good, particularly the wine. The patron has a real enthusiasm for wine and passes it on in some astounding prices – Chateau Haut Beychevelle Gloria 1994, £19.95, Chateau Margaux 1993, £23.50! He has a wide selection of really great Spanish whites too – I chose the wonderful, lightly oaked Sauvignon from Torres Fransola. The place looked a bit like a Spanish bodega with sawdust everywhere, low beams and rough plastered walls, albeit in a lock-up shop that could have been a Woolwich Building Society branch or a Mothercare. My oysters were a little on the dry side, but the hake, floured and shallow-fried and served with plenty of lemon, was moist and full of flavour.

Aberdovey, Gwynedd
Penhelig Arms Hotel and Restaurant
Terrace Road
Aberdovey LL35 0LT
Tel: (01654) 767215
E-mail:
penheligarms@saqnet.co.uk

Directions
On the A493 between Machynlleth and Tywyn, just past the railway station.

We arrived after dark, at the small estuaryside town of Aberdovey just on the southern edge of the Snowdonia national park, and checked into the Penhelig Arms Hotel, very tired and without much enthusiasm for that evening's dinner. But as soon as I walked in I had the feeling that things were going to be good. A really genuine welcome is more indicative of the general commitment of the owners and staff of a place than any amount of fancy décor and slick service. From the moment he greeted us until the moment we left, Robert Hughes was charming, and the hotel was comfortable and cheerful and the small rooms warm and cosy. But it was the food that really surprised me. I started with seared fillets of red mullet, with chilli, ginger and garlic. I've become so used to scoffing at British attempts to fuse various culinary ideas that I'd forgotten that it is possible to do it well. My next course, the Mediterranean fish stew with crevettes, garlic bread and aïoli, was really chunky, both the fish and the

flavour. I met the chef, Janie Howkins, briefly; my generation, I thought she had probably spent a lot of time in Spain or at least had a great enthusiasm for that pungent style of cooking using loads of garlic, olive oil and saffron. Then Robert sat down with us, produced a second, different bottle of Chablis Premier Cru Montmains just to see how the different vintage compared with the one we had chosen. Then he produced two splendid bottles of red burgundy, and the Chambolle Musigny 1990 Ghislaine was brilliant. We didn't drink all of those bottles either, honestly.

FISH AND CHIP SHOPS AND CAFÉS

Blackpool, Lancashire
The Cottage
31 Newhouse Road
Marton
Blackpool FY4 4JH
Tel: (01253) 764081

Directions
Near the Oxford Square junction, on the corner past the HSBC bank.

Ask anyone in Blackpool where the best fish and chips are and they'll say 'The Cottage'. It's about two miles inland so it's a bit tricky to find but it's well worth the trip. In addition to the usual cod, haddock and plaice, you can have hake, Dover sole or halibut and a whole side of haddock battered and deep-fried for about £10.

Blackpool, Lancashire
Robert's Oyster Bar
92 The Promenade
Blackpool FY1 1HE
Tel: (01253) 621226

Directions
On the promenade between the tower and the North Pier.

I was perfectly happy to sit in this dark, nineteenth-century seafood bar, divided up into tearooms with stained glass and wood panels. I ordered half a dozen Anglesey oysters, a soused herring, a cup of tea and some bread and butter and was happy as Larry.

Lytham St Anne's, Lancashire
Whelan's
26 Clifton Street
Lytham St Anne's FY8 5EW
Tel: (01253) 735188

Directions
In the main shopping street in the town centre.

It's quite unusual to find a licensed fish and chip restaurant but I think a nice glass of Chardonnay goes well with cod, chips and mushy peas. Certainly if the fish and chips are of the quality of Whelan's. Unusually for the north they used vegetable oil and, while my heart will always lean towards good dripping for fish and chips, I had to admit there was a cleanness and crispness to both the fish and the chips which pleased me greatly. Not so, however, the can of dandelion and burdock I took away with me. It used to taste so good when I was a kid, though.

Letterston, Pembrokeshire
Something's Cooking
The Square
Letterston SA62 5SB
Tel: (01348) 840621

Directions
On the A40 between Haverfordwest and Fishguard.

It doesn't matter how a restaurant is decorated or in what style – if the welcome and the underlying care for

customers are sound, you'll feel relaxed, happy and cheerful, whatever the surroundings. It would be nice one day to do a long article about the place of fish and chip restaurants in popular culture, and Something's Cooking would be an interesting case study. Everything about it was satisfying: the staff, the manager, but above all the fish and chips. The ubiquitous potato for fish and chip shops is the Maris Piper, sometimes known as Links Piper. Not a lot of people know this, but potatoes require more careful handling than grapes. If you drop them or bruise them at all, or subject them to extremes of temperature, the starch in them converts to sugar, which goes all black and caramelly on deep-frying and leads to greasy chips. The chips at Something's Cooking were a vibrant yellow – I should have asked which variety, because they were unusually full of flavour. The fish was spot-on and the

mushy peas sweet and intense.
I had tea, bread and butter and a nice
chat with the manager and left
contented, full of good feelings
for Wales.

FISHMONGERS

Cardiff
Ashton's
Central Market
Cardiff CF10 2AU
Tel: (029) 2022 9201

Directions
The market is right in the centre of the
town. The best entrance to use is the
one in Trinity Street by St John the
Baptist Church.

I hope there's a society of sensible
citizens in Cardiff whose job is to
preserve their wonderful market. Even
in Lyons, France, I noticed the central
market was suffering from the
predations of big supermarkets all
around the *périférique*. Markets are
civilized and interesting places to
shop for fresh produce, and much as I
use supermarkets too they don't
quite match up for a sense of surprise
and excitement and an enthusiasm to

get home and start cooking what
you've just bought. For me this stems
back to my days as a student in
Oxford when the covered market
there was a wondrous Aladdin's cave
of smells and displays of food. Alas,
now that market has seemed to have
become gift-orientated and less and
less the serious shopping experience
it once was. Cardiff is still bustling and
no stall more so than the
fishmongers, Ashton's. They had,
among other things, cuttlefish, squid,
octopus, conger eel, sprats, turbot,
brill, giant raw prawns, gilt head
bream, and even a pile of scads, also
known as horse mackerel, a bit bony
but not bad carefully filleted and
deep-fried as beignets.

Swansea
Coakley-Greene
Stall 41C The Market
Oxford Street
Swansea SA1 3PF
Tel: (01792) 653416

Directions
The market is right next to the
Quadrant shopping precinct. Use
the Union Street entrance.

It's amazing how good both the

markets in Cardiff and Swansea are;
I wish we could have markets like this
in all similar-sized towns. As with
Cardiff, the star attraction in Swansea
Market is the fishmongers – apart,
that is, from the cockle and
laverbread stalls right in the middle.
The two brothers who run Coakley-
Greene, Adrian and Nick, are a mine
of information about local supplies of
fish. Most of their fish comes from day
boats and it really showed in their
display – everything looked clear and
bright-eyed. I was particularly keen on
the pin hake (small hake), some
great-looking swordfish steaks and
some good-sized wild sea bass. If
you're in the market, do try a tub of
laver and some cockles – it's a flavour
that really grows on you.

Blackpool, Lancashire
The Fish Plaice
Abingdon Street Market
Blackpool
Tel: (01253) 293687

Directions
In the one-way system, Abingdon
Street links Church Street with Clifton
Street heading towards the
promenade and North Pier.

I thought I was going to hate
Blackpool but how wrong can you
be? Yes, it is pretty garish, but it's got
quite an exciting energy about it.
You're never going to be bored and
actually it's got some pretty good
shops and a covered food market.
I normally judge the quality of the
market by the fishmongers, of course,
and the Fish Plaice (good old British
puns) was very good. Well-informed
staff and a source of supply just up
the coast at the fishing port of
Fleetwood. On the day we went
there, there were whole black bream,
skate wings and skate knobs
(cheeks), octopus, Dover soles,
mackerel, skinned huss, West African
grouper, red snappers, cockles and
mussels to name but a few. They've
also got another shop of the same
name at Unit 19, Wyre Dock,
Fleetwood (Tel: 01253 772167).

SEAFOOD SUPPLIERS

Morecambe, Lancashire
James Baxter & Son
Thornton Rd
Morecambe LA4 5PB
Tel: (01524) 410910
Fax: (01524) 833363

Directions
Take a side road off the promenade

by a red-brick apartment block called The Sands. Take the next on the right after the garage; Baxter's is on your right.

I have to admit that Bob Baxter makes better potted shrimps than I make at home. He says it's all to do with carefully selecting the shrimps, a secret recipe for the spice, and the quality of the butter he sets them in. His client list is impeccable and like all successful small producers, he's utterly dedicated to what he does. Potted shrimps are a true British gourmet delicacy, emphasized by the fact that they don't sell them in the Morecambe branch of Morrisons supermarket. You can buy them from the door and you might be lucky, if he takes pity on you, to get on his mail-order list, but don't hold your breath.

Morecambe, Lancashire
Raymond Edmondson
32A York Street
Morecambe
Tel: (01524) 412828

Directions
In the west end of town. York street is one street back from the promenade and runs parallel with it.

Raymond nets the shrimps, his wife Pat peels them and his son Paul, pots them in the back of the shop. There's always a heavy demand so get there early. They're excellent.

Neyland, Pembrokeshire
Oneida Viviers Ltd
Brunel Quay
Neyland SA73 1PY
Tel: (01646) 600220
Fax: (01646) 602240

Directions
Right on the quay in Neyland.

David and Madeline Moore are a mine of information about the shellfish of Pembrokeshire. Their business is entirely to do with trucking all the lobsters and crabs and whatever spiny lobsters are left overland to Spain. They say that the Spanish laugh at us for not eating our own seafood but are quite delighted to take it off us and pay handsomely for it. Oneida are, however, quite happy to sell live lobsters, crayfish, velvet crabs, and brown crabs to the public from their vivier tanks. They also sell a rare delicacy, Cardigan Bay shrimps, in season from September to May. I can testify to their deliciousness for I had a bowl with some damn-fine

mayonnaise at Franco and Ann Taruschio's restaurant, the Walnut Tree at Abergavenny (see below), the day before.

Penclawdd, Swansea
Penclawdd Shellfish Processing Ltd
Unit 28
Crofty Industrial Estate
Crofty
Gower SA4 3YA
Tel: (01792) 851678

Directions
The industrial estate is two miles outside the village of Penclawdd, on the road towards Llanmorlais.

Here you can buy freshly cooked and shelled cockles and fresh laverbread.

OTHER PLACES WHERE I'VE EATEN GOOD FISH RECENTLY

Llandewi Skirrid, Monmouthshire
Walnut Tree Inn
Llandewi Skirrid
Nr Abergavenny NP7 8AW
Wales
Tel: (01873) 852797

SO.712

AS DAWN BREAKS AT DINGLE HARBOUR IN COUNTY KERRY, THE FISHERMEN GET THEIR NETS READY TO GO OUT TO SEA ONCE MORE.

northern ire

'It's absolute cats in England,' said Fergus O'Mahony, the landlord of Mary Ann's in Castletownshend, with great enthusiasm. Sunlight was streaming through the small-paned windows over the slate floor across the dark wooden bar and catching the silver of the beer taps and thick, straight pint glasses on the shelves. It was a place to gladden the heart; a plaque on the wall had a quote from James

land & eire

Joyce's *Ulysses*: 'A good puzzle would be to cross Ireland without passing a pub.'

I walked up the hill to the post office to send a postcard to Jill. It was a glorious, sparkling morning. Is there any more delightful prospect for a man with an enthusiasm for a pint than a short walk in the sunshine down an Irish village street to an old, wood-panelled bar where he will savour the first pint of the day?

A FISHING BOAT PREPARES TO LEAVE THE HARBOUR AT COBH IN CORK. YEARS AGO THOUSANDS OF FAMINE-STRICKEN EMIGRANTS LEFT THIS PORT FOR A NEW LIFE IN AMERICA.

A green post office van picked up the mail from a green postbox, a sort of alternative world to the red vans and boxes back home. I had lunch at the pub: fat scallops landed at Union Hall, sold on the market in Skibbereen and served in a nice, cheesy velouté sauce, a welcome change from pan-fried scallops with rocket or chilli or soy or ginger. Pubs generally do these fusion-cooking ideas badly. No, here was the sort of food you expect to get with a slow-poured pint of Guinness on a sunny morning.

It hadn't rained in west Cork for four weeks, but it's hard not to feel optimistic in Ireland even when it is raining. You feel a bit boring coming from Britain, heavy-handed, serious. It's almost as if we've lost the art of having fun. There's a lightness about life in Ireland, a feeling that anything is possible. Out in the bars of Cork on a Saturday night there's room only to squeeze through crowds of animated people to find some space by the Brazilian salsa band. The Murphy's is coming thick, black and fast, but nowhere – not in the bars or on the street or late at night in the Imperial Hotel after we'd got back from the Van Morrison concert at Blackrock – was there any sign of bad temper.

Everyone is having a thoroughly good time. A country that has a word for it, the *craic*, has got to be different. Where else too can you walk down the main street of a city in mid-afternoon and smell cows and green grass from the surrounding pastures, then dive into the best covered market in these islands for salt ling, live lobsters, turbot and some of Frank Hederman's smoked eel, which is unquestionably one of the foods I'd feature in my world top ten: it's creamy, subtle and delicately smoked. It's just the sort of thing to put on my menu, the skin peeled off at the last minute and the fillet thinly sliced and served with a warm potato salad, a few dandelion leaves and some snipped chives.

It's hard to believe how different Frank's smoked eel is from anyone else's. It's all to do with attention to detail. He uses wild silver eels from the River Shannon. Before smoking, the eels are salted with Spanish sea salt, which doesn't leave a bitter aftertaste as other salts can. He smokes the eels vertically to let some of the oil run out, and uses beechwood chippings rather than oak. The smoke wafts through the smoking chamber slowly and gently, gradually curing and flavouring the rows of eels and wild salmon hanging on tenterhooks.

I suggested to Frank that he look to Lough Neagh in County Antrim for possible supplies of eels. We went there last year to film the eel fishermen, leaving Ardboe before a cold, clear, pasture-scented dawn in July. We started hauling in the delicate long lines baited with earthworms while the sky was still dark, lit up in the eastern distance by the lights of Belfast. The fishermen were men of few words as each eel was brought writhing aboard and they flicked the cotton trace against a knife tied to the side of the boat and swung the eel into a blue plastic barrel. Without observing the action, I never would have understood Seamus Heaney's poem 'Lifting'.

The line's a filament of smut
Drawn hand over fist
Where every three yards a hook's missed
Or taken and smut thickens, wrist
Thick, a flail lashed into the barrel
with one swing.

The next day, I drove from Cork to Castletownbere, where Mike Sullivan picked us up in his fishing boat to take us over to Bere Island. We stopped by the wreck of a Russian ship to haul some prawn pots, a haven for fish and shellfish.

ALL QUIET ON THE HARBOUR FRONT. FISHING BOATS TIE UP AT COBH AFTER A GRUELLING TRIP TO SEA TO KEEP THE ENGLISH MARKET AT CORK STOCKED WITH LING, TURBOT AND LOBSTER.

Any old wreck, even a car, has the same attraction. In Japan they create coastal wrecks to increase the density of fish; sadly, it doesn't happen over here.

The first pot contained seven flapping langoustines and three velvet crabs. The ship at low tide looked like a scene from a Famous Five adventure: red-brown with rust, trailing green weed all around, its hatches and companionways dark holes filled with water, mussels growing on the sloping decks and in the ventilation shafts, the masts, still painted white and spattered with seagull droppings, leaning right over above the high-water mark.

I had gone to try the food at Lawrence Cove House and to talk to Mike about fishing. He buys Bantry Bay scallops from all the local fishermen, which he sells to top restaurants in Dublin. They are something to see; the best in the world, says Mike. Each shell is about six inches wide, the meat delicately sweet. The dredging for them is heavily controlled, and the other way of fishing for them – shading – is so naturally occasional that conservation is inbuilt. In order to catch scallops by shading, you must have a sunny day with no breeze so that you can see the bottom easily. You view the seabed on the shaded side of the boat, when the outline of any live scallop just under the sand can be seen as a white crescent. The scallops are scooped up in a small net on the end of a long pole.

Mike told me of one local fisherman who had fished 20 bags of scallops by shading and earned himself £2000, but it had taken two weeks. He said a diver (banned in the bay) could find the same amount in a day. He was very worried about the mussel farming in the bay, saying that plans to expand the existing and highly successful mussel farms would inevitably lead to a shortage of plankton on which the scallops also feed. He felt that the government, in the need to create more jobs in the area, would allow more mussel farming and jeopardize the existing jobs of the scallop fishermen.

A similar two-sided tale occurs out in Connemara at Delphi Lodge in County Galway. There a friend of my sister's, Peter Mantle, runs a fishing lodge near Leenane. I was dapping for sea trout with Peter on a soft, muted, watery afternoon in a boat on the lake outside the lodge, which, though a substantial building, is dwarfed by the heather-clad mountains behind. Dapping is like fly-fishing, but you hover the fly over the water rather than flick it across the surface. Peter talked about the plight of wild sea trout and salmon decimated by the build-up of sea lice around the salmon farms further down towards the sea. These lice burrow through the skins of the fish and, in quantity, kill them. Without the farms, the lice would be merely a pest, but fish farms create jobs in wild rural areas. Yet Peter pointed out that the jobs created by sport fishing far outweigh those created by salmon farming. The value of a salmon as a sporting fish is ten times its value as food when you consider the economic benefit to the area of a popular leisure activity.

Everywhere you go in Ireland the conflicting interests of fishing are manifest. It's a labyrinth of twists and turns in which one point of view is countered by another.

It seems too much of a jerk to bring some pleasant seafood thoughts out now, but it's not my wish to paint a constantly disturbing picture. After all, I'm

**NORRIE DOUGAN FISHES
STRANGFORD LOUGH,
SOUTH-EAST OF BELFAST,
FOR DUBLIN BAY PRAWNS.**

scribbling this in Myrtle Allen's kitchen in Ballymaloe. She's just cooked a thick
turbot fresh out of Ballycotton Bay this morning. It's been baked in the oven and
finished with butter, parsley, thyme, chives and chervil, and will be served as part
of a hot buffet lunch with a roast leg of lamb, some boiled ham, fish pies, darnes
of salmon and new potatoes, mayonnaise, green salads and tomatoes from
Darina Allen's garden at the cookery school just down the road, all swiftly cooked
by Rory O'Connell, Darina's brother, who's the chef at Ballymaloe. Myrtle's just
been made an honorary doctor. She deserves it. No one has been more
influential in championing the cause of locally produced ingredients cooked
without unnecessary adornment. She often says that it's all just a matter of good
common sense, but she also adds that good common sense is not very
common any more.

Great materials in cooking are what matter most. I made a trip to Strangford
Lough just outside Belfast because I had heard about the legendary mussels,
clams, lobsters, oysters and prawns from that pure and fertile sea lough.
I imagined a rugged Scottish-type stretch of water with mountains rolling down
to the sea. Instead I found soft, undulating farmland bordering a vast stretch of
inland water filled with small islands and tidal rocky outcrops, just blues and
greens on a sunny day. We went fishing there with Norrie Dougan and caught
Dublin Bay prawns the size of small lobsters. We ate a sumptuous lunch of
Portaferry mussels from the lough at the Narrows in Portaferry. Later we filmed

on the empty beaches at sunset all around Ardglass and Coney Island, nearby. It was August, but so few people go on holiday in Northern Ireland that it was like summer in Cornwall 40 years ago. That night we repaired to the Dufferin Arms at Killyleagh for more prawns, oysters and lobsters, all from the lough. So taken was I with the prawns on that day that I found a recipe for a sauce to go with them in one of Elizabeth David's books, *An Omelette and a Glass of Wine*: it's called *Grilled Dublin Bay Prawns with a Pernod and Olive Oil Dressing* (see page 163).

DULSE – A REDDISH-PURPLE SEAWEED – IS COLLECTED FROM THE MID-SHORE LINE AT BALLYWALTER. SORTED, CLEANED AND COOKED, IT'S ADDED TO MASHED POTATOES TO MAKE DULSE 'CHAMP'.

miso soup with dulse, scallops and cod

This delicate Japanese soup is, I think, the perfect way to serve up a variety of edible seaweeds. You almost have to think Japanese to appreciate the texture, colours and flavours of seaweed. The finished dish looks like an oriental abstract painting, and only in that delicate, smoky miso- and dashi-flavoured broth can the textures and flavours be fully appreciated. Curiously enough, these will-o'-the-wisp soups are often served as the last course, coming as a light surprise at the end of a multi-course Japanese meal.

SERVES 4

7 G (1/4 OZ) MIXED DRIED SEAWEED (E.G. DULSE,
   WAKAME, AGAR AGAR AND WHITE MOSS)
50 G (2 OZ) PIECE OF THICK COD FILLET, SKINNED
3 SCALLOPS
2 TABLESPOONS WHITE MISO PASTE
7 G (1/4 OZ) BABY LEAF SPINACH
7 G (1/4 OZ) MIZUNA LEAVES
2 SPRING ONIONS, THINLY SLICED ON THE DIAGONAL
2 BUTTON MUSHROOMS, THINLY SLICED

FOR THE DASHI (STOCK):

1.2 LITRES (2 PINTS) WATER
5 CM (2 INCH) SQUARE OF DRIED KOMBU SEAWEED
3 TABLESPOONS BONITO FLAKES

Drop the dried seaweed into a large bowl of cold water and leave to rehydrate for 8–10 minutes.

For the dashi, put the water and dried kombu into a pan and slowly bring to a simmer. Strain immediately, return the liquid to the pan, bring back to a simmer and add the bonito flakes. Bring to the boil, then remove the pan from the heat and allow the flakes to settle for 1 minute. Pour the dashi through a very fine or muslin-lined sieve into a clean pan.

Cut the cod into 2.5 cm (1 inch) cubes and then into very thin slices. Slice the scallops very thinly horizontally. Drain the seaweed.

Bring the dashi back up to a gentle simmer. Mix a ladleful of the hot liquid into the miso paste until smooth. Return the mixture to the pan and add the scallops and cod. Cook for 30 seconds, then add the drained seaweed, spinach leaves and mizuna and simmer for a few seconds only.

Ladle the soup into bowls and garnish with the sliced spring onions and mushrooms. Serve immediately.

grilled oysters
with parmesan cheese

If you're going to cook oysters, you'd better make sure you keep it dead simple, and I always think they've got to be served in the shell. Here, we've got just four ingredients plus the oysters but they're very good. There's no point in using natives for this dish – they're far too expensive and best served naturally to appreciate their flavour. Use Pacifics instead, which are half the price and just perfect.

SERVES 4

24 PACIFIC OYSTERS

175 ML (6 FL OZ) DOUBLE CREAM

25 G (1 OZ) PARMESAN CHEESE,
  FRESHLY GRATED

50 G (2 OZ) BUTTER, MELTED

FRESHLY GROUND BLACK PEPPER

METHOD

Pre-heat the grill to high. Open the oysters (see page 188), release them from the deeper bottom shells and then pour off most of the liquor. Put them on a baking tray or the rack of the grill pan. Spoon about 1$\frac{1}{2}$ teaspoons of the cream over each oyster and season with a little black pepper. Sprinkle over the Parmesan cheese and then drizzle with the melted butter.

Grill the oysters for 1 minute, until the cheese is golden brown. Serve straight away.

monk's seafood chowder

Irish seafood chowder is a dish imported from the New World to the Old, and changed slightly in the move. I found this at Monk's Pub in the village of Ballyvaughan in County Clare. In the pubs on the western shores of Ireland it has become as natural and local a dish as it is in New England. What more convivial thought could there be than a warm pub overlooking a sparkling bay, a bowl of chowder with soda bread and the Guinness on the way?

SERVES 6

25 G (1 OZ) DRIED BORLOTTI OR HARICOT BEANS,
   SOAKED OVERNIGHT
600 ML (1 PINT) *FISH STOCK* (SEE PAGE 185)
750 G (1½ LB) SKINNED WHITING FILLETS,
   CUT INTO BITE-SIZED PIECES
600 ML (1 PINT) CREAMY MILK
100 G (4 OZ) CARROTS, CUT INTO SMALL DICE
150 G (5 OZ) CELERY, CUT INTO SMALL DICE
450 G (1 LB) POTATOES, CUT INTO SMALL DICE
½ SMALL ONION, CUT INTO SMALL DICE
25 G (1 OZ) GREEN BEANS, CUT INTO SMALL DICE
25 G (1 OZ) CANNED SWEETCORN, DRAINED
40 G (1½ OZ) FRESH OR FROZEN PEAS
40 G (1½ OZ) PLAIN FLOUR
300 G (11 OZ) COOKED PEELED NORTH ATLANTIC PRAWNS
175 ML (6 FL OZ) DOUBLE CREAM
SALT AND FRESHLY GROUND BLACK PEPPER
A LITTLE LIGHTLY WHIPPED CREAM AND SMALL
   SPRIGS OF DILL, TO GARNISH

METHOD

Drain the soaked beans, put them into a pan with plenty of fresh water, then bring to the boil and cook for 40–50 minutes until just tender. Drain and set aside.

Bring the fish stock to a gentle simmer in a large pan, add the whiting pieces and poach for 5 minutes, until only just cooked. Transfer to a plate with a slotted spoon and keep warm.

Add three-quarters of the milk to the pan with the carrots, celery, potatoes and onion, bring to the boil and simmer for 10 minutes. Add the green beans, sweetcorn, peas and borlotti or haricot beans and simmer for another 5 minutes.

Gradually mix the remaining milk into the flour to make a smooth paste. Stir it into the soup and simmer for 4–5 minutes, until the flour has cooked out and the vegetables are tender. Stir in the prawns, poached whiting and cream and simmer for 1 minute. Season well with salt and pepper and serve in warmed soup bowls, garnished with a little lightly whipped cream and some dill sprigs.

stir-fried eel with black bean sauce

It's not for no reason that the Chinese love cooking with eel. They just seem to have the best recipes. I'm particularly fond of the fresh, oily flavour of eel but it needs careful handling. Generally, any dish that includes butter, cream and eel doesn't work, apart from the recipe for *Anguilles au Vert* in my last book, *Seafood Odyssey*, where I drastically cut the richness. But this dish, an imaginative rendering of my many trips to Chinese restaurants all over the world, is what stir-fried eel with black bean sauce is all about.

SERVES 2

225–275 G (8–10 OZ) EEL FILLET, SKINNED

1^1/$_2$ TEASPOONS CORNFLOUR

1^1/$_2$ TABLESPOONS CHINESE FERMENTED
    SALTED BLACK BEANS

^{1}/$_2$ TEASPOON CASTER SUGAR

2 TABLESPOONS SESAME OIL

2 GARLIC CLOVES, CUT INTO FINE SHREDS

2.5 CM (1 INCH) PIECE OF PEELED FRESH GINGER,
    CUT INTO VERY THIN SHREDS

1 MEDIUM-HOT RED FINGER CHILLI, THINLY SLICED

3 TABLESPOONS CHINESE RICE WINE OR
    DRY SHERRY

1 TEASPOON DARK SOY SAUCE

4 SPRING ONIONS, CUT ON THE DIAGONAL
    INTO LONG, THIN SLICES

SALT

METHOD

Cut the eel diagonally into pieces 2.5 cm (1 inch) wide. Toss with a little salt and then the cornflour. Put the black beans, sugar and 2 tablespoons of cold water into a small bowl and crush to a coarse paste.

Heat a wok over a high heat until it is smoking hot. Add the sesame oil and garlic, quickly followed by the ginger, red chilli and black bean paste. Stir-fry for a few seconds, then add the eel pieces and stir-fry for 1 minute. Add the rice wine or sherry, soy sauce and 3–4 tablespoons of water and cook for 2 minutes, until the eel is cooked through.

Add the spring onions to the wok and stir-fry for about a minute. Serve immediately with some steamed rice.

grilled dublin bay prawns
(langoustines) with a pernod and olive oil dressing

I got the sauce for this from re-reading Elizabeth David's *An Omelette and a Glass of Wine*. Some recipes just jump off the page at you as essential to do now – this is particularly common with recipes from Elizabeth David's books. It's the sort of sauce I would love to have invented for all members of the lobster family. The combination of the aniseed flavours of the Pernod and tarragon, salted with a little soy and sharpened with lemon juice, serves to 'tease you out of thought', as Keats might have said.

For the photo, we used very large prawns, weighing about 350 g (12 oz) each; if you come across any this size, you will need only one per person. You could also substitute two 450 g (1 lb) cooked lobsters for the Dublin Bay prawns, serving half a lobster per person.

SERVES 4

16 LARGE OR 24 SMALLER COOKED DUBLIN
  BAY PRAWNS (LANGOUSTINES)
2 SMALL SHALLOTS, FINELY CHOPPED
1/2 TABLESPOON ROUGHLY CHOPPED
  TARRAGON
1/2 TABLESPOON ROUGHLY CHOPPED
  FLAT-LEAF PARSLEY
1 TEASPOON DIJON MUSTARD
1 TEASPOON DARK SOY SAUCE
85 ML (3 FL OZ) EXTRA VIRGIN OLIVE OIL
1 1/2 TABLESPOONS FRESH LEMON JUICE
1 TEASPOON PERNOD
50 G (2 OZ) BUTTER, MELTED
SALT AND FRESHLY GROUND BLACK PEPPER

METHOD

Pre-heat the grill to high. Cut the Dublin Bay prawns open lengthways and scoop out the creamy contents of the heads and any red roe with a teaspoon. Put this into a small bowl and stir in the shallots, tarragon, parsley, mustard, soy sauce, oil, lemon juice, Pernod and a little salt and pepper to taste.

Place the halved prawns cut side up on a baking tray or the rack of the grill pan and brush with the melted butter. Season lightly and grill for 2–3 minutes, until the shells as well as the meat are heated through. Put the prawns on 4 serving plates and spoon over a little of the dressing. Divide the rest of the dressing between 4 dipping saucers or small ramekins and serve.

braised trout with mint,
parsley and caper sauce

It's a real pleasure to discover a really old recipe that has a modern feel about it. This particular recipe is just headed 'housekeeper's recipe' and is dated 1820. The extraordinary thing is that the sauce elements are like the very fashionable Italian sauce, *salsa verde*, and they have the same function – to partner a nice plump trout or freshwater pollan with some piquant flavours.

SERVES 4

4 RAINBOW TROUT

50 ML (2 FL OZ) DRY WHITE WINE

50 ML (2 FL OZ) WATER

50 G (2 OZ) BUTTER

1/2 TABLESPOON MINT LEAVES

A SMALL BUNCH OF CHIVES

1 1/2 TABLESPOONS FLAT-LEAF
   PARSLEY LEAVES

1 1/2 TABLESPOONS CAPERS IN BRINE,
   DRAINED AND RINSED

3 ANCHOVY FILLETS IN OLIVE OIL, DRAINED

1 GARLIC CLOVE, ROUGHLY CHOPPED

1/2 TEASPOON DIJON MUSTARD

1/2 TABLESPOON FRESH LEMON JUICE

1 TEASPOON PLAIN FLOUR

SALT AND FRESHLY GROUND
   BLACK PEPPER

METHOD

Pre-heat the oven to 200°C/400°F/Gas Mark 6.

Season the trout lightly inside and out and put them in a shallow baking dish. Pour over the wine and water and dot the fish here and there with half the butter. Cover with foil and bake for 25 minutes.

Meanwhile, pile the herbs, capers, anchovy fillets and garlic on to a board and chop together into a coarse paste. Scrape the mixture into a bowl and stir in the mustard and lemon juice.

Beat the remaining butter in a small bowl to soften it and then mix in the flour to make a smooth paste. Remove the trout from the oven and carefully pour off the cooking liquor into a small pan. Cover the trout again and keep them warm. Place the cooking liquor over a medium-high heat, bring it to a simmer and then whisk in the butter and flour paste. Leave it to simmer for 1 minute, stirring until smooth and thickened. Stir in the herb mixture and take the pan off the heat.

Put the trout on 4 warmed plates, spoon over the sauce and serve.

myrtle's turbot

Myrtle Allen at Ballymaloe House in County Cork has been more influential than anyone else in stressing the importance of great produce simply prepared as the essence of Irish cooking. She cooks the sort of food I love to eat – it's like my mother's cooking really. The day we filmed in her kitchen, the chef, Rory O'Connell, was roasting poultry and local lamb, boiling hams, making fish pies, sautéing potatoes and tossing soft green lettuce salads for lunch, while Myrtle baked a turbot fresh from Ballycotton Bay that morning. The recipe for it is very easy, so if you can get a suitable-sized turbot, you must try it and marvel at what a fantastic fish it is when cooked on the bone.

SERVES 4

1 X 1.5 KG (3 LB) TURBOT
A SMALL BUNCH OF THYME
A SMALL BUNCH PARSLEY
A SMALL BUNCH OF CHIVES
75 G (3 OZ) BUTTER
SALT AND FRESHLY GROUND BLACK PEPPER

Pre-heat the oven to 200°C/400°F/Gas Mark 6.

With a sharp knife, cut through the skin on the top (dark) side only of the turbot, all the way around the fish, close to the frill-like fins. Season on top with some salt and pepper.

Pour 85 ml (3 fl oz) water into a roasting tin large enough to hold the turbot. Put the fish in the tin and bake for 30 minutes. Meanwhile, finely chop half the herbs. Gently melt the butter in a small pan, stir in the chopped herbs and set aside.

Remove the fish from the oven and carefully peel away the top skin. Lift the fish on to a warm serving plate, then pour the cooking juices and the warm herb butter over the white flesh of the turbot. Shape the rest of the herbs into a bouquet and lay them near the head as a garnish. Serve with plenty of boiled new potatoes.

roast monkfish with crushed potatoes, olive oil and watercress

The idea of roasting a fillet of fish sounds appetizing. I have an image of a crisp, brown crust and succulent white fish underneath. The reality, though, is that unless you are cooking a large whole fish, it doesn't spend enough time in the oven to achieve the required caramelized colour. Much better, therefore, to sear the fillet in a pan on a hot stovetop, then transfer it to the oven. Incidentally, it's not a bad idea to deal with fried fish this way, too, because if you're busy getting other things ready, once the pan's in the oven, you don't have to keep a careful eye on it.

SERVES 4

2 X 350 G (12 OZ) PIECES OF THICK
MONKFISH FILLET
750 G (1^1/$_2$ LB) NEW POTATOES,
SCRAPED CLEAN
2 TABLESPOONS OLIVE OIL
85 ML (3 FL OZ) EXTRA VIRGIN OLIVE OIL,
PLUS EXTRA TO SERVE
50 G (2 OZ) WATERCRESS SPRIGS,
VERY ROUGHLY CHOPPED
BALSAMIC VINEGAR, SEA SALT FLAKES
AND COARSELY CRUSHED BLACK PEPPER,
TO SERVE

METHOD

Pre-heat the oven to 200°C/400°F/Gas Mark 6.

Season the monkfish with some salt and set it aside for 15 minutes. Cook the potatoes in well-salted boiling water until tender. While the potatoes are cooking, heat the 2 tablespoons of olive oil in a large, ovenproof frying pan. Pat the monkfish dry on kitchen paper, add to the pan and sear for 3–4 minutes, turning it 3 or 4 times, until nicely browned on all sides. Transfer the pan to the oven and roast for 10–12 minutes, until the fish is cooked through but still moist and juicy in the centre. Remove from the oven, cover with foil and set aside for 5 minutes.

When the potatoes are done, drain them well and return them to the pan with the extra virgin olive oil. Gently crush each potato against the side of the pan with the back of a fork until it just bursts open. Season with salt and pepper, add any juices from the fish and the watercress and turn over gently until the watercress is well mixed in.

Cut the monkfish across into thick slices. Spoon the crushed potatoes on to 4 warmed plates and put the monkfish on top. Put your thumb over the top of the bottle of extra virgin olive oil and drizzle a little of it around the outside edge of each plate. Do the same with the balsamic vinegar and then sprinkle around a few sea salt flakes and coarsely crushed black pepper.

salt ling, tomato and potato pasties

We don't seem to have much enthusiasm in this country for salted fish, yet the tradition of salting cod and haddock and, in Cornwall, pollack and ling goes back a long time. The trick with salt fish is to combine it with something sweet and fresh, in this case tomatoes and onions. I like to think of this pasty as similar to the *empanadas* of Northern Spain – the common food of two places with strong Celtic traditions.

If you can't get salt ling, any dried salt fish would do – most fishmongers stock it, whether it be cod, ling or pollack. Or you could prepare your own fresh salted cod (see page 186).

MAKES 9

550 G (1¼ LB) SALT LING OR POLLACK OR
  750 G (1½ LB) FRESH SALTED COD
1.5 KG (3 LB) CHILLED FRESH PUFF PASTRY
225 G (8 OZ) PLUM TOMATOES, ROUGHLY CHOPPED
275 G (10 OZ) POTATOES, PEELED AND CUT INTO SMALL PIECES
1 ONION, CUT INTO QUARTERS AND THINLY SLICED
100 G (4 OZ) CHORIZO SAUSAGE, FINELY DICED
2 GARLIC CLOVES, FINELY CHOPPED
15 G (½ OZ) CHOPPED PARSLEY
SALT AND FRESHLY GROUND BLACK PEPPER
2 TABLESPOONS OLIVE OIL OR 25 G (1 OZ) BUTTER, MELTED
1 EGG, BEATEN

METHOD

Rinse the excess salt off the salt ling or pollack and place the fish in a large bowl. Cover with plenty of cold water and leave to soak for 24 hours, changing the water once half-way through.

The next day, divide the pastry into 9 pieces and roll them out on a lightly floured surface. Cut a 19 cm (7½ inch) circle out of each one, using an upturned bowl or small plate as a template. Keep cool while you prepare the filling.

Drain the soaked fish and remove the skin and any bones. Cut the flesh into 2.5 cm (1 inch) pieces and mix with the tomatoes, potatoes, onion, chorizo, garlic, parsley, a little salt and plenty of black pepper. Gently stir in the olive oil or melted butter.

Divide the mixture between the pastry circles. Brush one half of the pastry edge with a little beaten egg, bring the sides together over the top of the filling and pinch together well to seal. Crimp the edge of each pasty decoratively between your fingers, then transfer them to a lightly greased baking sheet and chill for 20 minutes.

Pre-heat the oven to 200°C/400°F/Gas Mark 6. Brush the pasties with the remaining beaten egg and bake for 30–35 minutes, until crisp and golden.

northern ireland & eire selection

RESTAURANTS SERVING GOOD SEAFOOD

Baltimore, Co. Cork, Eire
Chez Youen
The Pier
Baltimore
Tel: (00 353) 282 0136
Fax: (00 353) 282 0495
E-mail: chezyouen@youenjacob.com
Website: www.youenjacob.com

Directions
Overlooking the harbour, just past the pub on the hill continuing into the village.

West Cork feels more like part of Europe than does any part of Britain; this is partly because the French, and particularly the Bretons, have taken to it as a second home. Youen Jacob, along with two or three other Breton chefs, has a simple seafood restaurant serving jolly good, classic French coastal fish dishes. I had langoustines with mayonnaise to start with. Then I had a lovely, plump piece of John Dory with a chive and butter sauce, and the sautéd potatoes with this were outstanding – sandy and perfectly seasoned. Debbie had scallops provençale. How often the scallops in this dish are just stewed in a rather indifferent tomato sauce, but this time they were seared and the sauce was an intense reduction of stock, red peppers, garlic, onion and cayenne. Youen's main course was small escalopes of monkfish cut to look like large conchiglia, the Italian shell-shaped pasta. Mention should be made too of the Jacobs' pizza café called La Jolie Brise (Tel: (00 353) 282 0600), The Pier, Baltimore, 50 metres from Chez Youen. To describe this establishment as laid-back is an understatement: you ask for everything three times, but this is Ireland, for God's sake – relax and enjoy it because the fish cooking and the pizzas are first rate.

Bere Island, Co. Cork, Eire
Lawrence Cove House
Bere Island
Beara
Tel/Fax: (00 353) 277 5063
E-mail: cove@indigo.ie

Directions
Catch the ferry to the island from the pontoon, 3 miles east of Castletownbere.

Ireland can sometimes be the most romantic place in the world. I took the early evening ferry from Castletownbere to Bere Island – there was me, David the director, Arezoo his researcher and a couple about my age from Italy. We were all going to Lawrence Cove House, where local farmer and fisherman Mike Sullivan runs a very well-regarded seafood restaurant, and his wife Mary cooks. We passed the sunken spars and partly submerged hull of a rusty Russian freighter. Our boatman explained that a few years ago the Russian crew had spent a year isolated on the boat, then had apparently jumped ship and scuttled it. We walked up the path to the restaurant and we ate grilled clams with garlic butter, Dublin Bay prawns and some of the best scallops I've ever tasted. They catch them there by 'shadowing'. The skill is to sit in your boat on a sunny day looking for the outline of the scallop under the sand below and you then hoick them up with a long pole. On the journey back in the moonlight, I talked about Dublin, and life in Venice and Milan; somehow you feel more European in Ireland than you do back home.

Cork, Co. Cork, Eire
The Ivory Tower
The Exchange Buildings
35 Princes Street
Cork
Tel: (00 353) 2127 4665
Fax: (00 353) 2127 2592

Directions
In the street running along the back of the English Market, between South Mall and St Patrick's Street.

In addition to The Yumi Yuki Club (see right) and The Ivory Tower, Seamus O'Connell is also opening a pizza warehouse which, when I peered through the window, looks as though it's going to be just as much fun as the others. This is how I found The Ivory Tower: I was walking through the English Market in Cork when I bumped into Frank Hederman, who produces the best smoked eel in the world (see Smokeries, page 175). He asked me where I was eating that night and I mentioned a seafood place just along the coast. 'You've got to be joking. Don't go there, come with me.' He took me through the narrow, old winding streets of Cork, through a scruffy doorway and up some rather grubby stairs, past a small, smoky kitchen and into a restaurant hung with paintings of strange figures in unrecognizable Celtic-influenced settings. He thrust a menu into my hand and I started to get very interested indeed; marinated rouget and bouillabaisse en gelée, escabèche of mackerel à la Roanne, scallops braised with a tagine of vegetables, spicy tuna ceviche, sushi roll and nigiri... There and then I decided I definitely wanted to come back. By the evening I'd met Seamus and talked about his cooking influences: Japan, Mexico and a long spell cooking in various restaurants in New York. He agreed to do a tasting menu for me and it was, as I'm fond of saying about great meals cooked by young, iconoclastic chefs, pure 'rock and roll'.

Cork, Co. Cork, Eire
The Yumi Yuki Club,
Triskel Arts Centre
Tobin Street
Cork
Tel: (00 353) 2127 5777
Fax: (00 353) 2127 2592

Directions
One of the narrow streets running between Grand Parade and South Main Street, close to the English Market.

Every year for the last five years Seamus O'Connell (see The Ivory Tower, left) has spent a month cooking in Japan, so he has a real understanding of that country's cuisine. His nigiri-sushi – hand-formed rice brushed with a little wasabi and topped with fish – is a revelation. The cooking of the rice is almost like a good risotto in that it has a definite but in no way assertive bite to it.

Kinsale, Co. Cork, Eire
Kinsale Gourmet Store & Seafood Bar
Guardwell
Kinsale
Tel: (00 353) 2177 4453
Website: www.dragnet-systems.ie/dira/gourmet

Directions
Next door to the police station and opposite St Multose Church.

At the time of writing this I'm planning to open a seafood deli. We'll sell lobsters, crabs, mussels, langoustines and oysters, a little wet fish, but mostly cooked fish dishes that people will want to take home and eat: things like fish pie, crab and Gruyère tartlets, fish tagine, even bouillabaisse and bourride to reheat carefully. When I walked into Martin Shanahan's Gourmet Store, I thought, these guys have stolen a march on me. They were doing exactly what I want to do, and in addition they had a few tables where you could eat too. I ordered a big plate of Dublin Bay prawns with garlic and chilli butter, and Debbie had a crab and avocado salad. This store is such a good idea and probably one that a lot of other fishmongers will try in the future.

Shanagarry, Co. Cork, Eire
Ballymaloe House
Shanagarry
Midleton
Tel: (00 353) 2165 2531
Fax: (00 353) 2165 2021
E-mail: bmaloe@iol.ie
Website: www.ballymaloe.com

Directions
Take the road just east of Midleton to Shanagarry and then follow signs to the house.

Lunch at Ballymaloe: fillets of monkfish, hollandaise sauce and the young shoots of sea kale. That was special, and then a dessert I'd never tasted before – carragheen moss pudding. Carragheen is a seaweed with similar properties to gelatine, but it flavours this pudding, made with milk, sugar and a vanilla pod, with a subtle undertone of iodine. You eat it with some farmhouse cream poured over and a spoonful or two of dark, soft brown sugar. These two dishes, and an hors d'oeuvre that contained some smoked mussels, salmon and eel, all from smokers within 20 miles of Ballymaloe, made for a memorable lunch with Darina and Tim Allen, whose cookery school just down the road is the one I aspire to with mine.

Greencastle, Co. Donegal, Eire
Kealy's Seafood Bar
The Harbour
Greencastle
Tel/Fax: (00 353) 778 1010
e.mail: kealys@iol.ie

Directions
On the seafront opposite the harbour.

One of the pleasures of my trip all around Ireland was to find seafood chowder in so many bars on the coast. I'd almost call it an Irish dish now because it's changed so much from the New England version. James and Patricia Kealy do a pretty mean chowder in their bar, but it was the really simple fish cooking that got me going. Simple grills of plaice, lemon sole, poached hake with saffron sauce and the dish that I had, grilled megrim sole with butter. It's a long old way up to Donegal, but it's beautiful and worth a trip when there are watering holes like Kealy's.

Portaferry, Co. Down, Northern Ireland
The Narrows Restaurant
8 Shore Road
Portaferry BT22 1JY
Tel: (028) 4272 8148
Fax: (028) 4272 8105
E-mail: info@.narrows.co.uk
Website: www.narrows.co.uk

Directions
The restaurant is a two-minute walk from Exploris (the aquarium centre) in Portaferry.

We got a lift by boat from Killyleagh across Strangford Lough to The Narrows with a local fisherman called Norrie Dougan. The payment was a bottle of rum, which we bought from The Dufferin Arms in Killyleagh (see page 173). In my top ten best ways to get to a restaurant, it's up there with the seaplane flight to Berowra Waters, north of Sydney. The meal completely lived up to expectations. Danny Miller's most famous dish is Portaferry mussels, cooked with smoked bacon, cream and garlic. The mussels, naturally, come straight out of the lough, and the sauce, with the cream and bacon, is just the thing you'd expect from Ireland. Danny, however, has a deft touch with modern ideas too, which was why my roasted cod with chargrilled Mediterranean vegetables was so very good. But the other thing about The Narrows is that it's such a nice-looking restaurant – lots of wood and right on the water.

Dublin, Co. Dublin, Eire
Caviston's Seafood Bar
Epicurean Food Hall
Liffey Street
Dublin 1
Tel: (00 353) 1878 2289
Fax: (00 353) 1878 2269

Directions
The hall is between Middle Abbey Street and Liffey Street in the centre of the city.

What a fantastic idea Caviston's Seafood Bar is. They have a very good wet fish shop, a small kitchen and a seating area with half a dozen tables serving what can be best described as seafood tapas – dishes such as shrimp ceviche, mustard and dill herring, lemon sole with chilli dressing, and queen scallops with lemongrass. Part of my enjoyment on both occasions I've been there was having long discussions with Stephen and Mary Caviston about fish and recipes. I'm sure Caviston's is the way forward for fish retailing. If you're in Dublin, don't miss it.

Dun Laoghaire/Sandycove,
Co. Dublin, Eire
Caviston's Restaurant
59 Glasthule Road
Sandycove
Tel: (00 353) 1280 9120
Fax: (00 353) 1284 4054
E-mail: caviston@indigo.ie
Website: www.cavistons.com

Directions
Between Dun Laoghaire (pronounced 'lairy') and Dalkey, or a five-minute walk from Glasthule Dart Station.

Peter, Stephen and Mary Caviston's fantastic food emporium has a simple philosophy: treat your customers as you would like to be treated, and serve them with food that you would like to eat. Theirs has to be one of the best fish counters in Dublin, and the restaurant matches it perfectly. Stephane McGlynn and Noel Cusack turn out fish that is always simple, colourful and perfectly cooked. Being a city restaurant, the menu is pretty funky, but my main course of seared tuna with mango and pear salsa was exciting and full of flavour. The wines on the list are well chosen and the whole place is alive with enthusiasm.

Howth, Co. Dublin, Eire
King Sitric
East Pier
Howth
Tel: (00 353) 1832 5235
Fax: (00 353) 1839 2442
E-mail: info@kingsitric.ie
Website: www.kingsitric.com

Directions
Situated on the East Pier of Howth Harbour, which is all the way across the harbour front and at the end of the road.

If you get a chance, do stay at the King Sitric – all of the eight bedrooms are named after lighthouses and have views over the harbour and out to

sea. But it's the restaurant that you'll be there for. Aidan and Joan MacManus have been turning out simple local seafood for ever: lobster and crab from Balscadden Bay, literally a stone's throw away from their front door, mussels from Mayo, oysters from County Cork, and all their smoked fish from McLoughlin's on the West Pier. I was pretty impressed with the fresh Howth prawns with aïoli and a darn of wild Irish salmon with braised endive and dill.

Leenane, Connemara, Co. Galway
Delphi Lodge
Leenane
Tel: (00 353) 954 2211
e.mail: delfish@iol.ie

Directions
From Leenane, head towards Westport. At the junction turn left and follow the road along Killary harbour until you reach the lodge.

You don't have to be a serious sea trout fisherman to stay at the Delphi Lodge, but if you are, you'll know about it anyway. Peter and Jane Mantle's delightful fishing lodge is comfortable, romantic and fascinating. Every time I've been there the food has been deliciously simple home cooking, even though there always seemed to be a different, nice Australian girl cooking. The fish to go for, obviously, is the salmon or sea trout, which will, like as not, have been caught in one of the chain of pools that run down the peaty lough on which Delphi Lodge stands. What is also remarkable is the size of the white burgundy list and the incredibly modest prices for some great wines to go with the great fish.

Dungarvan, Co. Waterford, Eire
The Tannery
Quay Street
Dungarvan
Tel: (00 353) 584 5420

Directions
At the end of Main Street, to the side of the Arts Centre.

Paul and Maire Flynn seem somewhat out of place in the rather lost-in-time town of Dungarvan, where you can still get coffee for breakfast in the local hotel in battered stainless steel pots that always pour through the lid on to the table cloth as you fill your cup. Paul cooked with Nico Ladenis before returning to his home town to set up a restaurant whose décor would look right in Dublin or London and with a menu to match. Everything on the

menu looked interesting. They really care about what they're doing – the cooking is spot on. I was heartened that a young couple should care so passionately about giving a nice place on the coast like Dungarvan a restaurant to be proud of. It took me back to our early days in Padstow.

PUBS SERVING GOOD SEAFOOD

Ballyvaughan, Co. Clare, Eire
Monk's Pub
The Quay
Ballyvaughan
Tel/Fax: (00 353) 6570 77059
E-mail: monkspub7@eircom.net

Directions
On the left-hand side of the harbour, and signposted.

A modern pub on the quayside in Ballyvaughan serving up good, honest seafood. It was packed on the lunchtime that we went. I don't recall it being a Sunday or any other particularly busy day; it's just the sort of place that's always going to be busy. If it's full up inside, you can sit on the harbour wall. For more impressions, have a look at the recipe for seafood chowder on page 160.

Burren, Co. Clare, Eire
Linnane's Lobster Bar
New Quay
Burren
Tel: (00 353) 6570 78120

Directions
Follow the signs from Ballyvaughan. Burren is half-way between Ballyvaughan and Kinvarra.

I was much taken with Linnane's and its location in a small hamlet on the edge of Galway Bay. It seemed to sum up everything I love about Ireland, which is described in the introduction to the chapter. However, I didn't mention the food that we ate there. Just a simple menu; I had a lovely dish of clams with pasta, but there were crab salads and sandwiches and cakes, moules marinières, oysters, both Pacific and native, smoked salmon and trout, Dublin Bay prawns and, of course, seafood chowder. The freshly cooked lobster came from tanks in a shed next door, and you can buy lobsters, crabs, oysters and mussels Monday–Friday, 9 a.m.–5.30 p.m. What I enjoy about bars like this is that there's no special restaurant – you can go in and have just a Guinness, or order a seafood

lunch as well, all in the bar. It would be just the place to go with a big group of friends. Quite special.

Killyleagh, Co. Down, Northern Ireland
Dufferin Arms
35 High Street
Killyleagh BT30 9QF
Tel: (028) 4482 8229
Fax: (028) 4482 8755
E-mail: dufferin@dial.pipex.com
Website: www.nova/dufferin/index

Directions
In a small street off the A22 running through town, leading up to the castle.

Actually the Dufferin Arms' menu isn't particularly seafood orientated, but it's such a brilliant pub, certainly one of the best I've ever been to, that I've got to include it. How could I not, having sat in the snug with an enormous plate of oysters from Strangford Lough and the odd pint or two of Guinness? In fact, Kitty and Morris will serve any seafood you like because most of the fishermen drink in the pub anyway. That night we had a couple of lobsters, which had been given to me by a fisherman called Jim Teggart. We also had a plate of enormous langoustines out of the lough, and then some large steaks, each one curiously garnished with a strawberry. Why, I don't know, but then that's the Dufferin Arms, always full of surprises.

Kilcolgan, Co. Galway, Eire
Moran's Oyster Cottage on the Weir
Kilcolgan
Clarinbridge
Tel: (00 353) 9179 6113
Fax: (00 353) 9179 6503

Directions
Follow the signs for the pub from the main N18 road in Kilcolgan.

Willie Moran believes passionately in one thing – oysters. Not just any oysters, but the natives from the creek at Kilcolgan which runs into

Galway Bay. We went out filming with one of his regular customers, Louis Hanley, and repaired to Moran's for a feast of oysters, soda bread and Guinness. Willie does other seafood well too; crab salads, seafood platters of crab, smoked salmon, oysters, Dublin Bay prawns with mayonnaise and more soda bread, but it's the oysters that keep bringing people back, and you wouldn't believe who's been there – Paul Newman, Roger Moore, Julia Roberts, Naomi Campbell and Pierce Brosnan, to name but a few. But is it the oysters that keep bringing them back, or is it the incredible conviviality of the place, or the pub's beautiful setting on the waterside with a derelict church on a hill on the opposite bank lending an air of sweet melancholy?

Castletownshend, West Cork, Eire
Mary Ann's Bar & Restaurant
Town Square
Castletownshend
Tel: (00 353) 283 6146
E-mail: golfer@indigo.ie
Website: maryanns.com

Directions
Go down the hill towards the water, and the pub is on the right, just past the two trees in the middle of the road.

What a lovely pub Mary Ann's is. Castletownshend is one of those unspoilt, idyllic estuary-side villages, whose property prices these days would really make you sweat. The landlord, Fergus O'Mahony, said that in the best street the houses were selling for between £300,000 and £400,000. Film director David Puttnam has a house on the other side of the water. Then there are all the American stars who have moved in. But it's still a lovely place, and the pub seafood added to the pleasure of being in such agreeable surroundings. We had some enormous, plump scallops in a cheese gratin, and fish cakes the size of cartwheels, made with cod and salmon, and homemade tartare sauce.

FISH AND CHIPS

Dublin, Co. Dublin, Eire
Leo Burdock's
2 Werburgh Street
Dublin 8
Tel: (00 353) 1454 0306
Fax: (00 353) 1490 9519
Website: www.leoburdocks.com

Directions
Just around the corner from Christchurch Cathedral.

This very well-known fish and chip shop is easy to find because of the almost never-ending queue outside. Classic fish and chips, but they also do lemon sole or salmon goujons and breaded Dublin Bay prawns, the breadcrumbs, though, being a rather garish bright orange. Nice to see bottles of their own malt vinegar on the counter. Needless to say of a shop with such enduring fame that all the fish is straight from the market and is excellent. Celebrity customers at this take-away (there is no restaurant) include Tom Cruise, U2 and Naomi Campbell.

Howth, Co. Dublin, Eire
Beshoff Brothers
Harbour Road
Howth
Tel: (00 353) 1832 1754
Fax: (00 353) 1833 9210
E-mail: beshoffbrothers@eircom.net

Directions
Along the Harbour Road, almost directly opposite the yacht club.

Last time I was in Sydney I wrote a little piece for a magazine about my two favourite fish and chip shops, The Magpie Café in Britain (see page 78), and The Bottom of the Harbour at Balmoral Beach in Australia. The brief was to explain the differences between the two, and the main one is that in Australia you get lemon wedges. It's only a small thing, but I wish it were universal in Britain and Ireland too. I mention this because Beshoff Brothers do serve lemon, and, like Australia, a comprehensive range of fish in batter: cod, smoked cod, haddock, plaice, lemon sole, salmon, hake, skate, scampi and calamari. They have another shop at 5 Vernon Avenue, Clontarf, Dublin 3. Tel: (00 353) 1833 9725, E-mail: beshoffbrothers@tinet.ie.

FISHMONGERS

Ballycastle, Co. Antrim, Northern Ireland
Mortons
9 Bayview Road
Ballycastle BT54 6BP
Tel: (028) 2076 2348
Fax: (028) 2076 3043

Directions
On the seafront, near the ferry terminal.

In his small, new, grey cement building on the quay, Sean Morton has a good but small display of selected fish, most of which is filleted, as is the Irish way. The selection includes plaice, sole, cod, haddock, skinned monkfish tails, whole trout and unskinned, butterflied trout fillets, salmon fillet and steaks, prepared scallops and some smoked fillets too.

Cork, Co. Cork, Eire
Eddie Sheehan
The English Market
1–2 Grand Parade
Cork
Tel: (00 353) 2127 0355

Directions
The English Market is situated in the centre of town between Grand Parade and Princes Street with entrances off both.

Eddie Sheehan's more modest fish counter opposite O'Connell's is to be taken seriously too, largely because of the thick fillets of salt ling that he does on the premises. It smells fresh and remarkably unfishy. Eddie is a charming man, passionate about this traditional Irish product.

Cork, Co. Cork, Eire
O'Connell's
The English Market
13–20 Grand Parade
Cork
Tel: (00 353) 2127 6380
Fax: (00 353) 2127 4532
E-mail: freshfish@eircom.ie

Directions
The English Market is situated in the centre of town between Grand Parade and Princes Street with entrances off both.

The fishmongers' corner of The English Market in Cork is the most exciting bit of that splendid gourmets' mecca. Eddie Sheehan's, Brandans and O'Connell's are all good fishmongers, but O'Connell's takes pride of place for variety. On the day I visited their enormous double-fronted stall they had the following selection: monkfish with the heads on, wild and farmed salmon, Dover and lemon soles, brill and turbot, oysters and mussels, cod, hake, haddock, coley and whiting, John Dory, red mullet and gurnard, pink shrimps, squid, three sizes of just-landed Dublin Bay prawns and some small dabs. There was a lot of smoked fish: salmon, sea trout, haddock and cod, dyed a rather off-putting deep brown, which the Irish seem to prefer. There were lobsters and brown crabs in the tanks, plus a lot of very good-quality filleted fish as well. This is one of the most important stalls in the market. No supermarket counter anywhere could come near to it. Incidentally, the words written in Gaelic on one side of the stall are the owner's name, K. O'Connell.

Midleton, Co. Cork, Eire
Ballycotton Seafood
46 Main Street
Midleton
Tel: (00 353) 2161 3122
Fax: (00 353) 2163 2101

Directions
In the main street running through the town.

Midleton is a pretty, thriving town just off Ballycotton Bay, and it's not for no reason that Ballymaloe House Restaurant and the Ballymaloe Cookery School buy from Ballycotton Seafood. It's a buzzing shop doing brisk business with the local retail trade and restaurants. Some of the good fish I noticed were whole, unskinned ray wings, some shiny Dover soles (called black soles in Ireland), and a lot of filleted fish. While I was there, they were taking a delivery of a few boxes of lovely looking monkfish and some lively brown crabs. They also do quite a lot of homemade fish pies and fish cakes.

Skull, Co.Cork, Eire
Normandy Island
The Pier
Skull
Tel: (00 353) 2828 599/638
Fax: (00 353) 2828 103
E-mail: normandyisland@tinet.ie

Directions
At the back of the harbour, opposite the quay.

There's a tiny but thriving fishing fleet at Skull, and they land to Normandy Island just at the top of the quay. When I went there, they were cleaning and packing some large monkfish and I instantly knew that it

was destined for Europe because the heads were being left on. You'll have no problem getting the very best here. The boats are all small and go out for only a couple of days; what you buy comes off them, and when the shop's shut, they'll willingly sell you something straight out of the fish boxes. Their fish and chip shop was shut when I went there, but it would be hard to imagine it being anything but excellent given the quality of the fish.

Bangor, Co. Down, Northern Ireland
McKeown's Fish Shop
14 High Street
Bangor BT20 5AY
Tel: (028) 9127 1141
Fax: (028) 9145 8751

Directions
In the centre of Bangor, at the bottom of the High Street near the McKee clock.

A small, local fishmonger's selling, among the more usual fish, local seafood such as Portavogie prawns, Donegal salmon, dulse, winkles, sometimes whelks and local herrings.

Howth, Co. Dublin, Eire
Nicky's Plaice
Howth
Tel: (00 353) 1832 3557
Fax: (00 353) 1832 0531

Directions
At the very end of the West Pier in Howth.

This is a modest little shop, but still the best place in the area to buy fresh fish. It has just yards to travel to the shop from where it is landed by the boats. Nicky McLoughlin, who owns the shop, is always behind the counter, and his knowledge is extensive. The shop also smokes its own salmon, which is delicious and very reasonably priced.

Galway, Co. Galway, Eire
McDonagh's Seafood House
22 Quay Street
Galway
Tel: (00 353) 9156 5001
Fax: (00 353) 9152 6246
E-mail: mcdonagh@tinet.ie

Directions
At the bottom of Quay Street.

I had a great afternoon in Galway City. It must have been the Irish Fisheries Board that had organized an oyster tasting, with oysters literally from all over Ireland. There was a general consensus among the assembled company that those from Clarinbridge were the best, having the right balance of sea flavour and creaminess. Afterwards I repaired to McDonagh's for some excellent fish and chips. The fish and chip shop was at the front and we sat down in a stone-floored, Celtic-influenced restaurant to the side, with plain wooden tables and folk music. On expressing an interest in their fish shop, I was taken through the kitchen to the shop. It was full of good things, including oysters from Clarinbridge and a couple of small sharks.

Cahersiveen, Co. Kerry, Eire
O'Donoghue's Fish Shop
Main Street
Cahersiveen
Tel/Fax: (00 353) 6694 72153
Website: http://www.java-site.ie

Directions
About half-way along the main street in the town.

I had a long chat with Patrick O'Donoghue about the supply of fish and the fish retail trade in Kerry. He had a wonderfully Irish turn of phrase – he regarded the average selection and quality of fish in supermarkets near him as 'brutal', and he explained that the staple diet of the locals in the past had been salt mackerel and potatoes, which he described as 'desperate stuff'. In my rather over-enthusiastic desire to revive local foods, I asked whether it wouldn't be possible to bring back salt mackerel, but it appears that no one would agree it was worth it. He had some excellent fish that day from Castletownbere market; most of it was filleted, but of a superb quality. I noticed a tendency in Ireland to cut small fish, such as herring, mackerel and whiting, into what they call butterflied fillets, which removes both fillets in one piece. Patrick also had whole fish, including some really fresh, small monkfish tails, which I think are better flavoured than the big ones. The shop is at the front of his small seafood restaurant, called the The Seahorse, rather charmingly decorated with marine blue tables, blue ceramic seahorses on the white walls, and plates hand-painted with fish. Unfortunately, they were closed for lunch, but the menu looked interesting: grilled fillet of hake with lemon butter, half a dozen local oysters with garlic crumbs and marinated citrus monkfish with basmati rice.

SEAFOOD SUPPLIERS

Glenarm, Co. Antrim, Northern Ireland
Glenarm Salmon
Glenarm BT44 0AA
Tel: (028) 2884 1691
Fax: (028) 2884 1637
E-mail: northern.salmon@btclick.com

Directions
Housed in a small factory on the side of the road as you drive into Glenarm from the south.

This salmon farmer's fish are some of the best farmed in Ireland, guaranteed chemical-free and as close to wild salmon as you can get. They are stocked by Harrods, Selfridges, The Bluebird and Harvey Nichols. The business has a small farm shop on the roadside open 12–6 p.m., Monday–Saturday, selling whole salmon, steaks, unskinned fillets and their own smoked salmon, produced at the Severn and Wye Smokery in Gloucester.

Toomebridge, Co. Antrim, Northern Ireland
Lough Neagh Fishermans Co-operative Society Ltd
Toomebridge BT41 3SB
Tel: (028) 7965 0618
Fax: (028) 7965 0240
E-mail: loughneagh-eels@ukgateway.net

Directions
On the bridge in Toomebridge.

You can buy live eels from here if you wish. They fly out 3 tons of eels each night, Monday–Friday, from Belfast to Holland.

SMOKERIES

Cobh Island, Cork, Eire
Frank Hederman
Cobh Island
Belvelly
Cobh Island
Tel: (00 353) 2148 11089

Directions
On the main road from Cork to Cobh. Look for the sign on the left. He also has a stall in the English Market in Cork (see O'Connell's and Eddie Sheehan under Fishmongers).

'You know,' Frank said, 'cheap smoked salmon is often done over chipboard sawdust, so in addition to wood, you get glue as well.' We were peering at the time into the dark depths of his traditional smoking kiln,

marvelling at the build-up of tar on all the surfaces, which he explained adds to the flavour in the smoking process. Frank's obsession is smoking eels. They are sublime, eaten with horseradish and a few slices of boiled potato. You should always buy them on the bone and take the fillets off just before serving. Frank also smokes mussels, mackerel and herrings.

Castletownshend, West Cork, Eire
Woodcock Smokery
Castletownshend
Skibbereen
Tel/Fax: (00 353) 283 6232

Directions
Between Castlehaven Creamery and Castletownshend.

Sally Barnes is Scottish and therefore known in nice local parlance as a 'lifestyler', or more colloquially in West Cork as a 'blow-in'. However, she's been there so long that even the locals say she's more local than they are. She's fantastically knowledgeable about local fishing matters, particularly the demise of the industry and the shrinkage of stocks. As she said to me, referring to the worrying trend to buy ever bigger and more expensive boats to catch ever more fish from a dwindling stock, 'My husband got fed up with killing fish to pay off the bank.' Is that the ultimate catch 22? Sally's smoked fish is legendary; she understands variability in the quality of fish, and how to apply the right cures and smoking process to each species. When I spoke to her, she was very excited about smoking some albacore tuna, which is caught off the coast of Southern Ireland during the summer months. She explained that it's ideal for smoking because, like salmon, it's an oily fish, which absorbs the flavour of smoke very well. She does a range of products, including smoked wild salmon, cod, hake and kippers.

OTHER PLACES WHERE I'VE EATEN GOOD FISH RECENTLY

Skibbereen, Co. Cork, Eire
Island Cottage
Hare Island
Skibbereen
Tel/Fax: (00 353) 283 8102

Dublin, Co. Dublin, Eire
Clarence Tea Room
6–8 Wellington Quay
Dublin
Tel: (00 353) 1670 7766

classic recipes

I've got to own up, all the recipes in this chapter have been in my previous books, but how could I not put these dishes that we know so well and love in a book about the seafood of Britain and Ireland? Fish and chips, grilled Dover sole with parsley butter, fish pie, cod in parsley sauce, they're all here. I've also included some classic stocks, sauces and basics, such as hollandaise sauce and mayonnaise, the quality of which can either make or break a dish. These are my recipes for them. What I've tried to do is produce a version of the recipe that highlights the essence of the dish and keeps the ingredients and method as brief as possible.

I still get excited every time I eat one of these dishes when it's well made with first-class ingredients. I think we've all been subjected to inferior versions of them for far too long. For many years I felt French ways with seafood were better than ours but that was largely because the cooking in France was better and the raw materials fresher. Once you change these shortcomings in our own seafood cooking, everything becomes a lot more optimistic.

These classics are what most of us have at home when we're cooking seafood – well, at least I do. Poached salmon or lobster with mayonnaise, fish cakes, plain grilled flat fish, fish pie, dressed crab – these are the dishes that my sons will make a point of getting back to for supper after surfing, and also the ones that I will be thinking of a nice bottle of white wine to go with.

It's sad, though, that we are constantly given inferior versions in pubs and restaurants and seem to put up with it. Think of tired Canadian lobster – 'previously frozen', as it ominously says on supermarket fish counters – with salads of sliced raw peppers and starfruit. Perhaps you've suffered salmon poached to dryness with that rancid tang of oily fish that has been long deep-frozen, or fish pies where the fish is soft and unidentifiable and topped with instant mashed potato. I have a horror of whitebait out of the deep-freeze with the smell of old sardines, and fish and chips, our prize dish, spoiled by thin old fillets of frozen fish and stale, dirty frying fat. Almost worse still is the current habit of dressing up perfectly good fresh fish with ideas from other countries – roasted red peppers with everything, sun-dried tomatoes, soy sauce, basil everywhere and buckets of balsamic vinegar. I have to admit I use all these ingredients with complete enthusiasm and all I can say, entirely arrogantly, is that I know what I'm doing but I also love plain British seafood, which is so hard to get.

There's a sensible old adage that runs, 'Plain cooking shouldn't be left to common cooks.' Our fish cooking may be plain but it needs the care and attention of intelligent cooks who understand the delight that these unadorned recipes can bring.

kedgeree of arbroath smokies

SERVES 4

25 G (1 OZ) BUTTER

1 SMALL ONION, CHOPPED

2 GREEN CARDAMOM PODS, SPLIT OPEN

1/4 TEASPOON GROUND TURMERIC

2.5 CM (1 IN) PIECE OF CINNAMON STICK

1 BAY LEAF, VERY FINELY SHREDDED

350 G (12 OZ) BASMATI RICE

600 ML (1 PINT) *CHICKEN STOCK*
  (SEE PAGE 185)

2 EGGS

450 G (1 LB) ARBROATH SMOKIES

2 TABLESPOONS CHOPPED FLAT-LEAF
  PARSLEY, PLUS A FEW SPRIGS TO
  GARNISH

SALT AND FRESHLY GROUND BLACK PEPPER

METHOD

Melt the butter in a large pan, add the onion and cook over a medium heat for 5 minutes, until soft but not browned. Add the cardamom pods, turmeric, cinnamon stick and shredded bay leaf and cook, stirring, for 1 minute. Add the rice and stir for about 1 minute, until it is well coated in the spicy butter. Add the stock and 1/2 teaspoon of salt and bring to the boil. Cover the pan with a close-fitting lid, lower the heat and cook very gently for 15 minutes.

Meanwhile, hard-boil the eggs for 10 minutes, then drain. When just cool enough to handle, peel them and slice them. Flake the Arbroath smokies into small chunks, discarding the skin and bones.

Uncover the rice and gently fork in the fish and the chopped eggs. Cover again and return to the heat for 5 minutes or until the fish has heated through. Then gently stir in the chopped parsley and season with a little more salt and black pepper to taste. Serve garnished with sprigs of parsley.

potted shrimps

SERVES 6

100 G (4 OZ) BUTTER

2 PIECES OF BLADE MACE

A GOOD PINCH OF CAYENNE PEPPER

FRESHLY GRATED NUTMEG

600 ML (1 PINT) PEELED COOKED
  BROWN SHRIMPS

6 TABLESPOONS *CLARIFIED BUTTER*
  (SEE PAGE 186)

METHOD

Put the butter, mace, cayenne pepper and a little grated nutmeg into a pan and leave to melt very slowly over a gentle heat, so that the butter becomes infused by the spices. Add the peeled shrimps and stir for a couple of minutes until they have heated through, but don't let the mixture boil.

Remove the mace and divide the shrimps and butter between 6 small ramekins. Level the tops and then leave them to set in the fridge. Spoon over a thin layer of clarified butter and leave to set once more. Serve with plenty of brown toast or crusty brown bread.

fish pie

SERVES 4

1 SMALL ONION, THICKLY SLICED

2 CLOVES

1 BAY LEAF

600 ML (1 PINT) CREAMY MILK

300 ML (10 FL OZ) DOUBLE CREAM

450 G (1 LB) THICK, UNSKINNED
  COD FILLET

225 G (8 OZ) UNDYED SMOKED
  HADDOCK FILLET

4 EGGS

100 G (4 OZ) BUTTER

45 G (1 3/4 OZ) PLAIN FLOUR

5 TABLESPOONS CHOPPED
  FLAT-LEAF PARSLEY

4 GRATINGS OF NUTMEG

1.25 KG (2 1/2 LB) FLOURY POTATOES,

SUCH AS MARIS PIPER OR KING EDWARD,
PEELED AND CUT INTO CHUNKS

1 EGG YOLK

SALT AND FRESHLY GROUND WHITE PEPPER

METHOD

Stud a couple of the onion slices with the cloves, then put the onion slices in a large pan with the bay leaf, 450 ml (15 fl oz) of the milk, the cream, cod and smoked cod. Bring just to the boil and simmer for 8 minutes. Lift the fish out on to a plate and strain the cooking liquor into a jug. When the fish is cool enough to handle, break it into large flakes, discarding the skin and bones. Sprinkle it over the base of a shallow 1.75 litre (3 pint) ovenproof dish.

Hard-boil the eggs for 8 minutes, then drain and leave to cool. Peel them, cut into chunky slices and arrange on top of the fish.

Melt 50 g (2 oz) of the butter in a pan, add the flour and cook for 1 minute. Take the pan off the heat and gradually stir in the reserved cooking liquor. Return it to the heat and bring slowly to the boil, stirring all the time. Simmer gently for 10 minutes to cook out the flour. Remove from the heat once more, stir in the parsley and season with the nutmeg, salt and white pepper. Pour the sauce over the fish and leave to cool. Chill for 1 hour.

Pre-heat the oven to 200°C/400°F/Gas Mark 6. Cook the potatoes in boiling salted water for 15–20 minutes, until tender. Drain well, then mash, adding the rest of the butter and the egg yolk. Season with salt and white pepper. Beat in enough of the remaining milk to form a soft, spreadable mash. Spoon the potatoes over the fish mixture and mark the surface with a fork. Bake for 35–40 minutes, until piping hot and golden brown.

lobster mayonnaise

SERVES 4

200 G (7 OZ) SALT

2 X 750-850 G (1¹/₂-1³/₄ LB) LIVE
  LOBSTERS

1 QUANTITY OF *MAYONNAISE*
  (SEE PAGE 186) MADE WITH OLIVE OIL

METHOD

Put 5.5 litres (10 pints) of water in a very large pan with the salt and bring to the boil. Lower in one of the lobsters, wait until the water comes back to the boil and then lower in the second one. Boil for 15 minutes. If you don't have a pan large enough to cook both lobsters at once, boil them one at a time, as they must be fully immersed in the water to cook properly.

Remove the lobsters from the water and leave to cool. Then place them on a chopping board and drive a large knife through the centre of the body section. Cut down through the head, between the eyes, then turn the lobster around and cut the tail section in half. Remove the rubber bands binding the claws together and crack the shells of the three claw sections with the thickest part of a large knife. Remove the stomach sac from just behind the mouth and then remove the intestine, which runs down the tail.

Put the lobster halves on 4 plates and serve with the mayonnaise, some minted new potatoes and a mixed green leaf salad.

poached salmon
with mayonnaise, new potatoes and cucumber salad

SERVES 4

2 CELERY STALKS, SLICED

1 CARROT, SLICED

1 ONION, SLICED

6 BAY LEAVES

¹/₂ TEASPOON BLACK PEPPERCORNS

65 ML (2¹/₂ FL OZ) WHITE WINE VINEGAR

1 X 1.5-1.75 KG (3-4 LB) SALMON, CLEANED

750 G (1¹/₂ LB) NEW POTATOES,
  SCRAPED CLEAN

3 SPRIGS OF MINT

1 CUCUMBER

1 QUANTITY OF *MAYONNAISE*
  (SEE PAGE 186) MADE WITH OLIVE OIL

SALT

Pour enough water into a fish kettle to cover the fish. Add the celery, carrot, onion, bay leaves, peppercorns and 50 ml (2 fl oz) of the vinegar. Bring to the boil and simmer for 20 minutes to make a court-bouillon. Carefully lower the salmon into the court-bouillon, increase the heat once more and poach gently for 16–18 minutes.

Meanwhile, boil the potatoes in salted water with one of the mint sprigs until tender, then drain and keep warm. Peel the cucumber and slice it as thinly as possible, preferably on a mandolin. Chop the leaves from the remaining mint sprigs and mix with the cucumber, the remaining white wine vinegar and a pinch of salt.

Lift the salmon, still sitting on the trivet, out of the fish kettle, and allow any excess water to drain away. Carefully lift it off the trivet with 2 fish slices and put it on a serving plate. Remove the skin by making a shallow cut through the skin along the backbone and around the back of the head and carefully peeling it back. Carefully turn the fish over and repeat on the other side.

To serve, run a knife down the length of the fish between the 2 fillets and gently ease them apart and away from the bones. Lift portion-sized pieces of the salmon on to each serving plate, then turn the fish over and repeat. Serve with the new potatoes, mayonnaise and cucumber salad.

herrings in oatmeal
with bacon

SERVES 4

4 X 225 G (8 OZ) HERRINGS,
   CLEANED AND FILLETED
100 G (4 OZ) MEDIUM OATMEAL
   (CALLED PINHEAD OATMEAL)
2 TABLESPOONS SUNFLOWER OIL
4 RASHERS OF RINDLESS STREAKY BACON,
   CUT INTO LARDONS (SHORT STRIPS)
SALT AND FRESHLY GROUND BLACK PEPPER
1 LEMON, CUT INTO WEDGES, TO SERVE

METHOD

Season the herring fillets on both sides with salt and pepper. Spread the oatmeal over a plate and coat the herring fillets in it, pressing it well on to both sides.

Heat the oil in a large frying pan. Add the streaky bacon strips and fry until crisp and golden. Remove from the pan with a slotted spoon and keep warm.

Add the herring fillets to the pan, flesh-side down, and fry for 1 minute. Turn over and fry for another 1–2 minutes, until the skin is golden brown. Put the fillets on 4 warmed plates and sprinkle over the bacon. Serve with the lemon wedges, and some boiled floury potatoes that have been tossed with a little chopped parsley.

freshly boiled and dressed crab

SERVES 1-3

1 X 900 G (2 LB) LIVE CRAB PER PERSON,
   OR 1 X 1.5-1.75 KG (3-4 LB) LIVE CRAB
   TO SERVE 2-3
FRESHLY GROUND BLACK PEPPER
MUSTARD MAYONNAISE (SEE PAGE 186),
   TO SERVE

METHOD

Crabs should be boiled in plenty of water, salted at the rate of 150 g (5 oz) salt to 4.5 litres (1 gallon) of water. Put the crabs in the cold salted water, bring to the boil and simmer the smaller ones for 15 minutes and the larger ones for 20–25 minutes. When the crabs are cooked, lift them out of the water and run them under the cold tap to make them easier to handle. Break off and discard the tail flap and the two flaps that cover the mouth on the under shell beneath the eyes.

Now insert the blade of a large knife between the body and the back shell and twist to release it. Pull off the feathery-looking gills or 'dead man's fingers' from the body and discard. Remove the stomach sac from the back shell by pressing on the little piece of shell located just behind the eyes. Discard both the bone and the stomach. Empty any excess water out of the back shell.

Cut the body into 4 pieces and crack each of the claw sections with the back of a large knife, but try not to shatter them completely, so that you can reassemble the crab to look much as it was.

Take a large plate for each person and put the 4 pieces of the body section back together again. Put the back shell back in place and rearrange any legs or claws, that may have fallen off.

If you wish to serve the crab dressed, break the legs away from the body section and discard all but the largest joints. Crack the shells with the back of a knife or a hammer and pick out the white meat from these joints with a crab pick. Break open the claws and remove this meat too, discarding the very thin flat bone from the centre of the claws. Then pick out all the white meat from the little channels in the body section, using a crab pick, taking care not to break off any pieces of the wafer-thin shell. Scrape out the brown meat from the back shell, chop it into small pieces if necessary and fold in a little of the mayonnaise and some freshly ground black pepper.

If you want to serve the crab in the back shell wash the shell out well under cold water. Dry. Spoon the white crab meat to either side of the shell. Spoon the brown crab meat down the centre, dividing the two with some finely chopped hardboiled egg yolk, egg white and chopped parsley if you wish. Serve with the mustard mayonnaise, some minted new potatoes and a mixed green leaf salad.

cod in parsley sauce

SERVES 4

1 LEMON, SLICED

750-900 G (1^1/$_2$-2 LB) THICK, UNSKINNED COD FILLET

75 G (3 OZ) UNSALTED BUTTER

15 G (^{1}/$_2$ OZ) PLAIN FLOUR

600 ML (1 PINT) CREAMY MILK

25 G (1 OZ) CURLY-LEAF PARSLEY, FINELY CHOPPED

SALT AND FRESHLY GROUND BLACK PEPPER

METHOD

Put 2.25 litres (4 pints) of water into a large pan with the lemon slices and a tablespoon of salt. Bring to the boil and simmer for 5 minutes. Add the cod, skin-side up, then cover and bring back to a simmer. Cook for just 2 minutes. Remove the pan from the heat and set aside while you make the sauce, during which time the cod will continue to cook.

Melt 25 g (1 oz) of the butter in a heavy-based pan, add the flour and cook until it starts to smell nutty but is not browned. Gradually add the milk, stirring all the time, until smooth. Add 300 ml (10 fl oz) of the fish cooking liquor and leave the sauce to simmer for 20 minutes, stirring now and then, until reduced and thickened to a sauce consistency.

Lift the cod out of the pan and drain away the excess liquid. Divide into 4 portions and put them on 4 warmed plates. Stir the chopped parsley and the rest of the butter into the sauce, season to taste and then spoon liberally over the cod. Serve with some minted new potatoes.

fish cakes

SERVES 4

900 G (2 LB) FLOURY POTATOES,
   SUCH AS MARIS PIPER OR KING EDWARD,
   PEELED AND CUT INTO CHUNKS
900 G (2 LB) WHITE FISH FILLET,
   SUCH AS COD OR HADDOCK
25 G (1 OZ) BUTTER, MELTED
15 G (1/2 OZ) CHOPPED PARSLEY
SUNFLOWER OIL FOR DEEP-FRYING
50 G (2 OZ) PLAIN FLOUR,
   SEASONED WITH SALT AND PEPPER
2 EGGS, BEATEN
150 G (5 OZ) FRESH WHITE BREADCRUMBS
1 QUANTITY OF *TARTARE SAUCE*
   (SEE PAGE 184)
SALT AND FRESHLY GROUND BLACK PEPPER

METHOD

Cook the potatoes in boiling salted water until tender. Drain well, tip back into the pan and mash until smooth. Leave to cool slightly.

Bring some water to the boil in a large, deep frying pan. Add the fish, bring back to the boil and simmer for 8 minutes. Lift the fish out on to a plate and, when it is cool enough to handle, break it into large flakes, discarding the skin and any bones.

Put the fish into a bowl with the mashed potatoes, melted butter, parsley and some salt and pepper and mix together well. Shape the mixture into 8 rounds, about 2.5 cm (1 inch) thick, cover with clingfilm and chill for 20 minutes.

Heat some oil for deep-frying to 180°C/350°F. Put the seasoned flour, beaten eggs and breadcrumbs in 3 separate shallow bowls. Dip the fish cakes into the flour, then into the egg and finally in the breadcrumbs, pressing them on well to give an even coating. Deep-fry in batches for about 4 minutes, until crisp and golden. Lift out with a slotted spoon and drain briefly on kitchen paper, then keep warm in a low oven while you cook the rest. Serve with the tartare sauce.

skate with black butter

SERVES 4

4 X 225 G (8 OZ) SKINNED SKATE WINGS
15 G (1/2 OZ) CAPERS IN BRINE,
   DRAINED AND RINSED

FOR THE COURT-BOUILLON:

300 ML (10 FL OZ) DRY WHITE WINE
1.2 LITRES (2 PINTS) WATER
85 ML (3 FL OZ) WHITE WINE VINEGAR
2 BAY LEAVES
12 BLACK PEPPERCORNS
1 ONION, ROUGHLY CHOPPED
2 CARROTS, ROUGHLY CHOPPED
2 CELERY STICKS, ROUGHLY CHOPPED
1 TEASPOON SALT

FOR THE BLACK BUTTER:

175 G (6 OZ) BUTTER
50 ML (2 FL OZ) RED WINE VINEGAR
1 TABLESPOON CHOPPED PARSLEY

METHOD

For the court-bouillon, put all the ingredients into a large pan, bring to the boil and simmer for 20 minutes. Set aside to cool, to allow the flavour to improve before using.

Put the skate wings into a large pan. Pour over the court-bouillon, bring to the boil and simmer very gently for 15–20 minutes, depending on the thickness of the skate, until they are cooked through. Carefully lift the skate wings out of the pan, allow the excess liquid to drain off and then place them on 4 warmed plates. Sprinkle with the capers and keep warm.

For the black butter, melt the butter in a frying pan. As soon as it starts to foam, turn quite brown and smell very nutty, add the vinegar, then the parsley. Let it boil down for a minute or so, until slightly reduced. Pour the butter over the skate and serve straight away.

crab pasties with leek and saffron

MAKES 6

900 G (2 LB) CHILLED FRESH PUFF PASTRY

$^1/_4$ TEASPOON SAFFRON STRANDS

350 G (12 OZ) FRESH WHITE CRAB MEAT

75 G (3 OZ) FRESH BROWN CRAB MEAT

225 G (8 OZ) LEEKS, CLEANED AND
  THINLY SLICED

50 G (2 OZ) FRESH WHITE BREADCRUMBS

1 TEASPOON SALT

10 TURNS OF THE WHITE PEPPER MILL

25 G (1 OZ) BUTTER, MELTED

1 EGG, BEATEN

METHOD

Pre-heat the oven to 200°C/400°F/Gas Mark 6.

Divide the pastry into 6 pieces. Roll out each piece on a lightly floured surface and cut into a 19 cm (7$^1/_2$ inch) disc, using an upturned bowl or small plate as a template.

For the filling, soak the saffron in 2 teaspoons of hot water for 5 minutes. Put the white and brown crab meat, leeks, breadcrumbs, salt and pepper into a bowl and stir together until well mixed. Crush the saffron a little into the water to release the colour and flavour, then stir it into the melted butter. Now stir this into the rest of the filling ingredients.

Divide the filling between the circles of pastry. Brush the edge of one half with a little water, bring both sides together over the top of the filling and pinch together well to seal. Crimp the edge of each pasty decoratively between your fingers. Brush with beaten egg. Transfer to a lightly greased baking sheet and bake for 35 minutes, until golden brown. Serve hot or cold.

VARIATION: Smoked Haddock Pasties with Leeks and Clotted Cream For the filling, cut 350 g (12 oz) skinned undyed smoked haddock fillet into 2.5 cm (1 inch) pieces and mix with 175 g (6 oz) thinly sliced cleaned leeks, 275 g (10 oz) peeled potatoes cut into 1 cm ($^1/_2$ inch) cubes, 4 tablespoons of clotted cream, 1 teaspoon of salt and some freshly ground black pepper. Fill and bake the pasties as above.

deep-fried whitebait with lemon

SERVES 4

550 G (1$^1/_4$ LB) FRESH WHITEBAIT

SUNFLOWER OIL FOR DEEP-FRYING

75 G (3 OZ) PLAIN FLOUR

$^1/_2$ TEASPOON CAYENNE PEPPER

1 TEASPOON SALT

1 LEMON, CUT INTO WEDGES, TO SERVE

METHOD

Wash the whitebait in plenty of cold water, then drain and shake vigorously in a colander.

Heat some oil for deep-frying to 190°C/375°F. Put the flour, cayenne pepper and salt into a large bowl and mix together well. Add the whitebait, toss together until they are all well coated, then lift them out and shake off the excess flour.

Deep-fry the fish in batches for about 3 minutes, until crisp. Drain briefly on kitchen paper, then tip into a large serving bowl and serve with the lemon wedges.

fish and chips with tartare sauce

SERVES 4

900 G (2 LB) FLOURY POTATOES,
  SUCH AS MARIS PIPER OR KING EDWARD

SUNFLOWER OIL FOR DEEP-FRYING

4 X 175 G (6 OZ) PIECES OF THICK
  COD FILLET FROM THE LOIN END,
  NOT THE TAIL

SALT AND FRESHLY GROUND BLACK PEPPER

FOR THE BATTER:

240 G (8$^1/_2$ OZ) PLAIN FLOUR

1 TEASPOON SALT

3$^1/_2$ TEASPOONS BAKING POWDER

270 ML (9 FL OZ) ICE COLD WATER

FOR THE TARTARE SAUCE:

1/2 QUANTITY OF *MUSTARD MAYONNAISE* (SEE PAGE 186)

1 TEASPOON FINELY CHOPPED GREEN OLIVES

1 TEASPOON FINELY CHOPPED GHERKINS

1 TEASPOON FINELY CHOPPED CAPERS

2 TEASPOONS CHOPPED FRESH CHIVES

2 TEASPOONS CHOPPED FRESH PARSLEY

METHOD

To make the batter, mix the flour, salt and baking powder with the water. Keep cold and use within 20 minutes of making.

Pre-heat the oven to 150°C/300°F/Gas Mark 2. Line a baking tray with plenty of kitchen paper and set aside. Mix together the ingredients for the tartare sauce.

Peel the potatoes and cut them lengthwise into chips 1 cm (1/2 inch) thick. Pour some sunflower oil into a large, deep pan until it is about a third full and heat it to 130°C/260°F. Drop half the chips into a frying basket and cook them for about 5 minutes, until tender when pierced with the tip of a knife but not coloured. Lift them out and drain off excess oil. Repeat with the rest of the chips and set aside.

To fry the fish, heat the oil to 160°C/325°F. Season the pieces of cod with salt and pepper and then dip them into the batter. Fry, 2 pieces at a time, for 7–8 minutes, until crisp and golden brown. Lift out and drain on the paper-lined tray. Keep hot in the oven while you cook the other 2 pieces.

Now raise the temperature of the oil to 190°C/375°F and cook the chips in small batches for about 2 minutes, until they are crisp and golden. Lift them out of the pan and give them a good shake to remove the excess oil, then drain on kitchen paper and keep them hot while you cook the rest. Sprinkle with salt and serve them with the deep-fried cod and tartare sauce.

grilled dover sole
with parsley butter

SERVES 4

4 X 350–450 G (12 OZ–1 LB) DOVER SOLE, CLEANED AND SKINNED

15 G (1/2 OZ) BUTTER, MELTED

SALT AND FRESHLY GROUND BLACK PEPPER

FOR THE PARSLEY BUTTER:

A SMALL BUNCH OF FRESH PARSLEY, LARGE STALKS REMOVED

5 ANCHOVY FILLETS IN OLIVE OIL, DRAINED

100 G (4 OZ) BUTTER, SOFTENED

2 TEASPOONS FRESH LEMON JUICE

5 TURNS OF THE BLACK PEPPER MILL

1/2 TEASPOON SALT

METHOD

For the parsley butter, chop the parsley and anchovy fillets together on a board into a coarse paste. Beat into the butter with the lemon juice, pepper and salt. Spoon the mixture into the centre of a sheet of clingfilm, shape into a roll 4 cm (1 1/2 inches) thick and then wrap in the clingfilm. Chill in the fridge or freezer until firm.

When the butter is firm, pre-heat the grill to high. Trim the tails and fins of the fish with kitchen scissors. Brush the fish on both sides with the melted butter and season with a little salt and pepper. Depending on the size of your grill, cook them 1 or 2 at a time, on a buttered baking tray or the rack of the grill pan, for about 10 minutes until the flesh is firm and white at the thickest part, just behind the head. Keep warm while you cook the rest.

Unwrap the parsley butter and slice it into thin rounds. Put the fish on warmed plates and lay a few slices of the butter down the centre of each one. Serve straight away.

fish stock

MAKES 1.2 LITRES (2 PINTS)

1 KG (2¼ LB) FISH BONES, SUCH AS
   LEMON SOLE, BRILL AND PLAICE

2.25 LITRES (4 PINTS) WATER

1 ONION, CHOPPED

1 FENNEL BULB, CHOPPED

100 G (4 OZ) CELERY, SLICED

100 G (4 OZ) CARROTS, CHOPPED

25 G (1 OZ) BUTTON MUSHROOMS, SLICED

1 SPRIG OF FRESH THYME

METHOD

Put the fish bones, vegetables and water into a large pan, bring just to the boil and then simmer very gently for 20 minutes. Strain through a muslin-lined sieve. Use as required. If not using immediately, leave to cool, then chill and refrigerate or freeze.

chicken stock

MAKES 1.75 LITRES (3 PINTS)

BONES FROM A 1.5 KG (3 LB) UNCOOKED
   CHICKEN, OR 450 G (1 LB) CHICKEN
   WINGS

1 LARGE CARROT, CHOPPED

2 CELERY STICKS, SLICED

2 LEEKS, SLICED

2 FRESH OR DRIED BAY LEAVES

2 SPRIGS OF FRESH THYME

2.25 LITRES (4 PINTS) WATER

METHOD

Put all the ingredients into a large pan and bring just to the boil, skimming off any scum from the surface as it appears. Leave to simmer very gently for 2 hours – it is important not to let it boil as this will force the fat from even the leanest chicken and make the stock cloudy. Strain the stock through a muslin-lined sieve and use as required. If not using immediately, leave to cool, then chill and refrigerate or freeze for later use.

hollandaise sauce

SERVES 4

2 TABLESPOONS WATER

2 EGG YOLKS

225 G (8 OZ) *CLARIFIED BUTTER*
   (SEE PAGE 186), WARMED

JUICE OF ¹/₂ LEMON

A GOOD PINCH OF CAYENNE PEPPER

³/₄ TEASPOON SALT

METHOD

Put the water and egg yolks into a stainless steel or glass bowl set over a pan of simmering water, making sure the base of the bowl is not touching the water. Whisk until voluminous, thick and creamy. Remove the bowl from the pan and gradually whisk in the clarified butter until thick. Whisk in the lemon juice, cayenne pepper and salt.

This sauce is best used as soon as it is made but will hold for up to 2 hours if kept covered in a warm place, such as over a pan of warm water.

SERVING SUGGESTION:
Samphire with Hollandaise Sauce

For 4 people you will need 350–450 g (12 oz– 1 lb) fresh samphire. Break off and discard the woody stalks from the samphire and break the rest into short pieces. Drop the samphire into a pan of boiling water and cook for 1 minute, then drain well and tip it into a warm serving bowl. Stir a few teaspoons of warm water into the sauce to loosen it a little, then spoon it over the samphire and serve.

quick hollandaise sauce

Using the same quantities as for *Hollandaise Sauce* (above), put the egg yolks, lemon juice and water into a liquidizer. Turn on the machine and then slowly pour in the warm butter through the hole in the lid until the sauce is thick. Season with the cayenne pepper and salt.

clarified butter

Place some butter in a small pan and leave it over a very low heat until it has melted. Then skim off any scum from the surface and pour off the clear (clarified) butter into a bowl, leaving behind the milky white solids that will have settled on the bottom of the pan.

beurre manié

Blend equal quantities of softened butter and plain flour together into a smooth paste. Cover and store in the fridge until needed. It will keep for the same period of time as butter.

mayonnaise

This recipe includes instructions for making mayonnaise in a liquidizer or food processor or by hand. It is lighter when made mechanically, because the process uses a whole egg, and it's very quick, but I still prefer making it by hand. You can use either sunflower oil or olive oil – or a mixture of the two, if you prefer.

MAKES 300 ML (10 FL OZ)

2 EGG YOLKS OR 1 EGG

2 TEASPOONS WHITE WINE VINEGAR

1/2 TEASPOON SALT

300 ML (10 FL OZ) OIL

METHOD

To make the mayonnaise by hand, make sure all the ingredients are at room temperature before you start. Put the egg yolks, vinegar and salt into a mixing bowl and then place the bowl on a cloth to stop it slipping. Using a wire whisk, beat the oil into the egg mixture a few drops at a time until you have incorporated it all. Once you have beaten in the same volume of the oil as the original mixture of egg yolks

and vinegar, you can add it a little more quickly.

To make the mayonnaise in a machine, put the whole egg, vinegar and salt into a liquidizer or food processor. Turn on the machine and then slowly add the oil through the hole in the lid until you have a thick emulsion.

This mayonnaise will keep in the fridge for about 1 week.

mustard mayonnaise

See the recipe for *Mayonnaise* (left) if you prefer to make it by hand.

MAKES 300 ML (10 FL OZ)

1 TABLESPOON ENGLISH MUSTARD

1 EGG

1 TABLESPOON WHITE WINE VINEGAR

3/4 TEASPOON SALT

A FEW TURNS OF THE WHITE PEPPER MILL

300 ML (10 FL OZ) SUNFLOWER OIL

METHOD

Put the mustard, egg, vinegar, salt and pepper into a liquidizer. Turn on the machine and then gradually add the oil through the hole in the lid until you have a thick emulsion.

The mayonnaise will keep for about 1 week in the refrigerator.

fresh salted cod

Sprinkle a 1 cm (1/2 inch) layer of salt over the base of a plastic container. Put a thick piece of unskinned cod fillet on top and then completely cover it in another thick layer of salt. Cover and refrigerate overnight. The next day, the salt will have turned to brine. Remove the cod from the brine and rinse it under cold water. Cover with fresh water and leave to soak for 1 hour. It is now ready to use.

rouille

MAKES ABOUT 300 ML (10 FL OZ)

1 RED PEPPER
1 TEASPOON TOMATO PURÉE
1 TEASPOON GROUND CORIANDER
A PINCH OF SAFFRON STRANDS
2 MEDIUM-HOT RED FINGER CHILLIES,
  ROUGHLY CHOPPED
1/4 TEASPOON CAYENNE PEPPER
1/2 TEASPOON SALT
25 G (1 OZ) SLICE OF DAY-OLD CRUSTLESS
  WHITE BREAD
A LITTLE FISH STOCK OR WATER
3 FAT GARLIC CLOVES, PEELED
1 EGG YOLK
250 ML (8 FL OZ) OLIVE OIL

METHOD

First roast the red pepper, which you can do in one of two ways. Either spear the stalk end on a fork and turn the pepper in the flame of a gas burner or blowtorch until the skin has blistered and blackened. Or pre-heat the oven to 220°C/425°F/Gas Mark 7 and roast the pepper for 20–25 minutes, turning once, until the skin is black. Leave to cool and then break in half and remove the stalk, seeds and skin. Put the roasted red pepper, tomato purée, ground coriander, saffron, red chillies, cayenne pepper and 1/4 teaspoon of salt into a food processor and blend to a smooth paste (this spice paste is known as harissa).

Cover the slice of bread with a little fish stock or water and leave to soften. Squeeze out the excess liquid and put the bread into a clean food processor or liquidizer with 2 tablespoons of the harissa, the garlic cloves, egg yolk and remaining salt. Blend until smooth, then with the machine still running, gradually add the oil through the hole in the lid as you would for mayonnaise, until you have a thick emulsion. Scoop into a bowl and store in the fridge for up to 1 week.

beurre blanc

This is my favourite sauce for fish. I like to serve it with sea bass which I grill simply and serve with samphire and new potatoes.

SERVES 4

50G (2 OZ) SHALLOTS (OR ONIONS),
  FINELY CHOPPED
2 TABLESPOONS WHITE WINE VINEGAR
4 TABLESPOONS DRY WHITE WINE
6 TABLESPOONS WATER OR FISH STOCK
2 TABLESPOONS DOUBLE CREAM
175 G (6 OZ) UNSALTED BUTTER,
  CUT INTO PIECES

METHOD

Put the shallots, vinegar, wine and water in a small pan, bring to the boil and simmer until nearly all the liquid has evaporated. Add the cream and reduce a little more, then remove the pan from the heat and whisk in the butter a little at a time until it has all amalgamated.

You can also make the sauce by reducing down and adding the cream as before then adding a couple of tablespoons of water. You then bring the sauce to a rapid boil and whisk the butter in while boiling. This method will produce a perfectly acceptable sauce but it will be a little less light than if you choose the first method. This second method is also the way to reconstitute a sauce which has got too hot and separated. At the restaurant we replace the water with well-reduced fish stock which gives the sauce a roundness but it still tastes good made with water.

fish preparation

CLEANING ROUND FISH

Cut off the fins with kitchen scissors. Then, working over several sheets of newspaper or under cold running water, remove the scales from the fish by scraping it from the tail to the head with a blunt, thick-bladed knife or a fish scaler.

To remove the guts, slit open the belly from the anal fin (situated two-thirds of the way down the fish) up towards the head. Pull out most of the guts with your hand and cut away any remaining pieces with a small knife. Wash out the cavity with plenty of cold water.

With large fish you may wish to remove the gills. Pull open the gill flaps and cut them away from the two places where they join the fish, at the back of the head and under the mouth.

FILLETING ROUND FISH

Lay the fish on a board with its back towards you. Cut around the back of the head, through the flesh of the fillet down to the backbone. Turn the knife towards the tail and, beginning just behind the head, carefully start to cut the fillet away from the bones, down towards the belly. Once you have loosened enough flesh to enable you to get the whole blade of the knife underneath the fillet, rest a hand on top of the fish and cut away the fillet in one clean sweep, down to the tail, keeping the blade close to the bones as you do so. Turn the fish over and repeat on the other side. Remove any small bones left in the fillets with tweezers.

CLEANING FLAT FISH

To remove the guts, locate the gut cavity by pressing on the white side of the fish just below the head until you find an area that is much softer. Make a small incision across this area (if you wish to remove any roe, make a slightly longer incision) and pull out the guts. Snip off the fins with kitchen scissors.

Dover sole and brill are the only flat fish that need scaling. Follow the method for round fish.

FILLETING FLAT FISH

You will get 4 fillets from one flat fish. Lay the fish on a board and cut around the back of the head and across the tail end, through the skin and flesh down to the bones.

Then cut through the skin down the centre of the fish from head to tail, very slightly to one side of the raised backbone. Starting at the head end, slide a knife under the corner of one fillet and carefully cut it away from the bones, keeping the knife as close to the bones as you can and folding the released fillet back as you go. Remove the adjacent fillet in the same way, then turn the fish over and repeat.

SKINNING FILLETS OF FISH

Place the fillet skin-side down on a board with the narrowest (tail) end nearest you. Angling the blade of the knife down towards the skin, start to cut between the flesh and the skin until a little flap of flesh is released. Flip this flap over and firmly take hold of the skin. Working away from you, continue to cut along its length, sawing with the knife from side to side and keeping the blade of the knife as flat and as close to the skin as you can.

PREPARING MONKFISH TAILS

First remove the skin from the tail. Grasp hold of the thick end of the tail in one hand and the skin in the other and briskly tear off the skin, which should come away quite easily. Fillet the monkfish by cutting along either side of the thick backbone. You now need to remove the thin membrane that encases the fillets. Pull off as much as possible with your fingers and then carefully cut away the rest with a sharp knife, taking care not to cut away too much of the flesh.

PREPARING COCKLES AND CLAMS

Wash the cockles or clams well in plenty of cold water and discard any that won't shut when lightly tapped on the work surface.

PREPARING MUSSELS

Clean the mussels by scrubbing them in plenty of cold water. Scrape off any barnacles with a knife and discard any open mussels that don't close when tapped lightly on a work surface. Pull out the tough, fibrous beards protruding from between the tightly closed shells.

OPENING OYSTERS

Hold the oyster flat-shell uppermost and push the point of an oyster knife or a small, thick-bladed knife into the hinge of the oyster at its narrowest point. Work the knife forwards and backwards to break the hinge. Slide the knife under the top shell and sever the ligament that joins the oyster to the shell. Lift off the top shell and, working over a bowl so that you collect all the juices, remove the oyster from its shell and pick out any little bits of broken shell.

REMOVING THE MEAT FROM A COOKED CRAB

Break off and discard the tail flap, then twist off the two larger claw arms and the legs. Break the legs at the joints and discard all but the first, largest joints. Crack the shells with the back of a knife or a hammer, then pick out the white meat with a crab pick. Break open the claw arms, crack the shells and remove this meat in the same way, discarding the very thin, flat bone from the centre of the claws.

Insert the blade of a large knife between the body and the back shell, twist to release the body and lift it out. Pull off the feathery-looking gills or 'dead man's fingers' from the body and discard. Cut the body into four and pick out all the white meat from the little channels. Remove the stomach sac from the back shell by pressing on the little piece of shell located just behind the eyes. Discard both the bone and the stomach. Scrape out the brown meat from the back shell and keep it separate from the white meat.

REMOVING THE MEAT FROM A COOKED LOBSTER

Twist off the claw arms and legs and discard the legs. Break the claw arms apart at the joints and crack the shells with the back of a knife or a hammer. Remove the meat in as large pieces as possible.

Cut the lobster in half lengthways and remove the intestine. Take out the meat from the tail section. Cut it into largish chunks. Remove the soft, greenish tomalley (liver) and any red roe from the head section and set them aside with the rest of the meat (they are both edible), but remove the little stomach sack just behind the mouth. If the lobster is large it is worth picking the meat out of the head in the same way as for the crab, above.

If you want to remove the tail meat in one piece, don't cut the lobster in half lengthways. Instead, detach the head from the tail and then cut the head in half and deal with as before. Turn the tail section over and cut along either side of the flat under-shell with scissors. Lift back the flap of shell and take out the meat. Remove the intestinal tract before or after slicing, with the tip of a small, sharp knife.

PREPARING RAW PRAWNS

Firmly twist the head away from the body and discard, or use for stock. Break open the soft shell along the belly and carefully peel it away from the flesh. For some recipes you may wish to leave the last tail segment of the shell in place.

With some large prawns you may need to remove the intestinal tract, which looks like a dark vein running down the back of the prawn flesh. Run the tip of a small knife down the back of the prawn, lift up the vein and pull it away.

CLEANING SQUID

Gently pull the head away from the body, taking the milky-white intestines with it. Cut off the tentacles from the head and squeeze out the beak-like mouth from the centre. Cut this off and discard it, along with the head. Pull out the plastic-like quill from the body, then pull off the fins from either side of the body pouch. Pull off the purple, semi-transparent skin from both the body and the fins and wash out the pouch with water.

CLEANING CUTTLEFISH

Cut off the tentacles just in front of the eyes, then remove and discard the beak-like mouth from the centre of the tentacles. Pull off the skin from the tentacles. Cut the head section from the body and discard. Cut open the body section from top to bottom along the dark-coloured back, then remove and discard the cuttlebone and entrails. If you want to use the ink for the recipe, be very careful not to pierce the small, pearly-white ink pouch in amongst the entrails. Wash the body well and then pull off the skin.

PREPARING SCALLOPS

Wash the scallops in plenty of cold water to remove any sand and weed from the shells. Hold the scallop flat-shell uppermost and slide the blade of a filleting knife between the shells. Keeping the blade flat against the top shell, feel for the ligament that joins the shell to the muscle meat of the scallop and cut through it. Lift off the flat top shell and pull out the black stomach sac and the frilly 'skirt' that surrounds the white scallop meat and orange coral. If you want to cook the scallop in the shell, rinse away any visible sand from the inside of the shell and drain away all excess water. Otherwise, cut the scallop meat away from the bottom shell and lift out.

alternative fish

I've compiled a list of alternative fish for both Great Britain and the main English-speaking countries. The suggested alternatives are not necessarily the closest biologically but those that I think will match the recipes best.

Fish from Recipe	Alternatives in UK	Australia	New Zealand	South Africa	USA/Canada
Abalone	Cuttlefish	Abalone	Paua	Abalone	Abalone
Black Bream	Grey Mullet	Black Bream	Sea Bream	Sea Bream	Snapper
Brill	Lemon Sole	John Dory	Brill	Sole	Mahi Mahi
Clam	Mussel	Clam, Pipi	Clam	Clam	Clam
Cockle	Small Clam	Pipi, Cockle	Cockle	Cockle	Cockle
Cod	Haddock	Murray Cod	Hake	Rock Cod	Cod
Crab	Crab	Crab	Crab	Crab	Crab
Cuttlefish	Large Squid	Cuttlefish	Cuttlefish	Cuttlefish	Cuttlefish
Dogfish	Shark, Tope	Gummy Shark	Elephant Fish	Dogfish	Spur-dog
Dover Sole	Which Sole, Grey Sole	Flounder	Brill	Flounder	English Sole
Dublin Bay Prawn, Langoustine	Tiger Prawn	Prawn	Langoustine	Prawn	Prawn
Eel, jellied	Conger Eel	Eel	Eel	Eel	Eel
Eel, stir-fried	Bream	Eel	Eel	Eel	Eel
Flounder	Plaice	Flounder	Flounder, Brill	Flounder	Flounder
Grey Mullet	Sea Bass	Grey Mullet	Grey Mullet	Grey Mullet	Gray Mullet
Gurnard	Bream	Gurnard, Snapper	Gurnard	Gurnard	Sea-robin
Haddock	Cod, Hake	Coral Trout, Murray Cod	Deep Sea Cod, Hoki	Rock Cod	Haddock
Smoked Haddock	Smoked Cod	Smoked Gemfish	Smoked Hake	Smoked Whiting	Smoked Haddock
Halibut	Salmon	Atlantic Salmon	Grouper	Salmon	Halibut
Herring	Mackerel	Herring	Pilchard	Herring	Herring
John Dory	Red Mullet	Silver Dory	John Dory	John Dory	John Dory
Ling	Hake	Ling	Hoki	Rock Cod	Cusk
Lobster	Spiny Lobster	Rock Lobster	Rock Lobster	Lobster	Lobster
Mackerel	Herring	Mackerel	Mackerel	Mackerel	Mackerel
Monkfish	Wolf Fish, Rock Turbot	Stargazer, Monkfish	Monkfish	Monk	Monkfish
Mussel	Cockle, Clam	Mussel	Mussel	Mussel	Mussel
North Atlantic Prawn	Pink Shrimp	Prawn	Prawn	Prawn	Prawn
Octopus	Cuttlefish, Large Squid	Octopus	Octopus	Octopus	Octopus
Oyster	Clam	Oyster	Oyster	Oyster	Oyster
Pilchard	Sardine	Sardine	Sardine	Sardine	Sardine
Plaice	Lemon Sole	Sand Whiting, Flounder	Orange Roughy, Flounder	Flounder	American Plaice
Red Mullet	Bream	Emperor, Snapper, Red Mullet	Snapper	Red Mullet	Goatfish
Salmon	Salmon Trout	Atlantic Salmon	Salmon	Salmon	Salmon
Scallop	Mussel	Scallop	Scallop	Scallop	Scallop
Sea Bass	Grey Mullet	Murray Cod, Hapuku	Hapuku	Sea Bass	Striped Bass
Sea Trout	Salmon	Ocean Trout	Trout	Atlantic Salmon	Sea Trout
Shrimp	Pink Shrimp	Small Prawn	Small Prawn	Small Prawn	Small Prawn
Skate	Ray, Angel Fish	Skate, Ray	Skate	Skate	Skate
Squat Lobster	Dublin Bay Prawn	Balmain Bug, Moreton Bay Bug	Prawn	Prawn	Shrimp
Squid	Cuttlefish	Squid	Squid	Squid	Squid
Trout	Pollen, Greyling, Smelt	Trout	Trout	Trout	Trout
Turbot	Brill	Greenback Flounder	Turbot, Sole	Sole, Flounder	Walleye
Whitebait	Whitebait	Whitebait	Whitebait	Whitebait	Whitebait
Whiting	Codling	Flathead	Blue Whiting	Rock Cod	Whiting
Wolf Fish	Monkfish, Haddock	Coral Trout	Hoki	Cape Hake	Wolf Fish, Tilefish

index

Acknowledgements

As ever, there are not enough hours in the day. A book with as much information as this one is bound to require lots of help. This has come mainly from Debbie Major who tested the recipes and typed them, prepared all the food for filming and did the lion's share of the research for the guide section of the book. She also accompanied me on many of the journeys in search of seafood. There is no question, I couldn't have done it all without her. Thanks too to Viv Bowler who ironed out so many of the uncertainties arising from tackling this new type of book and quietly, but determinedly, kept me going and kept me confident. I love Paul Welti's design and also appreciate the input of Lisa Pettibone. Many thanks too for the editing of Rachel Copus and Jane Middleton. Thanks to the TV crew, Chris Topliss, Peter Underwood and Arezoo Farahzad whose incredibly detailed research has been very valuable when writing this book. Lastly, a big glass of Shiraz for the Director, David Pritchard, who's my chum.